PC DOS

A Self-Teaching Guide

Related Titles of Interest from Wiley:

WordStar Without Tears, Ashley and Fernandez

Using dBASE IV: Basics for Business, Brownstein

R:BASE for DOS: A Business User's Guide, Condliffe

The PC Upgrader's Manual: How to Build and Extend Your System, Held

IBM PS/2: A Business Perspective, Revised Edition, Hoskins

The New DOS 4.0, Christopher, Feigenbaum, and Saliga

DOS 4.0 Reference, Christopher, Feigenbaum, and Saliga

DOS Productivity Tips & Tricks, HELD

Quick C DOS Utilities, Alonso

Turbo C DOS Utilities, Alonso

Lotus 1-2-3 Release 2.2., Williams

Lotus 1-2-3 Release 3, Williams

Lotus Agenda, Goodman and Wolf

Inside ALLWAYS: The Spreadsheet Publisher, Sandler and Bagett

PC DOS

A Self-Teaching Guide

Third Edition

Ruth Ashley
Judi N. Fernandez

WILEY

John Wiley & Sons, Inc.

New York • Chichester • Brisbane • Toronto • Singapore

Editor: Therese A. Zak
Managing Editor: Ruth Greif
Copy Editor: Ron Pronk
Design and Production: Rob Mauhar and Lenity Himburg, The Coriolis Group

Library of Congress Cataloging-in Publication Data

Ashley, Ruth.
PC DOS : a self-teaching guide / Ruth Ashley, Judi N. Fernandez. -
- 3rd ed.
p. cm.
Includes bibliographical references.
ISBN 0-471-51355-5
1. IBM Personal Computer--Programming. 2. PC DOS (Computer operating system) I. Fernandez, Judi N., 1941- . II. Title.
QA76.8.I2594A83 1990
005.4'46--dc20 89-16752
CIP

Printed in the United States of America
90 91 10 9 8 7 6 5 4 3 2 1

Contents

About This Book

This guide consists of 12 chapters that have been carefully sequenced to introduce you to your personal computer and its operating system and to help you develop a useful set of skills. We have made every effort to organize the material in the best possible learning sequence, so that you can begin using your machine as quickly as possible. We strongly recommend that you study the chapters in order. You will learn to do easy tasks, then successively more complex tasks, until you have mastered the system.

Each chapter begins with a short introduction followed by objectives, which outline what you can expect to learn from the chapter, and ends with Exercises to guide you in transferring your new knowledge to the computer.

The body of each chapter is divided into short sections in which information is presented or reviewed, followed by questions that ask you to apply the information. A line across the page separates the questions from their correct answers. As you work through the book, use a folded sheet of paper or a card to cover the correct answers until you have written yours. Be sure you actually write each response, especially when the activity asks you to create a command. Only by writing out the commands and checking them carefully can you get the most from this book. Similarly, be sure to do each Exercise section at your computer. The real way to learn DOS is to use it, hands-on.

This book is written for beginning computer users—people with no previous personal computer experience. If you have some experience with another computer, you will still benefit from this book. The book assumes you have a personal computer available, along with DOS 3.3. Either the IBM or the Microsoft version of DOS will do. Both versions are identical except for an occasional difference in messages. If you have a fixed (hard) disk, we assume it has not been prepared for use. For Chapters 1 through 4, you will boot from diskette. After Chapter 4, the book assumes you are booting from fixed disk. However, if you don't have a fixed disk, you can continue to boot from diskette.

This is an introductory book and does not teach everything there is to know about DOS. Most of the commands are mentioned, but advanced options are not explained. It is meant to get you started with DOS. Once you are comfortable with the system, you can learn about advanced facilities yourself by studying your DOS reference manuals.

Throughout the book are command format statements. This hypothetical one shows how you should read a format statement:

Format:

READ [/S | /V] [filespec]

Any term in all uppercase letters must be entered character for character as it appears in the command format. All special characters except square brackets ([ ]) and the vertical line (|) must be entered as shown. Any term in lowercase letters indicates an item for which you must supply a value. Items outside of brackets are required. Items inside brackets are optional. A vertical line indicates a choice between items. Thus, the above format indicates that you must enter the word READ. (You don't have to type it in all capital letters.) You can also enter either /S or /V, but not both. You can also provide a filespec. You don't enter the word "filespec"; instead you enter a phrase, such as CHAPTER1, that is used by DOS to find a file.

Introduction: The Personal Computer and DOS

Before you can study DOS commands, you should know a bit about your hardware (the machinery) and your software (the DOS programs). This introduction briefly describes both. You'll learn about the various IBM (and compatible) personal computers and their major components. You'll learn what DOS is, what it does (in general terms), and how it relates to all those computers. You'll also learn many terms used in the book, such as *byte*, *track*, *batch*, and *environment*.

Your Hardware

IBM has developed a complete line of personal computers. First came the PC, a basic but expandable microcomputer designed to meet the needs of a wide variety of home and business users. The PC/XT (eXTended) was designed for those who needed more facilities than the basic PC offered. As personal use grew, so did needs and expectations. The PC/AT (Advanced Technology), built around a faster microprocessor with more capacity, permitted both the home and the business user to have larger, more complex programs and files. And now the PS/2 serves modern business users who need networking, massive data bases, advanced graphics, and other features approaching mainframe computer capabilities.

Many competitors have introduced microcomputers that are compatible with these IBM machines, although the degree of compatibility varies. This book uses the term *personal computer* to mean any of the IBM microcomputers or compatibles. DOS is basically the same on all of them.

The System Unit

The heart of your personal computer is the *system unit*, which contains the microprocessor and memory. The *microprocessor* is a set of miniaturized circuits that does all the "thinking." It processes programs and gives orders to the rest of the computer.

Figure 1. An IBM PC System Unit

Memory is another set of miniaturized circuits (on several chips) where the microprocessor stores the programs and data it is working on. The more memory your machine has, the better. A small memory means the computer can't handle long programs, which may prevent you from using some of the more interesting software available. Also, if memory can't hold much data, the microprocessor must constantly use disks for storage, which slows processing tremendously.

Memory is divided into *bytes*. A byte is like a cell where one thing (such as the letter A) can be stored. Memory sizes are usually given in *kilobytes*, abbreviated as K. One K is 1,024 bytes, but you can think of it as approximately 1,000 bytes. A 64K memory has approximately 64,000 bytes, which is fairly small for a personal computer today. A more typical memory size is 640K. Your computer's memory might be stated in *megabytes* (MB), which are kilobytes squared. There are 1,048,576 bytes in a megabyte, which you can round off to one million bytes for casual conversations.

The Keyboard

The *keyboard* lets you enter data into your computer. When you're using DOS, you type commands on the keyboard. DOS reads and executes the commands. Your keyboard resembles a typewriter keyboard, but it has a lot more keys. Some of the extra keys have special uses in DOS, and you'll learn in this book what they do.

Figure 2. An IBM PC Keyboard

The Monitor

Your *monitor* is a television-like device that the computer uses to communicate with you. When you give DOS a command, the results are displayed on the monitor. Several types of monitors are available. Whichever type you've chosen, DOS can use it. (You'll learn later a command to adjust the data on your monitor.)

Figure 3. An IBM PC Monitor

The Diskette Drive

The system unit, the keyboard, and the monitor are the required parts of a personal computer. Virtually all computers have at least one *diskette drive,* also known as a floppy disk drive. In fact, a diskette drive is required for DOS.

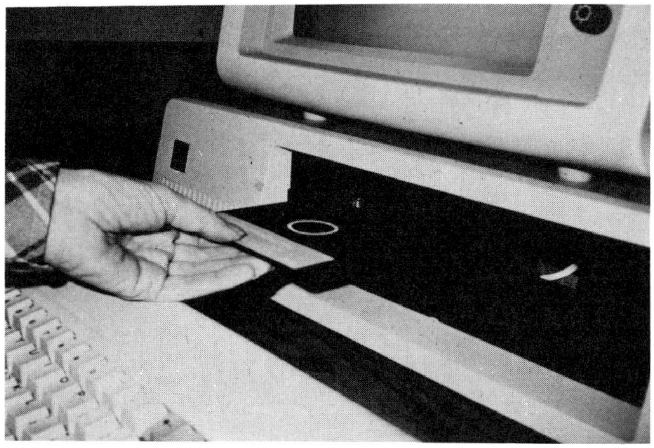

Figure 4. A 5.25-inch Diskette Drive

Each diskette drive has a name. The first one (on the left or top) is called A:. The second is called B:. If you have only one drive, it is named both A: and B: so that you can perform two-drive operations such as copying a diskette. DOS keeps track of when it's drive A: and when it's drive B: and tells you which diskette to insert. If you have more than two diskette drives, their names depend on whether you have fixed disk drives and, if so, what names are given to the fixed drives. In all cases, though, a drive name is a single letter followed by a colon.

Several types of diskette drives are available. You might have a 5.25-inch double-density drive, which can store 360K of data on a diskette. A 5.25-inch high-density drive can store 1.2MB of data per diskette. The newer, smaller 3.5-inch drives are not smaller in capacity. One type stores 720K, and the other stores 1.44MB.

Diskettes store data more permanently than memory does. Since diskettes are interchangeable in the drive, you might have hundreds of diskettes containing data and programs. Your personal computer (under the direction of DOS) transfers the information it needs from the diskette into memory. At your command, it saves new information on the diskette.

On diskettes, data is stored in concentric rings called *tracks*. The drive accesses the tracks through an opening in the disk covering. The drive spins the diskette inside its covering so the read/write heads can access the full circle. The heads move in and out to access the various tracks. The number of tracks depends on the size and density of the diskette.

The tracks are divided into *sectors*. The drive accesses one sector at a time. If a track has nine sectors, sector 1 might belong to file A, sector 2 to file B, sector 3 to file C, sector 4 to file B, and so on. The number of bytes in a sector depends on the type of diskette. A sector size of 512 bytes (.5K) is typical. The number of sectors per track also depends on the diskette type. A 5.25-inch double-density diskette has nine sectors per track, while a 3.5-inch 1.44MB diskette has 18 sectors per track.

The diskette surface is coated with a magnetizable material, just like the surface of audio tape. The read/write heads can magnetize and demagnetize this surface repeatedly. Thus, a diskette can be used, erased, and reused. (It will wear out eventually, but a high-quality diskette lasts a long time.)

Diskettes need care. They can be damaged by dust, smoke, oil from your fingertips, liquids, scratching, bending, heat, and the low-level magnetic fields in speakers, lamp cords, telephones, and so forth. Keep your diskettes in sturdy, closed containers when not in use. And avoid touching the recording surface.

Figure 5 shows the write-protection features on diskettes. For the 5.25-inch diskette, if the notch in the upper right corner is open, the computer can write on the diskette, perhaps erasing valuable data. For the 3.5-inch diskette, if the write-protection window is closed, the computer can write on the diskette. To protect valuable programs and data from accidental erasure, write-protect the diskette as shown in Figure 5. (You'll find pieces of tape, usually black or silver colored, in a box of new 5.25-inch diskettes. The write-protection tab is built into the 3.5-inch diskette's plastic cover.)

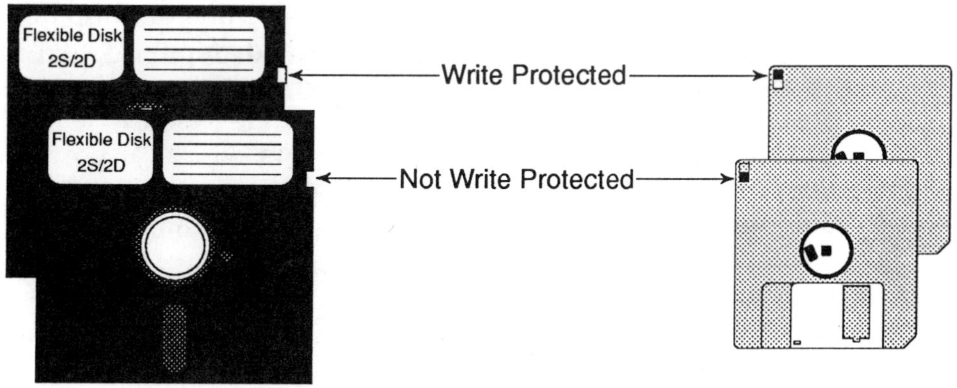

Figure 5. Disk Write Protection

Fixed Disk Drive

Many users also get a *fixed (hard) disk drive* for their personal computers. The fixed drive is usually named C:. You might partition the hard disk into more than one drive. For example, you might partition a 60MB disk into three 20MB drives, C:, D:, and E:. DOS treats the three drives as if they were three different hard disks, even though they're all contained on one device.

A fixed disk drive is like a stack of diskettes, all accessible at once. (You can't see them, however, unless you open the case, which is not a good idea.) The unit has several read/write heads, attached to a comb-like arm, that move between the disks; each recording surface has its own head.

The disks are stacked so that all the tracks are aligned. Looking down through the top, if you imagine all the track 0's connected to each other vertically, they would form a cylinder; the track 1's form another cylinder, and so forth. If the disks have 400 tracks, the unit has 400 cylinders.

Typical fixed disk capacities are 10MB, 30MB, and 40MB. That's enough space for most individual users' total storage needs. Business computers often have 60MB or even 100MB fixed disks. And it's all available at once, without changing disks as you do in a diskette drive.

The disadvantage of fixed disk drives is that, if something goes wrong physically, you stand to lose all your data at once. You'll learn in this book how to minimize that kind of catastrophe (you can't prevent it completely).

The Printer

Most users have at least one *printer* for their computers. Dot-matrix printers are inexpensive and fast and can provide nice-looking copy. They can also be driven by today's advanced word processing and desktop publishing software to produce typeset-looking material and graphics. Letter-quality printers are usually more expensive and slower, but they create printed pages that are better than typewritten. However, they are less flexible in terms of fonts and cannot do graphics at all. Laser printers, which can cost as much as the rest of the computer combined, can create letter-quality print with a nearly unlimited variety of fonts and graphics. Plotters can produce drawings and whatever lettering goes with the drawing, but most of them do not furnish the same quality as a laser printer.

DOS can drive most dot-matrix and letter-quality printers. Its capacity to drive a laser printer is limited; it can produce fixed-pitch text, but it cannot handle proportional fonts or graphics without special software. Often the laser printer must emulate a dot-matrix printer for DOS to interact with it. DOS cannot drive a plotter. This does not mean that your laser printer and plotter are useless under DOS. Many programs that run under DOS—including word processors, desktop publishers, and CAD programs—include software to drive these output devices to their full capacity. But the DOS output commands, such as TYPE and PRINT, will furnish only basic output on these devices.

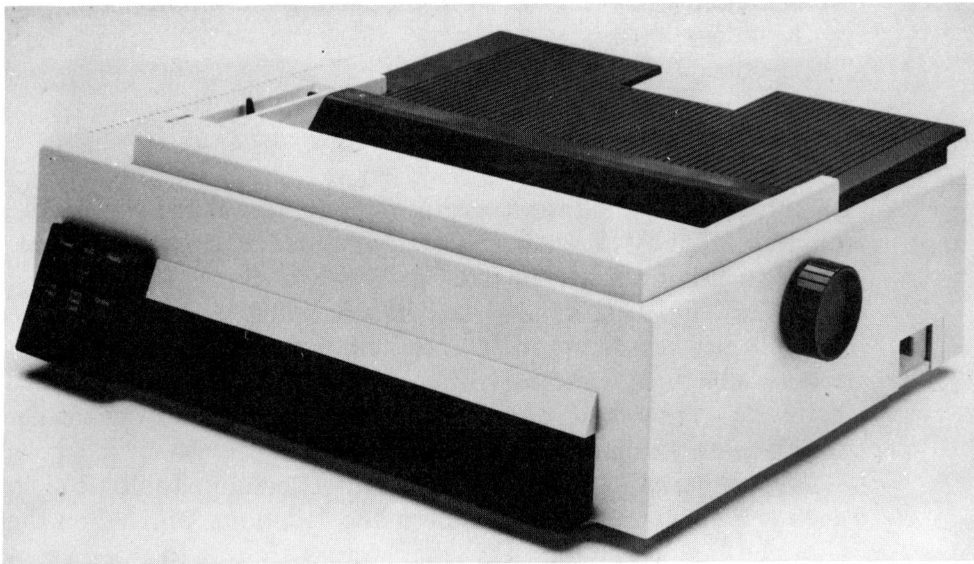

Figure 6. A Dot-Matrix Printer

Other Devices

You may have also chosen other devices for your personal computer, such as joysticks or modems. These devices require additional software, not included in DOS, so we won't cover them in this book.

Your Software

A computer without software is like a car without fuel: It has lots of potential, but there's nothing to make it go. An operating system is a software package that lets you operate a computer. Several types of operating systems are available for your personal computer; by far the most popular of these is DOS.

You might have heard of MS-DOS and PC-DOS. They are essentially the same program. PC-DOS is the version provided by IBM with the true IBM PC. MS-DOS is the version distributed by Microsoft and provided by most manufacturers of IBM PC compatibles.

Perhaps the best way to understand an operating system is to look at what it does. The following paragraphs highlight some of the most important functions of DOS. We won't cover them all here, since many of them won't have meaning to you now. You'll learn to use them in detail as you continue with this book.

Managing Your Diskettes and Fixed Disks

DOS has some functions for your diskette, some for fixed disks, and several functions that pertain to both diskettes and fixed disks. This book uses "disk" to mean either diskette or fixed disk.

DOS helps you manage your diskettes and fixed disks in several ways. In general, it lets you organize your data into *files*. A file might be a letter, a report, a balance sheet, a mailing list, a grocery list, a tax form, or any other item you want to save on the disk. You decide what to put in each file. Each program you have is also a file.

DOS maintains a directory and File Allocation Table (FAT) on each disk showing all file names, their sizes and locations, and when they were last changed. The FAT tells DOS what sectors are free to store a new file.

DOS provides several commands for managing your diskettes and fixed disks. You will learn how to use all these commands later in this book; here's a summary list for now:

- DIR shows you a directory of the files stored on a disk.
- VOL shows you the disk's name.
- LABEL lets you change the disk's name.
- DISKCOPY copies a diskette.
- DISKCOMP compares two diskettes.
- FORMAT prepares a new disk (which puts the directory and FAT on it).
- CHKDSK checks a disk for errors.
- RECOVER rescues data from a disk that has developed bad sectors.
- SYS puts the DOS system files on a diskette.
- BACKUP makes a backup copy of files for safekeeping.
- RESTORE restores backup files to a usable form.

A fixed disk or a high-capacity diskette can hold hundreds of files, and any directory containing more than 30 or so files is too large for easy use. DOS lets you break a directory into reasonable-sized chunks by establishing subdirectories. Since the main directory, called the *root directory*, branches into two or more subdirectories (which can in turn branch into two or more subdirectories, and so forth), subdivided directories are called tree-structured directories. DOS gives you several commands to create and control tree-structured directories:

- MKDIR creates a new subdirectory.
- CHDIR lets you access a subdirectory.
- TREE shows the structure of the entire directory.
- RMDIR removes a subdirectory.

File Management

Several commands let you manage your files (no matter what type of device they're on). Here are some of them:

- COPY copies a file from one place to another.
- COMP compares two files.
- TYPE displays a file's contents on your monitor.
- PRINT prints a file's contents on your printer.
- RENAME changes a file's name.
- DEL deletes a file.
- SORT sorts a file.
- FIND displays file lines containing whatever phrase you specify.

```
 Volume in drive B is L&C BACKUP
 Directory of  B:\

CHAP01          38093   4-14-90    6:41p
CHAP00          20847   4-14-90    2:26p
CHAP02          55993   4-16-90    5:13p
CHAP04          15348   4-17-90    8:21p
CHAP03          77144   4-17-90    6:25p
OUTLINE          2517   1-06-90    6:22a
PREFACE          7243   1-04-90   11:23a
CHAP05          87097   1-03-90   11:00a
        8 File(s)     17408 bytes free
```

Figure 7. A Typical Diskette Directory

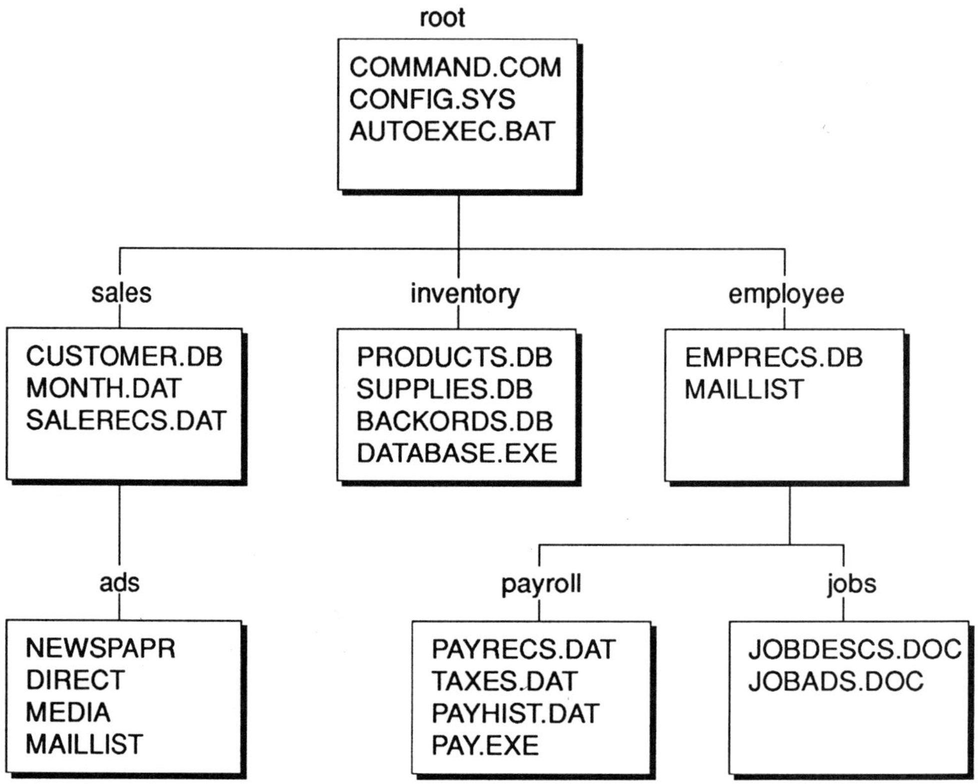

Figure 8. Diagram of a Tree-Structured Directory

Controlling the Environment

To function properly, DOS must establish certain conditions that are so basic to every move it makes that we call them the DOS *environment*. For example, DOS assumes you will enter commands from the keyboard as opposed to some other device. It displays messages on the monitor. The current date and time are part of the environment, as are many other factors.

You can change the DOS environment if you need to. Here are a few of the commands you can use:

- CTTY changes the standard input/output device from the keyboard/ monitor combination to any device you specify.
- DATE changes the date.
- TIME changes the time.
- GRAPHICS tells DOS that your printer can produce graphics.

Batch Processing

When you first start using DOS, you'll type a command on the keyboard and press the Enter key, and DOS will read and obey the command. After a while, you'll begin to recognize certain routines consisting of a series of commands that you use frequently. You can save typing time and speed processing by creating *batch files* for these often-used routines. A batch file contains several DOS commands. The file's name becomes another DOS command. You enter the batch file's name, and DOS executes the entire series of commands. Thus, with one command you can tell DOS to COPY a file, SORT the copy, and PRINT the sorted output. Or you can create one batch file that issues all the commands necessary to set up the environment the way you like it.

All the commands you've seen so far can be used in batch files. In addition, DOS has several commands that pertain only to batch files, to help you control the batch processing and make it as useful as possible. Some of the batch commands are:

- ECHO controls messages on the monitor.
- PAUSE displays a message and waits for you to respond.
- IF decides which commands to execute.

Command Processing

At the very heart of DOS is the command processor, named COMMAND. This program is placed in memory when you start up DOS, and it makes everything else happen. It is COMMAND that reads and processes the commands you type on the keyboard.

Some of the programs we've mentioned here, such as TYPE, DIR, and COPY, are built into the command processor and are called *internal* programs. An internal program is always available whenever DOS is running, since COMMAND is always in memory.

The DOS programs you use most often are internal programs. Most of the file management and directory handling programs are internal, as are many of the environment control programs.

Other programs, such as FORMAT and SORT, are *external* programs, meaning they are not part of COMMAND. They have their own files on the DOS diskettes. When you enter an external command, COMMAND causes the appropriate file to be read into memory. However, it doesn't stay in memory. The next time you enter the same command, the program must be read into memory again. Thus, the external programs tend to be slower than the internal programs.

If you buy a program outside of DOS, such as an accounting program or a word processor, it's an external program. You still use DOS to run it, just as if it were a DOS external program.

Programmer Services

DOS offers some special services to people who want to write their own programs. BASIC, BASICA, and GWBASIC let the programmer develop programs using the BASIC language. LINK prepares a program for execution. DEBUG helps a programmer find and fix errors in a program. We assume you are not a programmer, so we do not cover the programming features in this book.

The Line Editor

DOS includes a program called EDLIN that lets you type files on your keyboard and save them on disk. However, EDLIN is awkward, and most people buy a more sophisticated editor or a word processor instead. Since almost no one uses EDLIN, we won't cover it in this book. Your reference manual includes the EDLIN commands and options if you want to try it out.

Versions of DOS

Several versions of DOS have been released over the years to accommodate advancements in personal computer hardware. This book is current with version 3.3. If you are using an older version, you might find that some of the commands and options discussed in this book do not work on your system. The reference book that came with your DOS software is the best guide to what does and does not work with your version of DOS.

1

Getting Started

You must learn several basic concepts and procedures before you can use DOS. You must know how to start up DOS through a procedure called *booting*, which also requires you to enter some data. And you should make a backup copy of your DOS diskettes, for safety's sake. Finally, you must know how to shut the system down again. This chapter shows you how to do these things.

When you have finished this chapter, you will be able to:

- Boot DOS
- Enter the date
- Enter the time
- Reboot DOS
- Use DISKCOPY to make backup copies of your DOS diskettes
- Interpret messages resulting from the above operations
- Shut down the system

Entering Data

Even before you boot DOS, you must be able to enter data, because the booting process requires you to enter some. We'll cover only the basics here; this book has two chapters about entering DOS commands later on.

You type letters on the keyboard pretty much the same as you would on a regular typewriter. DOS doesn't care whether you use uppercase or lowercase characters, so you might as well save a few keystrokes by using lowercase characters. We'll show all uppercase characters in our examples so you can tell the difference between what we type and what DOS displays, which is usually in mixed upper- and lowercase.

Type numbers using the number keys on the top row of your keyboard. You'll learn how to use your numeric keypad in Chapter 2.

If you need to type an uppercase symbol, such as a colon (:), hold down a Shift key while you press the appropriate character key. Can't find the shift keys on your keyboard? On many personal computer keyboards, they are labeled with an outlined arrow pointing up, like this: ⇑.

DOS doesn't read characters while you're typing. It won't read them until you press the Enter key, which is the same as the Carriage Return key on a typewriter. (It's called Enter because it "enters" data from the keyboard into the computer.) On many keyboards, the Enter key is labeled with a bent arrow, like this: ↵.

Before you enter the data, you can correct mistakes by pressing the Backspace key. Each time you press Backspace, one character is erased. On many keyboards, the Backspace key is directly above the Enter key and labeled with a left arrow, like this: ←.

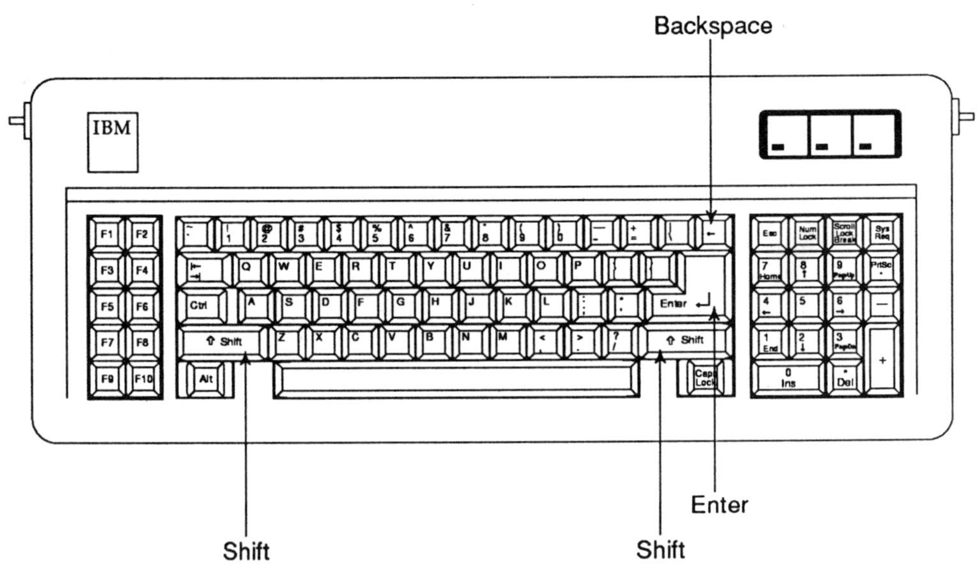

Figure 1.1. Shift, Enter, and Backspace Keys on an AT Keyboard

So, type data on your keyboard using the letter, number, symbol, and shift keys just as you do on a regular typewriter. Use Backspace to erase a character so you can overtype it. When the data is correct, press Enter to enter it.

(a) True or false? DOS doesn't care if you enter upper- or lowercase letters.
(b) What key do you press to erase characters you have typed?
(c) What key do you press to enter data?
(d) Find these keys on your keyboard. Show how they're labeled.
  A. Backspace
  B. Enter
  C. Shift

(a) True
(b) Backspace
(c) Enter
(d) The correct answers depend on your keyboard. On the IBM PC, they're labeled like this: A. ← B. ↵ C. ⇑

Sometimes DOS tells you to "press any key." However, the key you press must be a *character* key. That is, it must be a key that sends a specific signal to the computer. A Shift key by itself, for example, won't work, since it must have another key to show an effect. When DOS tells you to press any key, press a letter, number, or symbol key. We usually press the Spacebar or Enter.

Suppose DOS tells you to:

```
press any key...
```

Which keys won't work?

Enter Spacebar Shift Ctrl 1 2 3 : + . A B C

Shift and Ctrl

Booting

Now you know how to use the keyboard, so let's get on to booting. As you read the instructions, please don't try them. Wait until you have learned all the details. You'll get a chance to try the entire process at the end of the chapter.

Now assume you're ready to start your system. It has been set up and all the necessary cables connected. The power is off. How do you get DOS up and running? Your fixed disk, if you have one, may not be ready to boot yet. This chapter shows you how to boot from diskette. You'll learn how to use the fixed disk in Chapter 4.

Step 1: You must use a diskette containing the DOS system. For now, you will use the original system diskette. Later, we'll show you how to create and use other diskettes.

Insert your system diskette in drive A:. (If you have more than one drive, A: is the one on the left or the top.) For 5.25-inch diskettes, be sure to close the latch. The drive won't work if the latch is open.

Step 2: Turn on your printer if you wish.

Step 3: Turn on your monitor (if it has its own power switch).

Step 4: Turn on the main power switch on the system unit.

Actually, Steps 2 and 3 may be done at any time, but Step 1 must precede Step 4.

When you turn the computer on, a small built-in program called ROM BIOS takes over. It does a memory test to make sure that there are no internal problems. With some systems, you can see messages from ROM BIOS and the memory check. The memory check can take a while (a minute or so, depending on the speed and memory size of your machine), so be patient. Then ROM BIOS accesses drive A:, looking for an operating system, finds DOS on the diskette in drive A:, reads it into memory (you can see the drive light and hear it working), and turns control of the computer over to DOS.

(a) What must you do before turning on the main power switch?

(b) What must be on the diskette you boot from?

A. BASIC

B. The DOS system

C. Nothing—the diskette must be blank

(c) In which drive do you put the boot diskette?

(a) Put the DOS system diskette in drive A:

(b) B

(c) Drive A: (if you try to boot from drive B:, it won't work)

A number of things can go wrong when you try to boot. For example, suppose you don't properly install a diskette in drive A: before turning on the power. What happens next depends on your computer setup. You might get a system booted from your fixed disk. You might get IBM's BASIC system. Or you might get an error message or nothing at all.

Suppose you properly install a diskette in drive A:, but that diskette doesn't contain the DOS system. You might get a message such as the following:

```
Bad or missing Command Interpreter
```

or

```
Invalid COMMAND.COM in drive A:
```

or

```
Disk boot failure
```

or

```
Nonsystem disk or disk error
Replace and strike any key when ready
```

In most cases, you'll need to put the correct diskette in drive A: and reboot. (In the next section, we'll show you how to reboot without using the main power switch.) If the message tells you to, just put in the DOS diskette and press any character key.

Sometimes you try to boot and nothing at all happens. If the cursor (the little blinking line) does not appear in about 5 to 10 seconds, or if it appears but nothing else happens after a minute or so, turn the system off again. Wait a few seconds, and then try again with a different diskette.

Suppose you try to boot DOS and get this message:

```
Bad or missing Command Interpreter
```

(a) What's wrong?
(b) How can you fix the problem?

(a) The diskette you tried to boot from is not a good boot diskette
(b) Install a proper diskette and reboot

Note Please don't try booting yet. Wait until the end of the chapter.

Sometimes you want to reboot; that is, you want to restart DOS without using the power switch or the reset button if you have one. You usually do this to get rid of a bad program or to recover from a bad initial boot. When you reboot, DOS stops whatever it is doing and goes back to the beginning.

You don't have to shut the power off to reboot. All you have to do is make sure a system diskette is in drive A: and press three keys simultaneously: Ctrl, Alt, and Del. These are three of the special keys on your personal computer keyboard. The names are abbreviations for Control, Alternate, and Delete. If you have an enhanced (101-key) keyboard, you can use either Ctrl key, either Alt key, and either Del key.

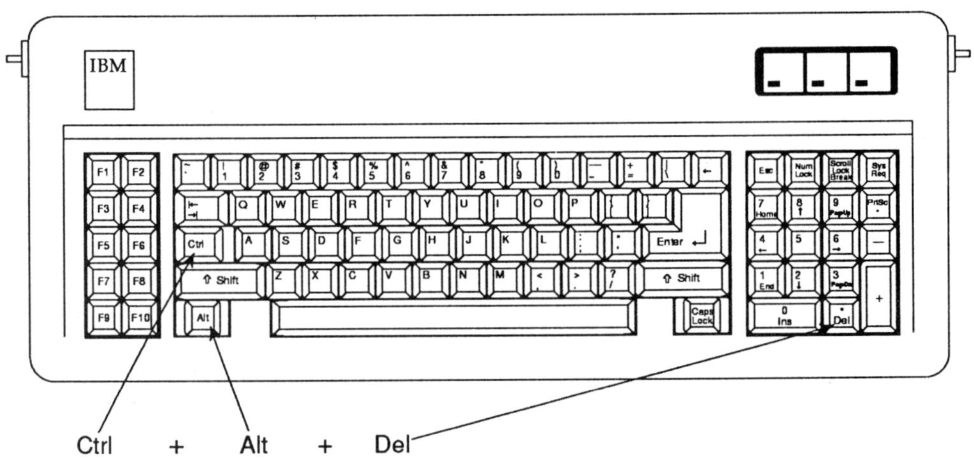

Figure 1.2. The Rebooting Keys on the AT Keyboard

Rebooting is faster than booting because it goes back to the beginning of DOS but not the beginning of ROM BIOS. Therefore, the memory checks are not repeated. Occasionally, a program is hung up and the system will not accept the reboot signals. In that case, just turn off the machine and start over or press the restart button if you have one.

(a) True or false? Rebooting interrupts (aborts) whatever the computer is currently doing.
(b) What keys are used in rebooting?
(c) In what order must they be pressed?

(a) True
(b) Ctrl, Alt, Del
(c) All together

Entering the Date

When the standard DOS system is booted or rebooted, a message similar to this is displayed:

```
Current date is Tue 1-01-1980
Enter new date (mm-dd-yy):_
```

This line represents the cursor

The date DOS displays depends on whether your system has an internal clock/calendar and whether it is set correctly. If the date is correct, all you have to do is press Enter. If the date isn't correct, you should correct it. DOS uses the date when it records data on a disk, so the date can be important to you.

You don't specify the day of the week; DOS figures that out from the date you enter. Dates are specified numerically, using either hyphens or slashes to separate the three parts. The month must be a number from 1 through 12. The day must be a number from 1 through 31. (You may omit leading zeros.) The year can be a two-digit number from 80 through 99, in which case 1980 through 1999 is assumed, or a four-digit number from 1980 through 2099. DOS cannot handle dates before 1980 or after 2099.

If you enter the date in the wrong format, such as Sept. 1, 1995, or use one outside the valid range, here's what you'll see:

```
Invalid date
Enter new date (mm-dd-yy):_
```

(a) Which of the following will DOS accept as legitimate dates?

A. 5/10/70	D. March 3, 2000	G. 12-1-1982
B. 6/19/81	E. 3-3-03	H. 12/9/1995
C. 20-1-99	F. 3/3/2003	I. 4/6

(b) Suppose today is June 5, 1995. Enter the new date.
(c) Suppose today is May 10, 2001. Enter the new date.
(d) True or false? It doesn't matter what date you enter because the system doesn't use it for anything.

(a) B, F, G, H (A—70 is not a legitimate year; C—20 is not a legitimate month; D—wrong format; E—03 is not a legitimate year, although 2003 is; I—needs a year)
(b) One possible answer is 6-5-95
(c) One possible answer is 5-10-2001 (be sure you used four digits for the year)
(d) False

Entering the Time

After the date has been entered, you'll see a message similar to this:

```
Current time is 15:00:12.02
Enter new time:_
```

The time DOS shows depends on whether your system has a built-in clock/calendar that has been set to the correct time. Like the date, the correct time is important when DOS is creating or updating files. Every file has a time and date associated with it in the directory. You will find the time and date handy in identifying various versions of a file and in deciding which files need to be backed up.

The time is expressed as hours:minutes:seconds.hundredths. To enter a new time, you can type hours between 0 and 23, minutes and seconds between 0 and 59. Leading zeros may be omitted. You must use colons between hours, minutes, and seconds, and a period between seconds and hundredths. Any value you omit will be assumed to be zero. You probably won't want to enter hundredths of seconds. Thus, 10:30 means 10:30:00.00 and 5 means 5:00:00.00. Twenty-four hour time is used, so that's 5 A.M. The entry 17:00:00.00 means 5 P.M.

If you enter an invalid time, you'll see this message:

```
Invalid time
Enter new time:_
```

To accept the default time (in computerese, "default" is the value that is used automatically if you don't change it), just press Enter and DOS uses the displayed time.

What would you type to enter the following times?
(a) 2 P.M.
(b) Three minutes and ten seconds after midnight
(c) Ten minutes after 9 A.M.
(d) The default time

(a) 14
(b) 0:3:10
(c) 9:10
(d) Enter

After you have entered a valid time, you will see a message similar to this:

```
Microsoft(R)  MS-DOS(R)  Version 3.30
              (C)Copyright Microsoft Corporation 1981-1987
A>_
```

This message tells you which version of DOS you have and that it is up and running. The symbol A> is the prompt that DOS gives you, telling you it is ready for your input.

```
Current date is Sun  2-18-90
Enter new date (mm-dd-yy):
Current time is 17:29:42.62
Enter new time:


Microsoft(R) MS-DOS(R)  Version 3.30
             (C)Copyright Microsoft Corp 1981-1987


A>_
```

Figure 1.3. A Successful DOS Boot

How can you tell when DOS has successfully booted and is ready for you to enter some commands?

The copyright message and the DOS prompt are displayed

Note

Disks can be arranged so that the Date and Time features are bypassed and another program is invoked as part of the booting process. In such cases, the booting procedure that we've described here does not take place. What actually happens depends on the program that is invoked. You'll learn about this DOS feature later in this book. For now, just be aware that you might boot with a diskette that bypasses the normal boot procedure. In any case, a new DOS system diskette will boot as we have described.

Using Your DOS Manual

If you have trouble remembering the boot procedure, you can look it up. You can come back to this book or use one of your DOS reference manuals. If you encounter a message you don't understand, look it up in your DOS manual. Use that manual now to look up this error message:

```
Syntax error
```

What does this message mean?
(a) DOS is not available
(b) The keyboard is not functioning properly
(c) A needed disk is missing
(d) The command is improperly formatted or mistyped

d

Copying a Diskette

Whenever you buy a new program diskette, always make a copy immediately unless the manufacturer explicitly forbids it and/or has copy-protected the diskettes. Put the original away and use only the copy. That way, if something happens to the copy, you still have the original to make a new copy from.

You can, and should, copy your DOS diskettes immediately. You'll use a program called DISKCOPY to do this. Here's how.

First, write-protect the original diskettes. This will prevent you from accidentally copying the blank diskettes onto the DOS diskettes.

After booting, DOS displays the A> command prompt and waits for you to enter a command. You type the command DISKCOPY and press Enter. This tells DOS you want to copy a diskette using your main (or only) diskette drive. DOS responds with this message:

```
Insert SOURCE Diskette in Drive A:
Press any key when ready...
```

Be sure you have the *source* diskette in drive A:—that is, the diskette to be copied. Double check it. Then you simply press any character key, and DOS will start copying data from the source diskette into memory.

DOS will read as much data as it can from the source diskette into memory; the larger your computer's memory, the more data DOS can read at once. Then DOS displays a message similar to this:

```
Copying 40 tracks
9 Sectors/Track, 2 Side(s)
Insert TARGET Diskette in Drive A:
Press any key when ready...
```

The first two lines are for your information only and vary with the type of diskette you are using. The next two lines appear when DOS is ready to write on the *target* diskette; that is, the one that will contain the copied data. Even if you have two diskette drives, you have to exchange the diskettes like this because the original DISKCOPY command didn't tell DOS to use both drives. You'll learn how to use both drives in the next section.

Now remove the source diskette and install a blank or reusable diskette in drive A:. Be sure to use a target diskette that contains no valuable data, because DOS will completely overwrite it. Also, be very careful not to confuse the two diskettes at this point. When you press a character key, DOS copies the first chunk of data from memory to the target disk, perhaps displaying this message:

```
Formatting while copying
```

This means DISKCOPY is preparing the disk at the same time it copies data.

What happens next depends on the computer's memory size. If DOS could not store the entire contents of the source diskette in memory, it displays:

```
Insert SOURCE Diskette in drive A:
Press any key when ready...
```

You continue exchanging diskettes when requested until the entire diskette has been copied. Once again, be very careful not to confuse the two diskettes as you exchange them. Then DOS says:

```
Copy another diskette (Y/N)?
```

The expression (Y/N)? means DOS is waiting for you to type Y for "yes" or N for "no." Any character except Y or y is interpreted as N. If you want to copy another diskette, type Y and DOS restarts the process. Otherwise, type N; DISKCOPY terminates and you'll see the command prompt.

```
A>DISKCOPY

Insert SOURCE diskette in drive A:

Press any key when ready . . .

Copying 40 tracks
9 Sectors/Track, 2 Side(s)

Insert TARGET diskette in drive A:

Press any key when ready . . .

Formatting while copying


Copy another diskette (Y/N)?N


A>_
```

Figure 1.4. Complete DISKCOPY Interaction

(a) What command causes DOS to copy a diskette?

(b) Identify the phrases that apply to each.

A. Target diskette	1. The diskette to be copied
B. Source diskette	2. A blank diskette or one with unneeded files
	3. Will be completely overwritten

(c) Why might some DISKCOPY messages be different from the ones we've shown here?

- A. Different memory size
- B. Different kind of diskette drive and diskette
- C. Target diskette already formatted
- D. Target diskette is write-protected

(a) *DISKCOPY*
(b) *A—2, 3; B—1*
(c) *All are valid reasons*

If you have two drives that handle the same type of diskette, DISKCOPY is easier than it is with one drive. You type this command:

```
A>DISKCOPY A: B:
```

This tells DOS to copy the diskette from drive A: (the source) to drive B: (the target). DOS responds:

```
Insert SOURCE diskette in drive A:
Insert TARGET diskette in drive B:
Press any key when ready...
```

You insert both diskettes as requested and press a character key. Be extremely careful not to confuse the two disks. Once again, write-protecting the source diskette is a good idea, to prevent the source diskette from being erased if you put it in the wrong drive. DOS makes the complete copy without any more bother. You don't have to exchange any diskettes. Figure 1.5 shows a complete interaction using two drives.

```
A>DISKCOPY A: B:

Insert SOURCE diskette in drive A:

Insert TARGET diskette in drive B:

Press any key to continue . . .

Copying 40 tracks
9 Sectors/Track, 2 Side(s)

Formatting while copying


Copy another diskette (Y/N)? N

A>_
```

Figure 1.5. A Two-drive DISKCOPY

(a) To use DISKCOPY with one diskette drive, what command do you enter?
(b) To use DISKCOPY with two diskette drives, what command do you enter?
(c) True or false? To use DISKCOPY with two diskette drives, both drives must handle the same type of diskette.

(a) DISKCOPY
(b) DISKCOPY A: B:
(c) True

Shutting the System Down

How do you shut the system down again? Turn off the power. You can remove the diskettes either before or after you shut it down. Be sure to store your diskettes carefully.

Some users like to leave the computer on at all times. They think turning it off and on puts more wear and tear on the hardware than just leaving it running. Some turn the computer off whenever they leave it. Others compromise, leaving it on for short absences but turning it off overnight. You'll have to make this decision for yourself. If you decide to leave your system running for several hours unused, turn down the brightness on the monitor so that you don't burn the current message into the screen. You can completely darken the screen with the brightness control or by turning off the monitor power switch (if your computer has one).

(a) True or false? You must remove the disks before you shut off the system unit.
(b) True or false? Floppy disks need to be handled and stored carefully.
(c) If you decide to leave your system running, what should you do to protect your monitor when not using the system?

(a) False—they can be removed either before or after the power is shut off
(b) True
(c) Darken the screen

Exercises

Each chapter in this book ends with exercises. If you have your personal computer and DOS diskettes available, work through these exercises. Hands-on practice is the best way to become comfortable with DOS.

If you don't know how to boot your system, this first exercise is vital, because you have to be able to boot in order to use your computer.

Your system must be set up before you work through these exercises. That is, it must be out of the box and all the cables must be hooked up properly. If your system has not been set up, follow the directions in your hardware manuals.

Make sure you have two blank diskettes on hand, then work through the exercises below.

What You Should Do	*How the Computer Responds*

1. Boot DOS.
a. Put your DOS diskette in drive A:.
b. Turn the power on.
	1. Performs an internal memory check for about a minute. Reads drive A:. Then displays:
	`Current date is date`
	`Enter new date (mm-dd-yy):_`

2. Press Enter to accept the default date.	2. Displays:
	`Current time is time`
	`Enter new time:_`

3. Press Enter to accept the default time.	3. Displays version and copyright information followed by the command prompt: `A>_`
4. Try rebooting. Hold down Ctrl and Alt and press Del.	4. Restarts DOS. (Reads drive A: but no internal memory check.) Then asks for the date.

5. Try entering these dates.
   1/1/21
   1-1-1921

5. Rejects each of these invalid dates with the message:

```
Invalid date
Enter new date (mm-dd-yy):_
```

6. Enter the correct date.

6. Asks for the time.

7. Enter the correct time.

7. Displays the copyright information followed by the command prompt.

8. Make a copy of your DOS diskette(s).
   a. For a one-drive system, enter

   ```
   DISKCOPY
   ```

   For a two-drive system (both drives the same type), enter

   ```
   DISKCOPY A: B:
   ```

8. Guides you through the process of copying your DOS diskette. (You'll be able to hear the drive reading and writing on the diskettes. You'll also see the red lights go on and off.)

   b. Use your DOS diskette as the SOURCE diskette. Just to be safe, write-protect the DOS diskette before you put it in drive A:. Use a blank diskette as the TARGET diskette. (Be sure it isn't write-protected.)

   Eventually displays a message similar to this:

   ```
   Copy another diskette (Y/N)?
   ```

9. If you have two DOS diskettes, type Y so you can copy your other DOS diskette. Use your second DOS diskette as the SOURCE diskette. (Write protect it before you put it in the drive.) Use another blank diskette as your TARGET diskette.

9. Guides you through the process again. Eventually displays:

```
Copy another diskette (Y/N)?
```

10. Type N.

10. Terminates DISKCOPY and displays the command prompt.

11. Attach label(s) to your backup diskette(s). (Write labels *before* you stick them on diskettes so you don't press on the diskettes with a pen.) Put your original DOS diskette(s) in a permanent storage container and use only the working copy or copies from now on.	11. Awaits your next command.
12. Turn off your system. (Do it this time for practice, even if you don't intend to turn off your computer most of the time.)	12. Shuts down.

What If It Doesn't Work?

1. If DOS won't boot, shut everything down, wait a few seconds, then try again. (Double-check: Are you really using the original DOS diskette?) If DOS won't boot a second time, turn the computer off and get help.

2. If DOS booted but didn't ask for the date, you didn't use your original system diskette. Find your original diskette and try again.

3. If DISKCOPY gives you any unexpected messages, your target diskette is probably faulty. Reboot. Then try DISKCOPY again with another target diskette. Be sure it isn't write-protected! If you can't make DISKCOPY work, get help. Don't continue to Chapter 2 without copying your DOS diskette(s).

2

Entering Commands—Basic Techniques

You use DOS programs by typing and entering commands. A typical command might be:

```
DISKCOPY A: B:
```

or

```
DEL JOHNSON.LET
```

The first example creates a complete copy of a diskette. The second asks DOS to delete a disk file named JOHNSON.LET. There are many commands corresponding to the various DOS programs. You'll learn the command details in later chapters. In this chapter, we will cover the general format of all DOS commands, what happens when a DOS command is entered, and some special keys you can use when typing DOS commands.

When you have finished this chapter, you will be able to:

- Identify the location of special keys on the personal computer keyboard
- Identify the control keys that invoke major DOS control functions
- Write a basic DOS command involving a program and a file
- Write DOS commands for files that are not on the default drive
- Use global filespecs
- Briefly describe what happens after a DOS command is entered
- Interpret error messages resulting from DOS commands

Using the Keyboard

Your personal computer keyboard has all the traditional typewriter keys, plus several special ones. If you are used to touch typing, you'll need a little practice to get used to this keyboard, not only because some of the keys are in different places, but also because all are repeating keys. That is, if you hold any key down, it repeats, so you might get DDDDDISKCOPPPY on the screen.

We'll go over the standard keys first and show you where they are on the standard AT keyboard. You'll have to locate them on your keyboard if you have a different one.

Letters: All the letters are in the same relative positions on the personal computer keyboard as they are on a standard typewriter keyboard. Also, each letter has an uppercase and a lowercase form. DOS doesn't care whether you type commands in uppercase or lowercase or even mixed case.

Numbers: The numbers in the top row are also in the same position here as on the standard keyboard, with number 1 included. They are all lowercase. Shifting a number produces a symbol, just as with a typewriter. Some of the symbols may be different from what you're used to. To type the number one, you'll have to use the digit 1 instead of a lowercase L. Both characters may look the same in print, but they're different characters to DOS. The same is true for the digit 0 and the letter O.

Symbols: Many symbols surround the letter keys. Again, most are in familiar positions, but there are also several extra ones, such as the vertical bar (|) and the backslash (\).

Enter: This key starts a new line, just like a carriage return on a typewriter. It is very important in DOS because it tells COMMAND that a command is ready to be processed. Therefore, we call it the *Enter* key, because it "enters" commands into the system. On most keyboards, it is located where the right-hand little finger can reach it and is labeled with a bent arrow (↲). The bent arrow shows the path of the cursor in starting a new line: down one line and over to the left margin. Other keyboards may label this key Enter or Return.

Backspace: This key backs up the cursor one position. In DOS it erases characters as it backs over them and is very useful in correcting errors while typing commands. On most keyboards, the backspace key is located above the Enter key and labeled with a backward arrow (←).

Tab: Tabs are not used in DOS commands, but you may need to use them with your application software. On most keyboards, the Tab key is located to the left of the Q and is labeled ⇆ to show that a lowercase entry jumps the cursor forward (regular tab) and an uppercase entry jumps it backward (backward tab).

Shift: This key selects the uppercase of any key pressed while it is held down, just like the shift key on a typewriter. (You'll learn an exception later.) On most keyboards the two Shift keys are in the familiar positions and are labeled like this: ⇑.

Select the true statements below.

(a) You can type DOS commands in uppercase or lowercase.
(b) DOS does not discriminate between the letter l and the number 1 or the letter O and the number 0.
(c) You press the Enter key to tell DOS that a command is ready to be processed.
(d) DOS commands don't use the Tab key.
(e) You never need the Shift keys with DOS.
(f) The Backspace key is used to make changes while typing DOS commands.

---

a, c, d, f (Shift keys are needed for many symbols, but not for typing commands)

Now that you know where the standard keys are on your keyboard, let's look at the special keys.

Function keys: The *function* keys are a set of ten or more keys that are controlled by software. Therefore, their function changes depending on which program you're using. DOS uses the first six of these keys; you'll learn what they do later. On the AT keyboard, the function keys are located on the left and are labeled F1 through F10. On many keyboards, they are in a separate row above the number keys.

Escape: This is another key that is controlled by software. Most programs use it to cancel whatever is happening, because it is called *Escape*. DOS uses it to abandon a command before it's entered. On the AT keyboard, the Escape key is located above the 7 on the numeric keypad; it's labeled Esc.

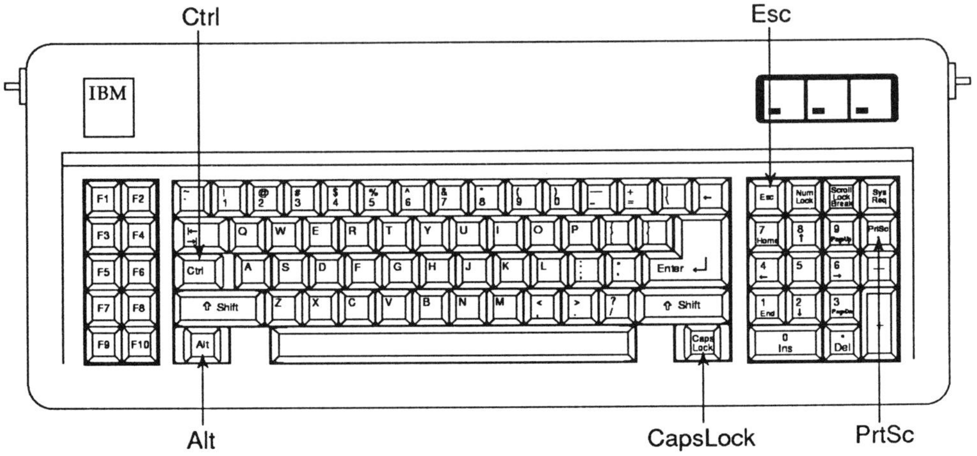

Figure 2.1. Escape, Control, Alternate, CapsLock, and Print Screen Keys

Control: The *Control* key functions like a Shift key because it changes the effects of keys that are pressed while it is held down, generating a *control character* rather than a letter, number, or symbol. What happens when you type a control character depends on the software, but usually the character acts as a command. You'll learn some of the DOS control characters in this chapter.

On the AT keyboard, the Control key is beneath the Tab key where you can reach it with the little finger of your left hand and is labeled Ctrl. When we want you to type a control character, we'll put Ctrl- before the key you should press. Thus, Ctrl-S means to hold down the Control key and press uppercase or lowercase S. Sometimes you will see the Control key represented by a caret, as in ^S.

Alternate key: The *Alternate* key is similar to the Control key because this key also affects the functions of other keys that are pressed simultaneously with it. DOS doesn't use the Alternate key except to reboot, which you have already learned. On the AT keyboard, the Alternate key is located to the left of the Spacebar and is labeled Alt.

CapsLock: The *CapsLock* key locks the letter keys only into uppercase, generating uppercase letters. It saves you from having to hold down the Shift key when you want to type two or more capital letters in a row. It's more useful than the shift lock on a standard typewriter because it affects only the letter keys, not the number and symbol keys.

CapsLock is a *toggle* key: press it once and it's on; it stays on until you press it again. Thus, you don't have to hold it down to use it. On the AT keyboard, this key is located to the right of the Spacebar and is labeled CapsLock. A light comes on when CapsLock is engaged. When CapsLock is on, the action of the Shift key is reversed for the letter keys: Unshifted letters are capitals and shifted letters are lowercase.

Once again, DOS doesn't care whether you use uppercase or lowercase characters in typing commands. However, you'll find the CapsLock key handy when you prepare files.

Print Screen: The *Print Screen* key sends an image of the monitor screen to the printer. It's very handy for documenting what you've been working on, including graphics if your printer can handle them. On the AT this key is the uppercase of the key directly beneath the SysReq key in the upper right corner of the numeric keypad; it is labeled PrtSc. (The lowercase character is an asterisk.) To print your screen, hold down a Shift key and press PrtSc.

Echo Print: *Echo Print* is another function of the PrtSc key. When it's on, everything that appears on the screen is printed at the same time. Every time you enter a command, it's echoed on the printer. Every time DOS displays a message or data, it's echoed on the printer. Echo Print is a toggle; it stays on until you turn it off again. The difference between Print Screen and Echo Print is that Print Screen captures things you've already done while Echo Print captures what you're currently doing. Also, Print Screen captures just one screenful at a time, while Echo Print can capture a single line or many pages. On the AT keyboard, Echo Print is toggled on and off with Ctrl-PrtSc. So Shift-PrtSc gives you a screen print, but Ctrl-PrtSc toggles echo printing on and off. (Ctrl-P also toggles Echo Print.)

Numeric keypad: The *numeric keypad* looks and works much like the keypad of a 10-key calculator. It's much handier than the number row for entering numeric data if you know how to use it. On most keyboards, the numeric keypad is located on the right side. All the number keys except 5 have an uppercase and lowercase character, and the numeric values are uppercase. Thus, you have to use a Shift key to access the numeric keypad; alternatively, you can turn on NumLock, a toggle key located directly above the keypad that locks the keypad into uppercase (like CapsLock does for letter keys). When NumLock is on, the action of the Shift keys is reversed for the numeric keypad.

Pause: When DOS displays a file or a directory containing more than 24 lines, it scrolls the top lines off the screen to make room for the bottom ones. If you're not a fast reader, you might miss the top lines. The *Pause* key halts the display for as long as you want. To resume, press any character key (except the Pause key). On most keyboards, the Pause key is Ctrl-NumLock. (Ctrl-S will also work.) Enhanced keyboards also have a separate Pause key. Later on, you'll learn some other ways to pause the display.

Cursor Movement Keys: These keys move the cursor around when you are typing a file. On most keyboards they are the lowercase characters of various keys on the numeric keypad. The enhanced keyboard has a separate set of cursor movement keys. Only two are used with DOS: the left arrow (←) has the same effect as the Backspace key, and the right arrow (→) is the same as F1, which you'll learn about in Chapter 8.

Insert: This toggle key lets you insert data into an existing line. If *Insert* is on, whatever you type is inserted into the line. If Insert is off, whatever you type overtypes (erases) the existing characters. You'll learn how to use Insert with DOS commands in Chapter 8. On the AT keyboard, Insert is the lowercase version of the 0 (zero) key on the numeric keypad and is labeled Ins. Many keyboards have a separate Insert key.

Delete: The *Delete* key erases the character at the cursor. You'll learn how to use it for typing DOS commands later in this book. For now, continue to use the Backspace key to erase characters. On the AT keyboard, the Delete key is the lowercase of the decimal point key on the numeric keypad, right next to the Insert key; it's labeled Del. Other keyboards have a separate Delete key.

Break: The *Break* key is used to interrupt programs and return to COMMAND. It is similar to reboot, but it doesn't restart DOS, which is nice because an interrupt doesn't turn off NumLock and CapsLock, reset the time and date, and so forth. On the AT keyboard, the Break key is located in the upper right corner, next to SysReq. The top of the key is labeled ScrollLock. You must press Ctrl to make it work. DOS and many other programs also recognize Ctrl-C as a break key.

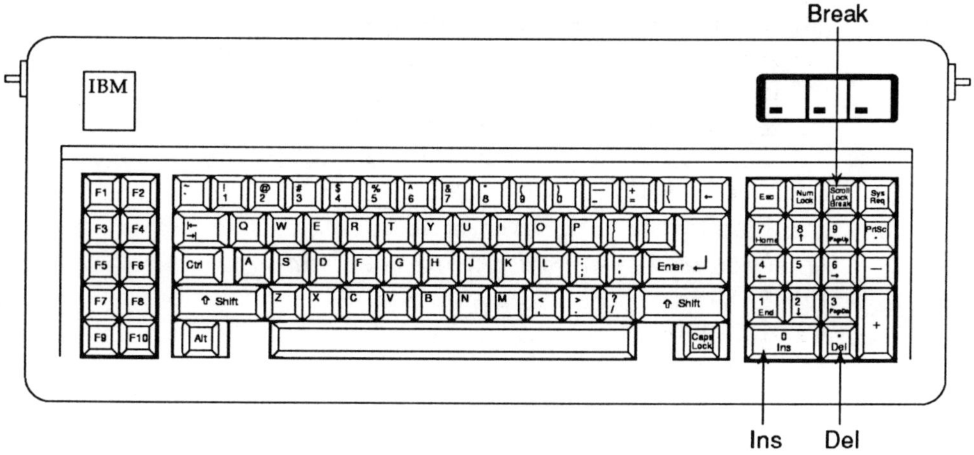

Figure 2.2. Insert, Delete, and Break Keys on the AT Keyboard

(a) How are these keys labeled on your keyboard?

A. Function keys
B. Escape
C. Control
D. Alternate
E. CapsLock
F. Print Screen
G. Numeric keypad
H. Cursor movement
I. Insert
J. Delete
K. Break

(b) What's a toggle key?

A. A key that turns a function on when you press it once and off when you press it a second time
B. A key whose function is software controlled
C. A key that changes the function of other keys

(c) Which keys are not character keys themselves but change the function of character keys when pressed simultaneously?

A. Shift
B. Enter
C. Control
D. Alt
E. Delete

(d) Identify the functions of these keys.

A. Ctrl-Alt-Del	1. Interrupts current program
B. Break	2. Abandons a command
C. Escape	3. Shifts the numeric keypad
	4. Reboots DOS

(a) The correct answers depend on your hardware
(b) A
(c) A, C, D
(d) A—1, 4; B—1; C—2

How to Type a Command

The DOS command prompt must be displayed before you type a command. When you first boot DOS from drive A:, the command prompt looks like this:

```
A>_
```

The cursor is positioned next to the prompt. Later you'll learn various ways to change the prompt, but when you first boot from drive A:, it will look like this. When you type your command, each character appears at the cursor.

As you type a command, the characters are stored in a special keyboard memory area called a buffer. They are not sent to the command processor until you release them by pressing the Enter key.

You might make typing mistakes or change your mind about a command. A few mistakes can be corrected by backspacing and retyping. If there are too many mistakes in the command, the best thing to do is start over. The Escape key eliminates the current line. When you press Escape, a backward slash is displayed on the canceled line, and the cursor moves to a new line. Suppose your display looks like this:

```
A>CPY B;TRX_
```

If you press the Escape key, your display looks like this:

```
A>CPY B;TRX\
  _
```

You can then type a corrected line.

(a) How do you send the line you have just typed to the command processor?
(b) How do you eliminate the line you just typed and start over?
(c) How do you backspace and erase one character in the line you are typing?
(d) Where do you type a DOS command?

(a) Press Enter
(b) Press Escape
(c) Press Backspace
(d) Next to the command prompt (or at the cursor)

The Default Drive

The command prompt tells you two things: the command processor is ready to receive a command, and the default disk drive is A:.

DOS looks for programs and data files on the default disk drive. For example, if A: is the default drive and you enter the command COMP SOURCE1 SOURCE2, DOS looks on drive A: for the COMP program as well as for the two files, SOURCE1 and SOURCE2.

You can change the default drive by entering the desired drive name, including the colon, as a command. If you type

```
B:
```

and press Enter, the command processor responds with this:

```
B>_
```

Now B: is the default drive and the command processor is ready for another command.

(a) Given the following prompt, which is the default drive?

```
B>_
```

(b) Write a command to make the first drive the default drive.
(c) When DOS is booted from drive A:, which default drive is selected for you?

(a) B:
(b) A:
(c) A:

The colon is a critical part of drive selection. If you enter a drivename without a colon, the command processor doesn't know you want to select a drive. It thinks you want to run a program named A, B, or whatever. If it can't find any program with that name, you'll get a message like this:

```
A>B
Bad command or file name
A>_
```

The new prompt indicates the default drive. Because the DOS system doesn't recognize B as a drive name, the A: drive remains the default drive.

If you enter an invalid drive name, you'll get an error message, as in:

```
A>H:
Invalid drive specification
A>_
```

For each example below, tell what happened.

(a)
```
A>B:
B>_
```
(b)
```
A>J:
Invalid drive specification
A>_
```
(c)
```
A>B
Bad command or file name
A>_
```

(a) Drive B: was selected; the new default drive is B:
(b) There is no J: drive and drive A: remains selected
(c) The colon was omitted and drive A: remains selected; also, no program named B exists on drive A:

File Specifiers

Every file on a disk has a unique specifier, often called a *filespec,* with up to four parts. Figure 2.3 shows an example. The first part is the *drivename.* This part of the filespec varies depending on which drive holds the disk. The drivename is not required. You need it only when the desired file isn't on the default drive. If used, the drivename includes the colon.

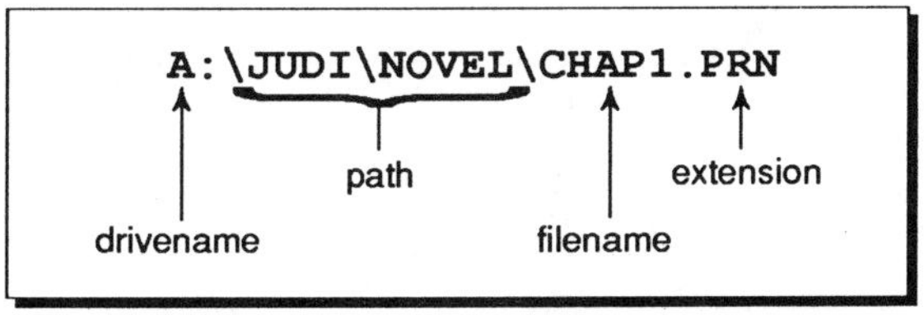

Figure 2.3. The Parts of a Filespec

The second part of a filespec is the *path,* which identifies the subdirectory containing the file. If the path is omitted, DOS looks in the default directory. If your diskettes aren't organized into subdirectories, you can ignore the path. We cover paths in Chapter 5.

The third filespec part is the *filename.* It must have from one to eight characters and is the only required part of the filespec. Most of the filenames you use will look like these examples:

JOHNSFIL	LASTWEEK	INFLIGHT	MEMOS583
X-15	CHAPTER1	OBASKET	T-BILLS

The fourth part of the filespec is the *extension.* If there is one, it has from one to three characters. The extension usually identifies the file's *type,* such as LET for letter, DAT for data, or TST for test. Not every file needs an extension. But if one is used, it is separated from the filename with a period. These filespecs all represent different files:

JOHNS.INT   JOHNS.6   JOHNS

If you type a filename longer than eight characters or an extension longer than three characters, DOS truncates (chops off) the extra characters. Thus, WEDNESDAYS.MENUS will be read as WEDNESDA.MEN.

The combination of filename and extension must be unique in each directory. Do not put spaces within the filespec.

Indicate whether each name below is a valid DOS filespec. If not, state why it is invalid.
(a) A:FILE6
(b) FILE6.SIX
(c) FILESIXTEEN
(d) A

(a) Valid
(b) Valid
(c) Valid, but will be read as FILESIXT
(d) Valid, but could be confused with drive A: by people

You can create filenames and extensions for files as needed. But DOS recognizes certain extensions and may treat them in a predetermined way. Here are a few of the standard extensions:

BAT a batch file containing a set of DOS commands
COM one kind of external program
EXE another kind of external program

DOS has other standard extensions also, such as BAS for BASIC programs.

Many files will have extensions needed by your software packages. For example, you may have an inventory program that will work only on a file with the extension INV. You may have a mailing label program that creates a file with the extension LAB. Many of your filespecs will have no extensions because none are needed.

Indicate whether each extension below is valid or invalid. If invalid, tell why.
(a) COM
(b) PRACTICE
(c) DOC
(d) 6X

(a) Valid
(b) Valid, but will be read as PRA

(c) Valid
(d) Valid

Each filespec must be unique. This means you can have only one file named TEXT1.DOC in a particular directory. Within one directory, you can have several files named TEXT1 if they all have different extensions. You may also have several files with the same extension as long as each has a different filename.

Which statements are true?
(a) Every filename must be unique
(b) Every filename.extension combination must be unique
(c) Every filespec must be unique
(d) Within one directory, every filename.extension combination must be unique

---

c, d

When you are creating a new file, make its name as meaningful as possible. You'll be glad later that you did. Imagine trying to find the file containing last year's income tax figures when your directory contains these filespecs: BC32R.C45, XT10BOB.FGP, MORE.FGP, and WKD. Think how much better these names are: CALTAX89, FEDTAX89, BUDGET89, and BALANCE.

You're limited to an eight-character filename, but you'd be surprised what you can do with eight characters. Try it.

(a) Create a filename (no extension) for the outline of your new novel, which is called *The Gray Psovrath.*
(b) Create a filename for your grocery list.
(c) Create a filename for your birthday card mailing list.

Of course, there are many correct answers to this exercise. Here are some suggestions:
(a) OUTLINE, GRAYOUT, PSOVRATH

(b) *GROCLIST, GROCERYS*
(c) *BDAYLIST, BCARDS, CARDLIST*

Many DOS commands include filespecs. For example, the TYPE command displays the contents of a specified file on the monitor. To display the OUTLINE file, you'd enter:

```
A>TYPE OUTLINE
```

A filespec must be complete enough for DOS to find the file. If the file is really named OUTLINE.F85, then you must enter

```
A>TYPE OUTLINE.F85
```

even if it's the only OUTLINE file in the directory.

If the file you want isn't in the current directory, then you must include the path in the filespec:

```
A>TYPE \JUDI\NOVEL\OUTLINE.F85
```

If the file is not on the default drive, then you must include the drivename in the filespec (or change the default drive):

```
A>TYPE C:OUTLINE.F85
```

You're going to study tree-structured directories in detail in Chapter 5. Until then, we won't ask you to use any paths.

If the file you specify isn't in the drive and directory you specify or imply, DOS responds:

```
File not found
```

This could mean you misspelled the filename, used the wrong extension, specified or implied the wrong drivename, or specified or implied the wrong directory.

(a) Write a command to type the file named GRADUATE. It's on drive A: in the default directory. This is the current prompt:
A>_

(b) Suppose GRADUATE is located in the default directory on drive B: instead.

```
A>_
```

(c) Suppose its name is GRADUATE.LST instead. (It's still on drive B:.)

```
A>_
```

(d) Suppose you have this interaction:

```
A>TYPE LOSTDOGS
File not found
A>_
```

What could be wrong?

A. The file you want might not be called LOSTDOGS.
B. LOSTDOGS might have an extension.
C. LOSTDOGS might not be on drive A:.
D. LOSTDOGS might be in another directory.
E. All of the above.

(a) `A>TYPE GRADUATE`
(b) `A>TYPE B:GRADUATE`
(c) `A>TYPE B:GRADUATE.LST`
(d) *E*

Global File Specifiers

A filespec is specific when it refers to a single file. All of the filespec examples used so far have been specific. However you can use a *global* filespec to refer to several files. One way of specifying a global filespec is to use an asterisk for either the filename or the extension. For instance, *.COM refers to all files in the directory that have extension .COM—no matter what the filename is.

Label the filespecs below as specific or global.

(a) B:INVENT.DEC
(b) INVENT.*
(c) A:*.DEC
(d) INVENT.DEC

(a) Specific
(b) Global
(c) Global
(d) Specific

A complete filespec may include a drivename and path as well as a filename and extension. Either the filename or the extension, or both, can be replaced with an asterisk. The asterisk means that any combination of characters will do. Neither the drivename nor path can be replaced with an asterisk.

Match these filespecs with their descriptions.

(a) *.PRN	1. Invalid filespec
(b) JOBTIME.*	2. Refers to all files in the default directory with extension PRN
(c) *:JOBTIME.PRN	3. Refers to all files in the default directory with filename JOBTIME
(d) *:*.*	4. Refers to all files on all disk drives
(e) *.*	5. Refers to all files in the default directory
(f) B:*.COM	6. Refers to all files in the default directory with extension COM
	7. None of these

(a) 2
(b) 3
(c) 1
(d) 1
(e) 5
(f) 7 (It refers to all files on drive B: with extension COM)

Write filespecs that refer to the files described below.
(a) All files that have PAYROLL as the filename
(b) All files that have COM as the extension

(c) The file with extension COB and filename PAYROLL
(d) All files on the disk

---

*(a) PAYROLL.**
*(b) *.COM*
(c) PAYROLL.COB
*(d) *.**

You have seen how the asterisk indicates a global filespec. The asterisk indicates any number of ambiguous characters—up to eight for the filename or three for the extension. Thus PAY*.COM refers to all files with extension COM and filenames starting with PAY.

You can also use a question mark (?) as a character in a global filespec. The question mark indicates just one ambiguous character. The reference ?TEST.DAT would match ATEST.DAT, BTEST,DAT, and CTEST.DAT, but it would not match NEWTEST.DAT or ALLTEST.DAT.

To answer the following questions, assume that your default disk contains these files:

PAYROLLS.COM
PAYROLL1.DAT
PAYROLL2.DAT
PAYTAXES.COM
PAYTAXES.DAT
PAYROLLS.COB
PAYTAXES.COB

(a) Name any files that match PAYROLL?.DAT
(b) Name any files that match PAY?????.COM
(c) Name any files that match PAYTAXES.CO?

(a) PAYROLL1.DAT and PAYROLL2.DAT
(b) PAYROLLS.COM and PAYTAXES.COM
(c) PAYTAXES.COM and PAYTAXES.COB

The question mark can be used to set any position in a filename or extension to refer to any character. The reference X?Z.* refers to any three-character filename that begins with X and ends with Z, no matter what the extension is. These files are all included:

XYZ
XYZ.TEM
X2Z.PRN
XAZ.B

Suppose a disk contains these files:

D330T1.WS
D330B1.WS
D330C1.WS
D331T1.WST
D331B1.WST
D330C1.TWS
COPY.COM
WS.COM

Write filespecs to refer to the groups of files indicated below.
(a) All files whose filenames end with T1
(b) All files whose filenames include 330
(c) All files with extension WS and filename ending with C1

(a) D33?T1. or ????T1.* (You can't use *T1.*)*
*(b) ?330??.**
(c) ????C1.WS

Under DOS, the filename has eight characters while the extension has three characters. A blank is considered a specific character. The filespec COMP.COM is really COMP~~bbbb~~.COM where ~~b~~ indicates a blank. The filespec TESTDATA is really TESTDATA.~~bbb~~.

If you use the global specifier P?.COM, you have really specified P?~~bbbbbb~~.COM. A matching filename will have blanks in positions 3 through 8; that is, it must be no more than two characters long. These filespecs would match: P1.COM, PT.COM, and P.COM. But the filespecs PIG.COM and

PAYROLLS.COM would not match. However they would if you specified P*.COM.

Suppose a disk contains these files:

(1) XYZ.A	(5) XYZ	(9) X006.A
(2) XYY.A	(6) XYX	(10) X007.A
(3) XYY.B	(7) WALL	(11) X008.B
(4) XYX.B	(8) ROOM	(12) X009.C

Which files are included by each filespec below? (Use the file numbers instead of the names.)
(a) ???.*
(b) ??X.*
(c) *.
(d) X???????.A
(e) X???.B
(f) X??.B

(a) 1, 2, 3, 4, 5, 6
(b) 4, 6
(c) 5, 6, 7, 8
(d) 1, 2, 9, 10
(e) 3, 4, 11
(f) 3, 4

In global filespecs the asterisk is really an abbreviation that fills the rest of the filename or extension with question marks. Look at these examples:

TE*.PRN is equivalent to TE??????.PRN
TE*.* is equivalent to TE??????.???

Characters following an asterisk are ignored. *EE.COM is treated the same as *.COM or ????????.COM. The asterisk causes the rest of the filename or extension to be filled with question marks, which will create the global filespec.

With some commands, if a filename ends with an asterisk and there is no extension, then a global extension is assumed. That is, DOS* is the same as

DOS*.*. A single asterisk is the same as *.*. To limit a filespec to files with no extension, include a period after the asterisk in the filename. For example, DOS*. means all files that start with DOS and have no extension, which may include fewer files than the DOS* filespec. The effect of *. is different in some commands. The example above is true with the DIR command, but not with other commands such as COPY and DEL.

When naming your files, keep global filespecs in mind. Give a group of related files filespecs that can be accessed globally. For example, a set of files containing student test scores from five different tests might be called TSCORES1, TSCORES2, TSCORES3, TSCORES4, and TSCORES5.

(1) TRY	(10) PLOT.COM	(19) CORRES.XX
(2) PRACTICE	(11) EDLIN.COM	(20) CORRES.DK3
(3) THIS.NOW	(12) COPE.COM	(21) BILLING.DT
(4) ONE.CH	(13) INVOICE.XX	(22) SUPPLIES.DT
(5) TWO.CH	(14) INVOICE.WI	(23) PROGRAM.COB
(6) THREE.CH	(15) INVOICE.DK	(24) PROGRAM.REL
(7) FOUR.CH	(16) CORRES.WI	(25) PROGRAM.PRN
(8) FIVE.CH	(17) CORRES.DK1	(26) PROGRAM.DAT
(9) INTRO.CH	(18) CORR.DK2	(27) PROGRAM.COM

Figure 2.4. Sample List of Files

The files in Figure 2.4 are numbered for your convenience. Indicate which files match each filespec below.

(a) *.
(b) T??.*
(c) T*.CH
(d) C*.*
(e) C*.D*
(f) *.WI
(g) *ES.D*
(h) P*.C*
(i) P* (on the DIR command)
(j) P*.

(a) 1, 2
(b) 1, 5
(c) 5, 6
(d) 12, 16, 17, 18, 19, 20
(e) 17, 18, 20
(f) 14, 16
*(g) 15, 17, 18, 20, 21, 22, 26 (Don't forget that DOS ignores characters following *)*
(h) 10, 23, 27
(i) 2, 10, 23, 24, 25, 26, 27
(j) 2

DOS Command Processing

A DOS command generally takes this form:

programname switches operands

The *programname* tells DOS what program you want to use. An *operand* is something that's operated on. The operands indicate what you want the program to work on. Frequently the operands are filespecs, as in:

```
TYPE JOHNSON.LET
```

or drivenames, as in:

```
DISKCOPY A: B:
```

Many commands have *switches*, which select optional features of the desired program. Switches usually begin with a slash, as in:

```
DIR /W /P
```

The /W asks for a "wide" directory and the /P asks for "paging" in the directory display. (Chapter 3 explains these terms.)

What happens when you enter a command? First, DOS searches for the program you named as program. If it's an internal program, it's already a part of the command processor. It was loaded into memory when the system was booted. Otherwise DOS looks for the appropriate file on the specified drive. (If no drive is specified, the default drive is assumed.)

If DOS can't find the correct program, the command processor returns an error message—`Bad command or file name`. Following is a sample interaction in which we mistyped the word DEL:

```
A>DELL INVENTY.DAT
Bad command or file name
A>_
```

This message means the system can't recognize the programname. Either we misspelled it or the appropriate file is not on the default drive in the default directory.

The DOS prompt is then repeated, as shown in the above example, so that we can enter another command.

Even though this error message mentions the filename, a different message is used when DOS can't locate an operand file. You'll see that message later. `Bad command or file name` always means DOS can't find the specified program.

(a) When you enter a DOS command, what's the first thing the command processor does?

(b) Suppose you have the following interaction:

```
A>TYP JOHNSON.PRN
Bad command or file name
A>_
```

What could be wrong?

A. TYP is not an internal command.

B. JOHNSON.PRN is not a file in the default subdirectory on drive A:.

C. TYP is not a program in the default subdirectory on drive A:.

(a) DOS searches for the programname program

(b) A, C

If the program you want to use isn't on the default drive, you can attach a drivename to the programname:

d:programname

For example, suppose drive A: is the default drive, and you want to use a program named CAROUSEL, which is in the default directory on drive B:. You could enter:

```
A>B:CAROUSEL
```

This causes DOS to look on drive B: for the CAROUSEL program. When you do this, drive A: remains the default drive, so it's different from entering

```
A>B:
B>CAROUSEL
```

in which case B: becomes the default drive.

Suppose the CAROUSEL program requires a filespec operand. If you enter

```
A>B:CAROUSEL JUNE90
```

DOS looks for the CAROUSEL program on drive B: and the JUNE90 file on drive A:, since A: is still the default. If you enter:

```
A>CAROUSEL B:JUNE90
```

DOS looks for the program file on drive A: and the JUNE90 file on drive B:. If you enter:

```
A>B:
B>CAROUSEL JUNE90
```

DOS looks for both the program and the file on drive B:, since B: is the default.

All this pertains only to external programs. Internal programs are located in memory, not on disks, and therefore drivenames and paths make no sense with them. If you attach a drivename or path to an internal command, DOS tells you `Bad command or file name.`

(a) Where will DOS look for the FOOTNOTE program in the following command?

```
A>C:FOOTNOTE QUARTER.REP
```

Where will it look for the QUARTER.REP file?

(b) In these commands, where will DOS look for the STARTOUT program?

```
A>C:
C>STARTOUT VARIBLES
```

Where will it look for the VARIBLES file?

(c) Write a command to use the TYPE program (internal) on the GOODLIST file (on drive C:).

```
A>_
```

(d) Write a command to use the SPELLING program (on drive B:) and the CHAPTER1 file (on drive A:).

```
A>_
```

(e) If CHAPTER1 is also on drive B:, how would you write the command?

```
A>_
```

(a) Drive C:; drive A:

(b) Drive C:; drive C:

(c) `A>TYPE C:GOODLIST`

(d) `A>B:SPELLING CHAPTER1`

(e) `A>B:SPELLING B:CHAPTER1`

or

```
A>B:
B>SPELLING CHAPTER1
```

If the command processor successfully locates your external program on the specified disk, it reads the program from the disk into memory. You can hear this happening. If it's a short program, it could take less than a second to load. Longer programs may take five seconds or longer.

DOS also stores any switches and operands in an area of memory where the external program can find them. Control of the computer is then given to the program.

What happens next depends entirely on the program. Most programs check the switches and operands and display error messages if they aren't correct. You'll be learning more about this when you study the internal and external programs later on. If the switches and operands are okay, the program may or may not display any messages. Many programs run perfectly without sending any messages to the user. Look at the example in Figure 2.5. During the five-second wait, the SORT program was located, loaded, and executed. It sorted the file named LEFTDATA and created the file named SORTDATA. Then SORT terminated, displaying no messages.

```
A>SORT <LEFTDATA >SORTDATA

        (five second wait)

A>_
```

Figure 2.5. No Message is a Good Message

When a program terminates, the command processor resumes control. You'll know when this occurs because you'll see the DOS command prompt. The terminated program is finished. Your next command may refer to any program, even the same program again.

(a) Following is a typical DOS interaction.

```
A>MERGE B A
(three-second wait)
A>_
```

Briefly describe what happened during the three-second wait. (MERGE is not an internal program.)

(b) Here's another interaction:

```
A>TYPE INVENTY.DAT
File not found
A>_
```

What program sent the error message—DOS or TYPE?
Can you enter a DOS command now?

(a) *DOS searched for and loaded the MERGE program, passed the operands to it, and gave it control; the MERGE program ran and terminated, and DOS resumed control*
(b) *TYPE; yes*

Exercises

To review this chapter, you're going to practice using a few very simple commands: VER shows you the version number of DOS and DIR shows you the directory of a disk. You'll also practice using some of your special keys.

What You Should Do	*How the Computer Responds*
1. Boot with your DOS work diskette in drive A:.	1. Boots and displays the command prompt.
2. If you have a drive B: and a second DOS diskette, put the second DOS diskette in drive B:. If you have a drive B: but only one DOS diskette, put any diskette in drive B:. If you don't have a drive B:, skip this step.	2. Awaits your next command.
3. Enter this command: `A>VER` You can use either uppercase or lowercase characters.	3. Displays a message similar to this: `MS-DOS Version 3.30`
4. Enter this command: `A>DIR` Don't be surprised when you get a lot of data back.	4. Displays the directory of the diskette in drive A:.

5. Try your Print Screen function.
   a. Make sure your printer is on.
   b. Hold down a Shift key and press PrtSc.
   c. Check your printout. Does it exactly match the screen? It should.

5. Copies the data from your monitor screen to your printer.

6. Now try Echo Print.
   a. Hold down Control and press PrtSc once. Don't hold PrtSc down for longer than a second or it may start repeating and you'll be toggling Echo Print on and off unintentionally.
   b. Now enter `DIR` again.

6. Displays *and prints* the directory. Notice how much longer DIR takes when echo printing is on. That's because printers are much slower than monitors.

7. Try the Pause function.
   a. With Echo Print still on, enter `DIR` again.
   b. Suspend the display by holding down Control and pressing NumLock.
   c. Resume the display by pressing any character key.

7.
   a. Displays and prints the directory.
   b. Pauses the display. Your printer might empty its memory before pausing.
   c. Resumes the display and Echo Print.

8. Turn off Echo Print (Ctrl-PrtSc again). Enter `VER` again to see that it is off.

8. DOS turns off Echo Print, but you won't see any result yet.

If you have a B: drive, continue with this exercise. If not, turn off your system if you like and go on to Chapter 3.

9. Switch to B: drive by entering B:.

9. Displays this prompt:

```
B>_
```

10. Now enter `DIR` again.

10. Displays the directory of the diskette in drive B:.

What If It Doesn't Work?

1. If your system won't boot, go back to Chapter 1 and follow the instructions in the exercise there.

2. If VER doesn't work, make sure you have a command prompt and that you typed the three letters VER and pressed the Enter key. However, if you happen to be working with a DOS version earlier than 2.0, then VER doesn't work; skip VER and go on. (You might want to upgrade to a more up-to-date version.)

3. If DIR doesn't work, make sure you booted with your DOS work diskette. It should have many files in its directory. Put a diskette in drive B: if you have one and try DIR B:. Keep trying until you can make DIR work.

4. If the print functions won't work, make sure your printer is (a) plugged in; (b) turned on; (c) cabled to the computer; and (d) on-line with the computer. The printer might have a button/light that says "on-line" or "select"; it should be on. If your printer has a button/light that says "local," it should be off. If you can't make DOS talk to your printer, get help.

5. If you have trouble switching to drive B:, be sure you put a colon after the drivename.

3

Managing Diskettes

Even if your system has a fixed disk, you must spend some time working with diskettes. This chapter covers all the DOS commands that pertain to diskette management. Most of these commands also apply to the fixed disk, as you'll learn later.

When you have finished this chapter, you will be able to:

- Use DIR's options to view various types of directories
- Use FORMAT to prepare a disk
- Use VOL to view a disk's name
- Use LABEL to change a disk's label
- Use SYS to make a preformatted disk bootable
- Handle problems with DISKCOPY
- Use DISKCOMP to compare two diskettes
- Interpret messages resulting from the above operations

Viewing the Diskette Directory

DIR causes a disk directory to be displayed. The basic form of the command is DIR with no operands, as you used it at the end of Chapter 2. This causes the complete default directory to be displayed, as shown in Figure 3.1.

```
 Volume in drive A is EXERCISE1
 Directory of  A:\

COMMAND  COM    25276   7-24-87  12:00a
4201     CPI    17089   7-24-87  12:00a
5202     CPI      459   7-24-87  12:00a
ANSI     SYS     1647   7-24-87  12:00a
APPEND   EXE     5794   7-24-87  12:00a
ASSIGN   COM     1530   7-24-87  12:00a
ATTRIB   EXE    10656   7-24-87  12:00a
CHKDSK   COM     9819   7-24-87  12:00a
COMP     COM     4183   7-24-87  12:00a
COUNTRY  SYS    11254   7-24-87  12:00a
DISKCOMP COM     5848   7-24-87  12:00a
DISKCOPY COM     6264   7-24-87  12:00a
DISPLAY  SYS    11259   7-24-87  12:00a
DRIVER   SYS     1165   7-24-87  12:00a
EXE2BIN  EXE     3050   7-24-87  12:00a
FASTOPEN EXE     3888   7-24-87  12:00a
FDISK    COM    48919   7-24-87  12:00a
FIND     EXE     6403   7-24-87  12:00a
FORMAT   COM    11671   7-24-87  12:00a
GRAFTABL COM     6136   7-24-87  12:00a
GRAPHICS COM    13943   7-24-87  12:00a
JOIN     EXE     9612   7-24-87  12:00a
KEYB     COM     9041   7-24-87  12:00a
LABEL    COM     2346   7-24-87  12:00a
MODE     COM    15440   7-24-87  12:00a
MORE     COM      282   7-24-87  12:00a
NLSFUNC  EXE     3029   7-24-87  12:00a
PRINT    COM     8995   7-24-87  12:00a
RECOVER  COM     4268   7-24-87  12:00a
SELECT   COM     4132   7-24-87  12:00a
SORT     EXE     1946   7-24-87  12:00a
SUBST    EXE    10552   7-24-87  12:00a
SYS      COM     4725   7-24-87  12:00a
FLAW1    MAP       55   3-16-89   6:59p
AUTOEXEC BAT      178   3-05-89   5:52p
       35 File(s)      3072 bytes free
```

Figure 3.1. Sample Directory Listing

The first line in Figure 3.1 gives the diskette's label. In this example, it is MS330PP01. You'll learn how to label a diskette later in this chapter. The second line shows the name of the directory being displayed. In this case, it is A:\, the only directory on drive A:.

The body of the directory lists files. The filename is in columns 1 through 8 and the extension is in columns 10 through 12. The dot that precedes the extension is not displayed. Thus, the first file in the directory shown in Figure 3.1 is 4201.CPI and the second file is 5202.CPI.

The next field in the directory shows the number of bytes in the file. The next two fields show the data and time the file was last changed. These reflect the values of the date and time fields the last time something was written in the file. The directory in the figure is of a DOS system diskette. That's why most of the files have the same date and time.

The last line of the display tells you the number of files that were listed and the number of bytes available on the diskette for storing more files.

DIR displays only the current directory, which might not include all files on the diskette.

(a) Write a command to get a full directory on the diskette in the default drive.

```
A>_
```

(b) In the sample directory in Figure 3.1, which is the largest file?
(c) Which is the smallest?
(d) How many files are listed?
(e) Can you tell from the directory when files were created?
(f) Which of the following is true?
  A. DIR always lists all files on a diskette
  B. DIR lists only one directory or subdirectory

(a) `A>DIR`
(b) FDISK.COM
(c) FLAW1.MAP
(d) 35
(e) No—you can only tell when they were last altered
(f) B

You've seen the basic format of the DIR command; now look at some variations. If you want to display the directory of a disk in a nondefault drive, you can add a drivename to the command, as in:

```
A>DIR B:
```

The above command displays the current directory of the diskette in drive B:.

If the directory requires more than 24 lines, you can display it one screenful at a time by adding /P (for page) to the command, as in:

```
A>DIR /P
```

Figure 3.2 shows what the screen looks like when you use the /P switch. DOS displays a screenful of directory entries and a line at the bottom that says `Strike a key when ready...` When you press any character key, the next part of the directory is displayed.

```
4201      CPI    17089  7-24-87  12:00a
5202      CPI      459  7-24-87  12:00a
ANSI      SYS     1647  7-24-87  12:00a
APPEND    EXE     5794  7-24-87  12:00a
ASSIGN    COM     1530  7-24-87  12:00a
ATTRIB    EXE    10656  7-24-87  12:00a
CHKDSK    COM     9819  7-24-87  12:00a
COMMAND   COM    25276  7-24-87  12:00a
COMP      COM     4183  7-24-87  12:00a
COUNTRY   SYS    11254  7-24-87  12:00a
DISKCOMP  COM     5848  7-24-87  12:00a
DISKCOPY  COM     6264  7-24-87  12:00a
DISPLAY   SYS    11259  7-24-87  12:00a
DRIVER    SYS     1165  7-24-87  12:00a
EDLIN     COM     7495  7-24-87  12:00a
EXE2BIN   EXE     3050  7-24-87  12:00a
FASTOPEN  EXE     3888  7-24-87  12:00a
FDISK     COM    48919  7-24-87  12:00a
FIND      EXE     6403  7-24-87  12:00a
FORMAT    COM    11671  7-24-87  12:00a
GRAFTABL  COM     6136  7-24-87  12:00a
GRAPHICS  COM    13943  7-24-87  12:00a
JOIN      EXE     9612  7-24-87  12:00a
Strike a key when ready . . .
```

Figure 3.2. First Page of a Paged Directory

If you don't need to see the size, date, and time, you can get a long directory in one screen by adding /W (for "wide") to the command, as in:

```
A>DIR /W
```

The /W switch causes the filespecs to be displayed five across, as shown in Figure 3.3.

/W and /P can be used in combination with operands, such as drive-names. Thus, you might enter:

```
A>DIR /P B:
```

This command produces a directory of the B: drive, pausing after every screenful.

For directories that contain more than 125 entries, you can use /W and /P together, in either order.

```
A>DIR /W

 Volume in drive A is MS330PP01
 Directory of  A:\

4201     CPI     5202     CPI     ANSI     SYS     APPEND   EXE     ASSIGN   COM
ATTRIB   EXE     CHKDSK   COM     COMMAND  COM     COMP     COM     COUNTRY  SYS
DISKCOMP COM     DISKCOPY COM     DISPLAY  SYS     DRIVER   SYS     EDLIN    COM
EXE2BIN  EXE     FASTOPEN EXE     FDISK    COM     FIND     EXE     FORMAT   COM
GRAFTABL COM     GRAPHICS COM     JOIN     EXE     KEYB     COM     LABEL    COM
MODE     COM     MORE     COM     NLSFUNC  EXE     PRINT    COM     RECOVER  COM
SELECT   COM     SORT     EXE     SUBST    EXE     SYS      COM     FLAW1    MAP
       35 File(s)      4096 bytes free

A>_
```

Figure 3.3. A Wide Directory

The location of switches in most commands is not important. You can put them before or after operands. (They must follow the command name, however.) You can put spaces around them or not, as you wish. All the following are legitimate commands.

```
A>DIR/P B:
A>DIR B:/P
A>DIR B: /P
A>DIR /P B:
```

(a) Write a command to obtain a directory of the diskette in drive B:.

```
A>_
```

(b) Change your above command so the directory entries will be abbreviated and displayed five across.

```
A>_
```

(c) Write a command to display a directory of the default drive, one screenful at a time.

```
A>_
```

(d) Which of the following commands are valid?

A. `A>DIR/P B:`
B. `A>DIR /W B:`
C. `A>DIR B: /P`
D. `A>DIR B:/W`
E. `A:>W/DIR B:`

(a) `A>DIR B:`
(b) `A>DIR /W B:` *(The /W can appear before or after B:.)*
(c) `A>DIR /P`
(d) A, B, C, and D; E is invalid because DIR must come first.

So far you have been dealing with full diskette directories. You can get a partial directory by using such filespecs as DIR COPY.COM or DIR BASIC*.*.

Suppose you want to find out the size of a particular file. You don't have to display the entire diskette directory. You can ask for the directory entry of that file only, as in:

```
A>DIR COMMAND.COM
Volume in drive A is MASTERDOS
Directory of A:\

COMMAND   COM   25276   7-24-87   12:00a
        1 File(s)      4096 bytes free
A>_
```

Suppose you want to find out what program (.EXE) files are on the current directory. You could use a global filespec, as in:

```
A>DIR *.EXE
```

You can even get the directory of a group of files with the same filename and different extensions by specifying just the filename, as in:

```
A>DIR B:LOCKMARK
 Volume in drive B is LOCKSMITH
 Directory of B:\

LOCKMARK DAT          631      5-10-89      3:14p
LOCKMARK              387      5-10-89      3:15p
LOCKMARK ASM         2485      5-10-89      3:15a
        3 File(s)           10310 bytes free
A>_
```

/P and /W can be used with filespecs, although they are rarely needed when you limit the directory. If there's no diskette in the specified drive, you'll see this message:

```
Not ready error reading drive x
Abort, Retry, Fail?_
```

This message (or an earlier one that uses Ignore instead of Fail) appears whenever you attempt to access an empty drive. You must respond with a single letter: A for abort, R for retry, or F for fail (or I for ignore). If you select F or I, DOS ignores the error and attempts to continue processing; this is not the proper choice when there is no diskette in a drive. Either select A for abort, which returns you to the command prompt where you can fix the situation, or put the correct diskette in the drive and select R for retry.

If no files exist in the directory, or no file matches the specified filespec, DOS tells you `File not found`. Suppose you are searching for a file called BUDGET90.GRP. You're not sure which diskette it's on. Place the first diskette in drive B: and enter DIR B:BUDGET90.GRP.

If the file is not there, you will see an interaction like this:

```
A>DIR B:BUDGET90.GRP
 Volume in drive B is INVENTORY
 Directory of B:\

File not found

A>_
```

When you reach the correct diskette, you will see:

```
A>DIR B:BUDGET90.GRP
 Volume in drive B is INVENTORY
 Directory of B:\

BUDGET90 GRP        4509    12-11-89  12:05p
        1 File(s)          69456 bytes free

A>_
```

Suppose you want to find out whether the diskette in drive B: is blank. You could ask to see the complete directory, as in:

```
A>DIR B:
 Volume in drive B has no label
 Directory of B:\

File not found

A>_
```

You can see that the root directory is listed. It contains no files (except perhaps the hidden files). It also contains no subdirectories, since none were listed. Therefore, the diskette is completely empty.

If the diskette has not yet been formatted, you'll see this message:

```
General Failure error reading drive B
Abort, Retry, Fail? _
```

This message means there is no root directory on the diskette.

(a) Write a command to find out the date that A:SYMBOL.DAT was last altered.
A>_

(b) Write a command to find out the size of B:CANCEL.COM.
A>_

(c) Write a command to list all files that have the filename ROBDOG on the B: drive.
A>_

(d) Write a command to find out the names, sizes, and dates of all COM files on drive A:.

```
A>_
```

(e) Suppose you have the following interaction:

```
A>DIR LINK.COM
 Volume in drive A is PGM SUPPORT
 Directory of A:\

File not found

A>_
```

What's wrong?

(f) Suppose you have the following interaction:

```
A>DIR
Not ready error reading drive A
Abort, Retry, Fail? _
```

What's wrong?

Suppose you forgot to attach a stick-on label to a diskette. You don't know what's on it, if anything. You place the diskette in drive B: and enter the command DIR B:. What would each of the following messages tell you?

(g) `File not found`

(h) `General Failure error reading drive B:`
`Abort, Retry, Fail? _`

(a) `A>DIR SYMBOL.DAT`
(b) `A>DIR B:CANCEL.COM`
(c) `A>DIR B:ROBDOG`
(d) `A>DIR *.COM`
(e) There is no file named LINK.COM on drive A:
(f) Drive A: does not contain a diskette
(g) The diskette is formatted but blank
(h) The diskette is not formatted

Here's the complete format of the DIR command:

Format (internal):
DIR [d:][filespec] [/P] [/W]

DIR is an internal command, so it's available whenever DOS is running. It displays the complete default directory of the default drive unless you limit it. In the format, square brackets ([ ]) indicate optional operands and switches. The d: operand specifies a drive. The filespec operand limits the listing to the specified file(s). The /P switch displays one screenful at a time. The /W switch displays five filespecs across. Be sure to use a colon when entering a drivename. Consider this interaction:

```
A>DIR B
 Volume in drive A is MS330PP01
 Directory of A:\

File not found

A>_
```

The message tells you there is no file named B in the default directory on drive A:. It doesn't tell you anything about the diskette in drive B:. You can save time by checking the first two lines of the directory listing to confirm the diskette and directory you have accessed.

(a) Write a command to display all files on drive B:, five across.
A>_
(b) Write a command to display all files on the default drive, pausing after each screenful.
A>_
(c) What does this interaction tell you?

```
A>DIR C
 Volume in drive A is MS330PP01
 Directory of A:\

File not found

A>_
```

A. There are no files on drive C:
B. There's no file named C on drive A:
C. There are no files in the current directory of drive C:

(a) `A>DIR B: /W` *or* `DIR B:*.* /W`
(b) `A>DIR /P`
(c) *B*

Preparing New Diskettes

The FORMAT program formats a disk. You cannot use any disk with the personal computer until it has been formatted. You can also reformat used disks at any time. However, reformatting erases all the data on the disk.

Suppose you buy a new box of diskettes. What program would you use to prepare them for use with your personal computer?

FORMAT

To format a diskette without using any options, you can enter this simple command:

```
FORMAT d:
```

You must specify a drivename, indicated by d: above. You will be told to put the target diskette in the specified drive. FORMAT always gives you a chance to install the desired diskette first. That's a safety measure to prevent accidental erasure. The message looks like this:

```
Insert new diskette for drive d
and strike ENTER when ready_
```

After you do so, you will see this message:

```
Head:   x Cylinder:   x
```

You will hear the drive working and see the numbers (indicated by x above) change in the message. (Earlier versions of DOS provide a different message.) It can take quite a while (several minutes) to format a large capacity diskette, so be patient. When the operation is complete, you will see this message:

```
Format complete

    xxxxxxx bytes total disk space
    yyyyyyy bytes in bad sectors
    zzzzzzz bytes available on disk
```

The last three lines give the status of the disk. The "bad sectors" line will be displayed only if some damaged areas were found. Bad sectors don't make the disk unusable. DOS simply marks those sectors off in the File Allocation Table so they don't get used for data. However, if your format message shows a high percentage of bad sectors, you might consider throwing the diskette away (or getting your money back if it's a new diskette).

The FORMAT program then asks you:

```
Format another (Y/N)?_
```

If you want to format another diskette using exactly the same switches and operands, enter the letter Y and the FORMAT program will be repeated. If you don't want to format another diskette, or if you want to use different switches and operands, enter the letter N and the system prompt will be displayed.

(a) Write a command to format a diskette on drive A:.
`A>_`
(b) Write a command to format a diskette on drive B:.
`A>_`

Suppose you get the following message:

```
   1213952 bytes total disk space
   1213952 bytes available on disk
Format another (Y/N)?_
```

(c) How many bad sectors are on the disk?
(d) Suppose you want to format another diskette using the same operands and switches. What do you enter?
(e) Suppose you don't want to format another diskette. What do you enter?

(*a*) `A>FORMAT` or `FORMAT A:`
(*b*) `A>FORMAT B:`
(*c*) *None*
(*d*) *Y*
(*e*) *N*

FORMAT can make a disk bootable if you wish. Not all your diskettes need to be bootable, especially if you'll usually boot from a fixed disk. But it never hurts to make a disk bootable; this just takes up some space.

You can boot with any diskette that contains the DOS *system files*. These are COMMAND.COM plus two program files that are stored on the diskette but don't show up in the directory listing and are thus called "hidden files." DOS uses them for its internal processing, but you never need to access them yourself. To cause FORMAT to copy the system files, use the /S switch, as in:

```
A>FORMAT B: /S
```

Figure 3.4 shows what the entire interaction looks like. You can see the "System transferred" message. We included a directory of the disk so you can see that the COMMAND.COM file shows up in the directory.

```
C>FORMAT A: /S
Insert new diskette for drive A:
and strike ENTER when ready

Format complete
System transferred

   1213952 bytes total disk space
     78336 bytes used by system
   1135616 bytes available on disk

Format another (Y/N)?N
C>DIR A:

 Volume in drive A has no label
 Directory of  A:\

COMMAND  COM    25276   7-24-87  12:00a
        1 File(s)   1135616 bytes free

C>_
```

Figure 3.4. Formatting a Bootable Diskette

(a) Write a command to format the diskette in drive A: so it can be used for booting.
`A>_`

(b) Write a command to format the diskette in drive B: so it can be used for booting.
`A>_`

(a) `A>FORMAT /S`
(b) `A>FORMAT B: /S`

By default, the FORMAT program always formats a diskette for the drive it's in. Thus, if it's a double-density drive, FORMAT prepares the diskette to be used in a double-density drive. If it's a 1.44MB drive, FORMAT prepares the diskette for a 1.44MB drive. If the diskette is incompatible with the drive, DOS displays an error message. A number of switches let you format diskettes in other formats. You might need these switches to prepare a diskette to send to a colleague who has a different type of drive.

The /1 switch prepares a 5.25-inch single-sided diskette. The original PCs had single-sided drives, but not many people have them anymore.

The /8 switch prepares a 5.25-inch diskette with eight sectors per track instead of nine. Versions of DOS before 2.0 formatted diskettes with eight sectors per track. The only reason to use this switch is to prepare a diskette for someone who is still using a DOS version earlier than 2.0.

The /B switch is just like the /8 switch, but DOS also leaves room on the diskette for the operating system files so the diskette can be made bootable. DOS doesn't actually copy the system files to the diskette, since it would make little sense to place the DOS 3.3 system on a diskette being prepared for an older version. The presumption is that someone will copy the correct system files on the diskette later with the SYS command (described later in this chapter).

The /4 switch causes a high-density 5.25-inch drive to format a double-density diskette. Unfortunately, this won't necessarily make the diskette usable by a double-density drive, as some high-density drives have difficulty formatting a double-density diskette accurately. The purpose of the /4 switch becomes clear if you have only high-density drives and want to use up some double-density diskettes left over from your old system. You can't format a double-density diskette for high-density use. But if you format it with the /4 switch, then you will be able to use it in the high-density drive. (The diskette will hold only 360K, however.)

The /N and /T switches are meant for use with 3.5-inch diskettes. The /N switch specifies the number of sectors per track, in this format: /N:nn. The /T switch specifies the number of tracks, in this format: /T:nnn. Both switches are used to format a 720K diskette in a 1.44MB drive. Since a 720K diskette has 80 tracks and 9 sectors per track, you will usually specify the following command to format a 720K diskette in a 1.44MB drive:

```
A>FORMAT B: /N:9 /T:80
```

These switches let you prepare diskettes for lower-capacity drives. You can never prepare a diskette for higher capacity than the drive you are using. And you can never force a diskette to be used for a higher capacity than it was manufactured for. FORMAT might experience problems if you try to format a double-density diskette as a high-density diskette or a 720K diskette as a 1.44MB diskette.

(a) Write a command to format a double-density diskette in drive A:, which is a high-density drive.
`A>_`
(b) Will the above diskette be usable in a double-density drive?
(c) Write a command to format a 720K diskette in a 1.44MB drive.
`A>_`
(d) Will the above diskette be usable in a 720K drive?

(a) `A>FORMAT /4`
(b) Probably not
(c) `A>FORMAT /N:9 /T:80`
(d) Yes

You can get various error messages when you use FORMAT.

```
Attempted write-protect violation
Format failure
```

You'll get this message if you try to format a write-protected diskette. If you really want to format the diskette, remove the write protection and try again. Otherwise, format a different diskette.

This next message covers several situations:

```
Invalid media or Track 0 bad - disk unusable
Format failure
```

It might be that track 0 of the disk is bad, in which case DOS can't write the root directory and File Allocation Table on the diskette, meaning that the diskette can never be used with DOS. It might be that you specified the wrong size diskette in the drive. For example, you put a high-density diskette in a high-density drive and specified the /4 switch. Whenever you get this message, check the diskette first. If it's the right diskette for the drive, then you have to suspect track 0. Try to format the diskette again. If it fails a second time, the diskette is no good. Throw it out or return it to the dealer.

This next problem crops up only when you have specified the /S switch:

```
Disk unsuitable for system use
```

The tracks to receive the system files are bad. DOS will format this diskette, but it can't put the system files on it.

Occasionally you'll see this message:

```
Insert DOS disk in x
and strike any key when ready
```

When DOS is ready to copy the system files to the new diskette, it must have the files available to copy from. If it can't find a source, it asks you to install one. When you see this message, put any bootable diskette in the indicated drive.

(a) Which message might mean the target diskette cannot be formatted and should be discarded?
   A. `Attempted write-protection violation`
   B. `Invalid media or Track 0 bad - disk unusable`
   C. `Disk unsuitable for system disk`

(b) Which message can result only from a FORMAT /S operation?
   A. `Insert DOS disk in x and strike any key when ready`
   B. `Invalid media or Track 0 bad - disk unusable`

C. `Disk unsuitable for system disk`
D. `Attempted write protection violation`

(a) B
(b) A, C

DOS lets you assign volume labels to your disks. These labels help in identifying disks, not only when you list a directory, but also when you accidentally try to reformat the hard disk. For your own protection, give every disk a meaningful volume label. (If you don't know the contents of the diskette when you format it, give it a general label; you can change the label with the LABEL command, discussed later in this chapter.)

To create the volume label, specify /V on the FORMAT command. The program asks you for the volume label, which can contain up to 11 characters, including spaces. If you enter more than 11 characters, only the first 11 are used. Some characters that DOS uses for specific purposes, such as * and ?, are forbidden. If you get the message `Invalid characters in volume label`, revise your label to get rid of such symbols.

Figure 3.5 shows an interaction that creates a diskette with the volume labeled PRACTICE 01. You can see the point in the dialog where FORMAT asked for the volume label in response to the /V switch in the original command.

```
A>FORMAT A: /V
Insert new diskette for drive A:
and strike ENTER when ready

Format complete

Volume label (11 characters, ENTER for none)? PRACTICE 01


   1213952 bytes total disk space
   1213952 bytes available on disk

Format another (Y/N)?N
A>_
```

Figure 3.5. Formatting a Disk with a Volume Label

(a) Write a command that formats a diskette with the label BUDGET DATA.
`A>_`
What will you enter for the volume label?
(b) Write a command that formats a diskette on drive B: without a volume label.
`A>_`
(c) Write a command that formats a diskette on drive B: with the label MASTERDISK.
`A>_`
What will you enter for the volume label?

(a) `A>FORMAT A: /V`; *the FORMAT command will ask you for the label and you then enter* `BUDGET DATA`.
(b) `A>FORMAT B:`
(c) `A:FORMAT B: /V`; *when asked, enter* `MASTERDISK`

Here's the complete format of the FORMAT command.

Format (external):
FORMAT d: [/S] [/V] [/1] [/4] [/8] [/B] [/N:nn] [/T:nnn]

Since this is an external command, the FORMAT.COM file must be available in the specified (or default) directory. Note that the drivename operand (d:) is required. If no switches are used, FORMAT formats the designated diskette according to the type of drive it's in. The /S switch tells FORMAT to make the diskette bootable. The /V switch tells it to give the diskette a volume label; if you're smart, you'll make this a habit. For 5.25-inch diskettes, /1 formats a single-sided diskette, /4 formats a double-density diskette in a high-density drive, /8 formats a nonbootable diskette for DOS 1.x systems, and /B formats a bootable diskette for DOS 1.x systems. For 3.5-inch diskettes, /N specifies the number of sectors per track and /T specifies the number of tracks when formatting a 720K diskette in a 1.44MB drive.

Assume the DOS system diskette is in drive A:.
(a) Write a command to format a diskette in the B: drive and to let you enter a label. In this example, the B: drive is the default. (The system diskette is still in A:.)
`B>_`

(b) Write a command to prepare a double-density diskette in the B: drive, which is a high-density drive.
```
A>_
```

(*a*) `B>A:FORMAT B: /V`
(*b*) `A>FORMAT B: /4`

Copying Your System Files onto a Previously Formatted Diskette

You've learned how to put the system files on a new diskette with FORMAT /S. But FORMAT erases and reformats a diskette. How do you put the system files on a diskette that you don't want to erase? The correct command is SYS. Its format is:

Format (external):
SYS d:

SYS exists solely to copy the system files from one disk to another. The default drive must contain the files to be copied. The SYS.COM file must also be available. The only operand you can specify is the destination drive. To copy the system files from drive A: to drive B:, you would enter:

```
A>SYS B:
```

You can't use SYS to put the system files on a diskette that doesn't have room for them. The two hidden files must be the first files in the root directory. This means that the diskette must have been formatted originally with the /S or /B switch, or it must have no files on it. If a diskette has even one file on it and was not formatted with /S or /B, there is no room for the system files. The primary use of SYS is to put your system files on a prerecorded diskette when the documentation for that diskette tells you to do so.

SYS can rarely be used to change the DOS version on a diskette. For example, if you have just upgraded to version 3.3 from 3.0, you could not upgrade your bootable diskettes by using SYS to overwrite the old system files because the new hidden files are larger than the old ones and they won't fit into the old space.

SYS copies the hidden files but not COMMAND.COM. You must complete the operation by copying COMMAND.COM to the target diskette. (The COPY command is discussed in Chapter 6.)

(a) Select the true statements below.
  A. SYS copies the system files from the default drive to the specified drive.
  B. If a diskette was formatted without the system files and now contains 20 files, SYS can be used to add the system files to it.
  C. Two ways to copy system files from A: to B: are SYS and FORMAT.
  D. SYS puts your system files on a prerecorded diskette (if room has been left for them).

(b) Write a command to copy the system files from A: to B:. Assume the diskette in A: contains the system files and SYS.COM.

```
A>_
```

(c) What's wrong with this command? `SYS B: A:`

(a) A, C, D
(b) `A>SYS B:`
(c) You can specify only one drivename with SYS—the destination drive

---

The SYS command can produce several messages you haven't seen before. This message means you have used an invalid drivename:

```
Invalid parameter
```

Perhaps you left out the colon or typed a wrong letter.

This message means that the diskette wasn't formatted for the system files in the first place and now contains at least one file, preventing SYS from putting the system files in their correct position:

```
No room for system on destination disk
```

Alternatively, the diskette might contain an earlier version of the DOS system files, and the new ones can't fit into the available space.

Identify the meaning of each message below.

(a) No room for system on destination disk
(b) Invalid parameter

A. You can't put the system files on this diskette (without reformatting it).
B. The diskette was formatted without the /S switch.
C. You didn't specify a correct drivename
D. The diskette was formatted by an earlier version of DOS and the system files won't fit.

(a) A, B, D
(b) C

Viewing a Diskette's Label

As you've seen, you can include a volume label with /V when you format a disk. It's a good idea to give every disk a volume label. Write its volume label on the outside of the diskette on the stick-on label.

The first line of the directory listing for an unlabeled disk is:

```
Volume in drive x has no label
```

This tells you that no name was assigned to the disk when it was formatted. If you were checking the directory of a disk in drive A: labeled DOSBACKUP, the first line of the directory display would be:

```
Volume in drive A is DOSBACKUP
```

You might want to know the label of a diskette without displaying the complete directory. Simply enter VOL or VOL d: as appropriate. The system responds with either

`Volume in drive A is INVENTORY` (for example)

or

```
Volume in drive A has no label
```

depending on whether the diskette has a label. The format of the VOL command is:

Format (external):
VOL [d:]

(a) How do you give a diskette a volume label? (Choose one.)
 A. Assign a label when you format the diskette
 B. Write a name on its stick-on label
 C. Use the VOL command

(b) Show two commands to find out the label of the diskette in drive A:.
`A>_`

(c) Write a command to display the volume label of the diskette in drive B:.
`A>_`

(a) *A*
(b) `A>DIR` or `A>VOL`
(c) `A>VOL B:`

Changing a Diskette's Label

Sometimes you want to change a diskette's label or add one to an unlabeled diskette without reformatting the diskette. Keeping the label current with the contents of the diskette is very appropriate. The LABEL command lets you do that. Here is its format.

Format (external):
LABEL [d:][volume label]

Since LABEL is an external command, the program must be available. If it's not on the default drive, you can precede LABEL with the correct drivename.

If you want to change the label on drive A: to WINTERCATLG, you would enter:

```
A>LABEL WINTERCATLG
```

To add a label to the currently unlabeled diskette in drive B:, you could enter:

```
A>LABEL B:FORTY YEARS
```

Don't put a space between the drivename and the volume label, or DOS won't "see" the volume label.

If you omit the volume label (or put a space after the drivename), DOS asks for the label:

```
A>LABEL
Volume in drive A is INV BACKUP
Volume label (11 characters, ENTER for none)?_
```

Now you can type the new volume label. If you press Enter without typing a label, LABEL asks if you want to delete the label:

```
Delete current volume label (Y/N)?_
```

If you say N, the current label is not changed. Figure 3.6 shows a complete interaction to delete a volume label.

```
A>LABEL

Volume in drive A is PRACTICE 01

Volume label (11 characters, ENTER for none)?

Delete current volume label (Y/N)? Y


A>_
```

Figure 3.6. Deleting a Volume Label

As with FORMAT /V, the label may contain spaces, but many special DOS symbols are prohibited. If you enter more than 11 characters, only the first 11 are used.

A volume label takes up an entry in the root directory. If the volume has no label and the root directory is full, there's no room to add a volume label. You will see this message:

```
No room in root directory
```

You can make room for the volume label by deleting one of the files in the root directory.

(a) Write a command to change the volume label in the default drive to SPECIALS.
`A>_`

(b) Write a command to change the volume label in drive B: to NONESUCH.
`A>_`

(c) How would you erase the label on drive B:?

(d) Write a command to view, not change, the label on the default drive.
`A>_`

(a) `A>LABEL SPECIALS`
(b) `A>LABEL B:NONESUCH`
(c) Enter LABEL B:; when it asks for a label, press Enter; then enter Y.
(d) `A>VOL` *(or* `DIR`*)*

Copying Diskettes

In Chapter 1 you learned the basics of copying a diskette. Here's the complete format of the DISKCOPY command:

Format (external):
DISKCOPY [d:] [d:] [/1]

Since DISKCOPY is an external command, it may be preceded by a drivename and path. If you omit all operands, the default drive is used for both the source and the target diskette. If you specify one drive, it's the source drive. Thus

```
A>DISKCOPY B:
```

copies the diskette from drive B: to drive A:. If you specify two drives, the first is the source and the second is the target. Thus

```
A>DISKCOPY A: B:
```

copies the diskette from drive A: to B:.

The /1 switch copies only the first side of the diskette. You might want to do this if you are making a copy to be used in a one-sided drive. Of course, you'll copy only half the diskette, so if the diskette has data on the second side, this might not meet your needs.

DISKCOPY destroys any existing data on the target diskette, so be sure to use a diskette that contains no valuable information.

Identify the commands on the right that have the same effects as those on the left.

(a) `A>DISKCOPY`	A. `A>DISKCOPY A:`
(b) `A>DISKCOPY B: A:`	B. `A>DISKCOPY B:`
	C. `A>DISKCOPY A: A:`
	D. `A>DISKCOPY B: B:`

(a) A, C
(b) B

If you have two different types of drives, you might have trouble copying diskettes from one to the other, since DISKCOPY requires both diskettes to be the same type. Suppose drive A: is a high-density drive and drive B: is a double-density drive. You could DISKCOPY a double-density diskette using both drives because the high-density drive can read a double-density diskette. Be sure to copy from A: to B:, since the high-density drive cannot reliably write a double-density diskette. You couldn't DISKCOPY a high-density diskette using both drives because the double-density drive can neither read nor write a high-density diskette. You'd have to back up your high-density diskettes with the slower, single-drive DISKCOPY.

Suppose you have one 5.25-inch drive and one 3.5-inch drive. All your DISKCOPY operations must use a single drive, because these two drive types are incompatible.

Suppose you have a 720K drive and a 1.44MB drive. You could do two-drive copies of 720K diskettes but not 1.44MB diskettes.

DISKCOPY works with diskettes only. It cannot be used to copy a diskette to your fixed disk, to back up a fixed disk, or to copy any simulated drives, such as a RAM drive (explained later). This message

```
Invalid drive specification
Specified drive does not exist,
or is non-removable
```

means you specified a simulated drive, a fixed drive, or a nonexistent drive.

DISKCOPY may discover bad sectors on the source or target diskette. It does a track-by-track copy, ignoring the information in the directory or File Allocation Table, so it doesn't know that bad sectors have already been identified. In fact, DISKCOPY copies the directory and File Allocation Table from the source to the target along with everything else. This message

```
Unrecoverable read error on drive A
Side x, track xx
Target diskette may be unusable
```

may or may not be a problem. If the bad sectors were identified when the source diskette was formatted, they don't contain data. In this case, the target diskette is an exact copy of the source diskette and no problem exists (except for some wasted sectors on the target diskette). However, if the bad sectors have developed after the diskette was formatted, then you have a problem that must be solved some other way. You can determine whether any bad sectors have been blocked out in the File Allocation Table with CHKDSK. You can copy individual files off the diskette with COPY. If some files won't copy, you can use RECOVER to rescue them. These commands are covered in later chapters.

If you see this message

```
SOURCE diskette bad or incompatible
Copy process ended
```

then you know that DISKCOPY was unable to read the source diskette due to bad sectors, lack of formatting, or other problems. This diskette cannot be used as a source diskette. If it contains the only copy of valuable data, you may need to get help from an expert.

When the bad sector is on the target diskette, you'll see this message:

```
Unrecoverable write error on drive B
Side x, track xx
Target diskette may be unusable
```

You might see this message instead:

```
TARGET diskette bad or incompatible
Copy process ended
```

The message tells you that the copy is no good. Make another copy using a different target diskette. You can probably still use the damaged diskette if you must by reformatting it with FORMAT (which sets aside the bad sectors) and using it for operations other than DISKCOPY.

(a) Suppose drive A: is a 1.44MB drive and drive B: is a 720K drive. You want to copy the 1.44MB diskette in drive A:. What command would you use?

```
A>_
```

(b) Suppose you have two diskette drives (A: and B:) and a fixed drive (C:). Examine this interaction:

```
A>DISKCOPY A: C:
Invalid drive specification
Specified drive does not exist,
or is non-removable.
```

What's wrong?

(c) Suppose you have this interaction:

```
A>DISKCOPY A: B:
Insert SOURCE Diskette in Drive A:
Insert TARGET Diskette in Drive B:
Press any key when ready...

Copying 80 tracks
9 Sectors/Track, 2 side(s)
```

```
Formatting while copying

Unrecoverable write error on drive B
Side 1, track 7
Unrecoverable write error on drive B
Side 1, track 8
Target diskette may be unusable

Copy another diskette (Y/N)?_
```

What should you do?

A. Don't worry about the unrecoverable errors; use the target diskette anyway.
B. Recopy the source diskette using a different target diskette; reformat the damaged diskette and use it for other things.
C. Throw out both the source and target diskettes immediately before they get mixed in with good diskettes.

(a) `A>DISKCOPY`
(b) You can't use a fixed drive with DISKCOPY
(c) B

Note Many prerecorded diskettes are copy-protected to protect the creator's copyright. Read the user's manual accompanying any software you buy to find out if, and how, you can back it up. If you try DISKCOPY and get negative messages, the source disk may be copy-protected.

Checking Your Copy

No computer copying operation is 100 percent reliable. Slight variations in electricity, read/write head tolerances, and the like can produce occasional errors. DOS gives you the opportunity to double-check a copied diskette with the DISKCOMP command, which compares two diskettes. Differences, if any, are reported on the monitor. You may want to use DISKCOMP after DISKCOPY. DISKCOMP is valid only to compare diskettes that were copied by DISKCOPY and have not been changed since.

The format of the DISKCOMP command is:

Format (external):
DISKCOMP [d:] [d:] [/1] [/8]

You can specify none, one, or two drivenames. You can specify /1 to limit the target comparison to the first side. You can specify /8 to compare eight-sector diskettes. Figure 3.7 shows a complete DISKCOMP interaction. The message `Compare OK` indicates that the two diskettes are identical in all respects.

```
A>DISKCOMP

Insert FIRST diskette in drive A:

Press any key when ready . . .

Comparing 40 tracks
9 sectors per track, 2 side(s)

Insert SECOND diskette in drive A:

Press any key when ready . . .

Compare OK


Compare another diskette (Y/N) ?N

A>_
```

Figure 3.7. DISKCOMP with Identical Diskettes

(a) Write a command to compare two diskettes—one on A: and one on B:.
A>_
(b) Which diskette should be in drive A: when you enter the above command?

(a) `A>DISKCOMP A: B:` *or* `A>DISKCOMP B:`
(b) The disk containing DISKCOMP.COM

You've seen an example of a successful comparison. Here are some other DISKCOMP messages.

Suppose the comparison identifies one or more mistakes:

```
A>DISKCOMP A: B:
Insert FIRST diskette in drive A:
Insert SECOND diskette in drive B:
Strike any key when ready...

Comparing 40 tracks
9 sectors per track, 2 side(s)

Compare error on side 1, track 7
```

This message means a difference was found; the two diskettes are not identical. If they are very different, the message will repeat over and over, indicating differences on different sides and tracks, accompanied by a beep each time. You can interrupt the process with Ctrl-Break.

Which statement is true?
(a) DISKCOMP displays a good or bad message about every side/track
(b) DISKCOMP displays errors only

---

b

Exercises

These exercises help you practice all the commands you have studied in this chapter. (You've used DIR before, but you'll practice using it here with some of its options.)

What You Should Do	*How the Computer Responds*
1. Boot with your DOS diskette in drive A:. Put another diskette in drive B: if	1. Boots as usual.

you have one. (You might want to turn on Echo Print now to document your work so you can review it later.)

2. Try these DIR commands:
   a. `DIR /W`
   b. `DIR /P`
   c. `DIR B:`
   d. `DIR *.EXE`
   e. `DIR COM*.*`

2.
   a. Displays filespecs five across.
   b. Displays one screenful at a time.
   c. Displays directory of drive B: (if present).
   d. Displays entries for EXE files, if any.
   e. Displays entries for COMMAND.COM and COMP.COM.

3. Now format two blank diskettes. Be sure they're blank or contain no valuable data. Any data on the diskettes will be destroyed.
   a. If you have two diskette drives enter

      ```
      A>FORMAT B: /S /V
      ```

      Otherwise enter

      ```
      A>FORMAT A: /S /V
      ```

   b. Follow the directions on your screen. Be sure to remove original diskettes from the drives and insert blank or reusable diskettes when prompted. Label the diskettes PRACTICE1 and PRACTICE2.
   c. Try booting with each diskette.
   d. Save the two formatted diskettes. You'll use them throughout this book. (Label each one with a stick-on label; be sure to mark on the label that the diskette is bootable.)

3. Guides you through the process.

4. Use the VOL command to view your two new diskette labels.
   a. Enter `VOL`.
   b. Enter `VOL B:` to see the label of the diskette in drive B:, if you have one.

4. Shows you the requested diskette labels.

5. Use LABEL to change the labels of your two new diskettes to EXERCISE1 and EXERCISE2.

5. Changes diskette labels as requested.

6. Use DISKCOMP to compare your DOS work diskette with your original DOS diskette.
   a. If you have two identical or compatible diskette drives, place your work diskette in drive A: and your original diskette in drive B:. Then enter `DISKCOMP A: B:`.
   b. If you have only one diskette drive, place your work diskette in drive A: and enter `DISKCOMP`.
   c. Follow the directions on the screen.
   d. If the two diskettes aren't identical, make another work diskette by copying the original diskette again. Use DISKCOMP on the new copy too. Keep trying until you have a perfect copy of your original DOS diskette. (If it takes more than two tries to get a perfect copy, there may be a problem with your diskette drives. Contact your dealer.)

6. Gives you on-screen instruction. Then compares the two diskettes and displays any discrepancies or tells you the diskettes compare okay.

What If It Doesn't Work?

1. If DIR won't work:
   a. Make sure you booted with a DOS system diskette in drive A:.
   b. Try again, making sure you type the command correctly.

2. If FORMAT won't work:
   a. Make sure FORMAT.COM is on the default drive. It should be on your DOS work diskette.
   b. Make sure you entered the command correctly.
   c. If FORMAT works but produces error messages (such as `Attempted write-protect violation`, refer back to the FORMAT error messages explained earlier in this chapter.
   d. Keep trying until you have two good, bootable, formatted diskettes.

3. If VOL won't work:
   a. Make sure you booted with a DOS system diskette in drive A:.
   b. Try again, making sure you type the command correctly.
   c. VOL doesn't work with DOS versions before 2.0.

4. If LABEL won't work:
   a. Make sure LABEL.COM is on the default drive. It should be on your DOS work diskette.
   b. Make sure you entered the command correctly.
   c. Make sure the target diskette is not write-protected.
   d. If error messages result, correct the error and try again.
   e. LABEL doesn't work with DOS versions before 3.0.

5. If DISKCOMP doesn't work:
   a. Make sure DISKCOMP.COM is on the default diskette. It should be on your DOS work diskette.
   b. Make sure you entered the command correctly.

4

Setting Up the Fixed Disk

A personal computer with a fixed disk requires special preparation before it can be used. If your system uses only diskettes, you can skip this chapter. If your fixed disk is already prepared—for example, if it contains files—you may also want to skip this chapter. However, you made need the information in this chapter someday. It includes methods for booting from a fixed disk as well as setting up and formatting it.

When you have finished this chapter, you will be able to:

- Use the FDISK command to set up a DOS partition
- Use the FORMAT command to prepare the DOS partition
- Boot the system from the fixed disk

Naming Your Fixed Disk

As you know, DOS uses the names A: and B: to refer to your diskette drives. If you have only one drive, both names apply to that drive. If you have two drives, the first is A: and the second is B:. If you have more than two diskette drives, the names of the extra drives depend on how your system is set up. If you have a fixed disk, it is generally named drive C:. If it is partitioned into logical drives, the extra drives are usually named D:, E:, and so on.

(a) If you have one diskette drive and two fixed drives, what are their names?
(b) If you have two diskette drives and one fixed drive, what are their names?

(a) The diskette drive is A: and B:, and the fixed drives are C: and D:
(b) The diskette drives are A: and B:, and the fixed drive is C:

Partitioning Your Fixed Disk

One primary difference between a diskette and a fixed disk is that you must *partition* the fixed disk. Partitioning physically formats the disk and optionally divides it into separate parts.

You must partition the disk before you can physically format it. If you want to establish more than one logical drive on it—drives C: and D:, for example—you can also divide the disk into parts. DOS cannot use more than 32MB in one partition; so if you have a larger fixed disk, you will definitely want to make it into at least two drives, or you will waste a part of your disk.

You can also divide the disk so that DOS uses part of it and another operating system uses another part. For example, suppose you have a 40MB disk and want to be able to use both DOS and XENIX on it. You could partition the disk so that DOS gets 20MB for drive C: and XENIX gets 20MB for its system. DOS will not be able to access the XENIX partition. (XENIX has special utilities that let it access files in the DOS partitions.)

(a) True or false? A fixed disk must be partitioned with FDISK regardless of whether you want to divide it into smaller parts.
(b) What is the largest size drive DOS can access?
(c) True or false? You can have more than one logical drive per fixed disk.
(d) True or false? Each fixed disk must be owned and completely controlled by only one operating system.

(a) True
(b) 32MB
(c) True
(d) False

If you try to use the fixed disk before it has been partitioned, DOS does not recognize the existence of the disk. For example, if you enter C:, DOS responds with `Invalid drive specification`. You partition your fixed disk with the FDISK command. To start the process, place your DOS diskette in drive A:, boot the system, and enter:

```
A>FDISK
```

The FDISK program takes over and displays a menu of options as shown in Figure 4.1. If you have more than one fixed disk, the menu includes Option 5, Select Next Fixed Disk Drive.

```
Fixed Disk Setup Program Version 3.30
(C)Copyright Microsoft Corp. 1987

FDISK Options

Current Fixed Disk Drive: 1

Choose one of the following:

    1. Create DOS partition
    2. Change Active Partition
    3. Delete DOS partition
    4. Display Partition Information



Enter choice: [1]




Press ESC to return to DOS
```

Figure 4.1. FDISK Option Menu

The FDISK menu choices let you perform several operations:

- You can create a DOS partition to store DOS programs and files on your fixed disk. A DOS partition must exist before you can use your fixed disk with DOS. FDISK destroys existing data, so don't use this program if you already have files on the fixed disk. (FDISK won't partition a fixed disk that has already been formatted unless you delete the DOS partition first.) If your fixed disk isn't partitioned yet, you can use FDISK during the exercises at the end of this chapter.

- You can change the partition that assumes control when booting from the fixed disk. Ordinarily, you would boot from the partition that is DOS drive C:. This is called the *primary DOS partition*. But if you have another operating system on the disk in another partition, and you want to boot that operating system, you use Option 2 to indicate that partition should be used when booting.
- You can delete a DOS partition. This destroys all the files in the DOS partition, so don't do it unless you are making drastic changes to your fixed disk and have already removed any valuable files. You might want to delete a DOS partition if you have decided to change the partitioning.
- You can display information about the fixed disk partitions, including their sizes, the active partition, the primary DOS partition, and lists of partitions that belong to each operating system. Displaying partition information doesn't harm or change the partitions in any way.
- If you have more than one fixed disk, you can switch to another fixed disk so that you can partition it.

If you want to set up your fixed disk with partitions for other operating systems, you should read the appropriate portions of the manuals for your other operating systems before proceeding. You can leave room for the other partitions when you set up your DOS partitions, but you cannot create the non-DOS partitions under DOS.

Which of the following are functions of the FDISK program?

(a) Display data about the partitions
(b) Create DOS partitions
(c) Create non-DOS partitions
(d) Delete DOS partitions
(e) Make a non-DOS partition the active partition
(f) Check the fixed disk for bad sectors

---

a, b, d, e

Suppose you intend to use only DOS on your computer. In that case, you want to use all the space for DOS partitions. The default option on the FDISK menu is 1, Create DOS Partition. When you press Enter, you see the menu shown in Figure 4.2. Now you can choose to create the primary DOS partition or an extended DOS partition.

The primary DOS partition is the one that becomes drive C:, from which DOS boots. It cannot be subdivided into logical drives. You can't boot from an extended DOS partition, but you can subdivide it into two or more logical drives.

Assuming that no partitioning has been done on your hard disk, you should start by creating the primary DOS partition. Press Enter to select the default option on the menu shown in Figure 4.2. If a primary DOS partition already exists, you will see an error message. If the primary DOS partition needs to be created, you will see the screen shown in Figure 4.3.

If you want to use your entire fixed disk (up to 32MB) as the primary DOS partition and make it active, then all you have to do is answer Y to this screen. This is the easiest way to create the primary DOS partition. However, if you don't want the maximum amount of space given to the primary DOS partition, enter N on this screen so that you can specify the partition size. DOS shows you the number of cylinders available and asks how many you want to include in the primary DOS partition.

```
Create DOS Partition

Current Fixed Disk Drive: 1



    1. Create Primary DOS partition
    2. Create Extended DOS partition





Enter choice: [1]




Press ESC to return to FDISK Options
```

Figure 4.2. Create DOS Partition Menu

```
Create Primary DOS Partition


Current Fixed Disk Drive: 1


Do you wish to use the maximum size
for a DOS partition and make the DOS
partition active (Y/N).........? [Y]




Press ESC to return to FDISK Options
```

Figure 4.3. Create Primary DOS Partition Screen

(a) Suppose you want to use your entire 20MB fixed disk as the primary DOS partition. What would you press to respond to this question?

```
Do you wish to use the maximum size
for a DOS partition and make the DOS
partition active (Y/N)?
```

(b) Suppose you want to create two logical drives on your fixed disk. How would you answer the question?

(a) Y
(b) N

Once the primary partition has been created, and if there are any cylinders left on the hard disk, you can use the remaining cylinders to create extended DOS partitions. This gives you more logical drives on the fixed disk. To create an extended DOS partition, select Option 2 on the menu shown in Figure 4.2. The screen shown in Figure 4.4 will appear. The number of remaining cylinders is filled in as the default. If you want to create a smaller partition, type the desired number of cylinders.

Once you have created an extended partition, you must designate one or more logical drives for it. The screen shown in Figure 4.5 appears. The maximum amount of space in the partition is filled in as the drive size. To make the entire partition into one drive, simply press Enter. To subdivide it, enter the number of cylinders for the first drive. Then FDISK will ask for the second drive, the third drive, and so forth until the entire partition has been used up. As you create drives, their drivenames appear on the screen.

If unused cylinders still are available on the disk, they can be used by another operating system. DOS permits only one primary and one extended partition.

```
Create Extended DOS Partition

Current Fixed Disk Drive: 1

Partition Status   Type  Start  End Size
 C: 1            PRI DOS     0  641  642





Total disk space is  819 cylinders.
Maximum space available for partition
is  177 cylinders.

Enter partition size..........: [ 177]


Press ESC to return to FDISK Options
```

Figure 4.4. Create Extended DOS Partition Screen

```
Create Logical DOS Drive(s)



No logical drive defined



Total Partition size is  177 cylinders.
Maximum space available for logical
drive is  177 cylinders.


Enter logical drive size.......: [ 177]



Press ESC to return to FDISK Options
```

Figure 4.5. Create Logical DOS Drive(s) Screen

(a) True or false? Both the primary DOS partition and extended partitions can be subdivided into logical drives.
(b) True or false? Extended partitions cannot be active partitions.
(c) True or false? If you create an extended partition, you must specify how many cylinders will be used for each logical drive.

(a) False
(b) True
(c) True

The FDISK command has some additional options. Suppose you want to find out whether or how your fixed disk has been set up for use. You can select Option 4, Display Partition Information, from the FDISK menu. Figure 4.6 shows an example of the screen you will see if the disk has been divided into two partitions. The active partition is marked with an A in the status column. When you don't follow the easy method of creating the primary partition, you have to use Option 2, Change Active Partition to designate the active partition. Until this is done, you can't boot from the fixed disk.

```
Display Partition Information

Current Fixed Disk Drive: 1

Partition Status   Type  Start  End Size
 C: 1        A   PRI DOS     0  641  642
 D: 2            EXT DOS   642  818  177


Total disk space is  819 cylinders.




Press ESC to return to FDISK Options
```

Figure 4.6. Display Partition Information Screen

(a) How can you find out how many partitions you have and which one is active?
(b) If no partition is active, how can you make one active?
(c) True or false? You can't boot DOS from the hard disk until the primary DOS partition has been designated as active.

(a) Display the partition information (Option 4 on the main FDISK menu)
(b) Change the active partition (Option 2 on the main FDISK menu)
(c) True

Formatting the Fixed Disk

Like a diskette, a fixed disk drive must be formatted with the FORMAT program before use. If you want to make the primary partition bootable, which you should, use the /S switch when you format it. The command you will most likely use to format drive C: is:

```
A>FORMAT C: /S /V
```

Extended drives cannot be made bootable, but they must be formatted before you can use them. The only FORMAT switch you can use with an extended partition is /V.

FORMAT behaves somewhat differently for a fixed disk drive than for a diskette. With a fixed disk, FORMAT presumes that you might have made a mistake and makes you confirm the FORMAT command. This helps to prevent you from wiping out 20MB, 30MB, or more, due to a careless mistake. If the disk drive has a volume label, you will see this message:

```
Enter current Volume Label for drive x:_
```

FORMAT uses the volume label as a password. If you can enter the exact volume label, the format proceeds. If you can't, it fails. If you don't know the correct volume label, press Ctrl-C, enter DIR or VOL to get the label, then restart the FORMAT process.

The next message appears regardless of whether the disk has a volume label:

```
WARNING! ALL DATA ON NON-REMOVABLE
DISK DRIVE x: WILL BE LOST
Proceed with Format (Y/N)?_
```

Whenever you see either of these messages, *stop!* and *think!* These are severe warning messages, indicating that you are about to erase all the data on the indicated drive, which is a fixed disk.

If you really want to reformat the disk, enter Y in response to the message. Anything else will abort the FORMAT command.

(a) Why should you not reformat the fixed disk unless absolutely necessary?

(b) What command formats drive D:?

(c) Identify whether each statement or message below pertains to diskettes (D), fixed disks (F), or both (B).

A. Must be partitioned before use

B. Must be formatted before use

C. Can be made bootable with the /S switch

D.
```
WARNING! ALL DATA ON NON-REMOVABLE
DISK DRIVE d: WILL BE LOST
Proceed with format (Y/N)?_
```

E. `Insert new diskette for drive d:`
`and strike ENTER when ready`
F. `Enter current Volume Label for drive d:`

(d) If your fixed disk is new, what steps must you take to make it usable and bootable?

(a) Because you will lose all the information on the drive
(b) `FORMAT D:`
(c) A—F; B—B; C—B; D—F; E—D; F—F
(d) 1. Create at least a primary DOS partition with FDISK; create extended partition and drives as desired
2. Make the primary DOS partition active with FDISK
3. Format the primary partition with the /S switch; also format each drive in the extended partition

---

Booting from the Fixed Disk

When you have a fixed disk, you can boot without using a diskette. When you use FORMAT C: /S, the DOS system files are written to your fixed disk. Once the primary DOS partition is made active with FDISK, you can boot DOS from the fixed disk.

When the computer is first turned on (or you reboot with Ctrl-Alt-Del), ROM BIOS examines drive A:. If no diskette is found in drive A:, it goes to the active partition of the first fixed disk drive. Assuming that's the DOS partition and the system files are available, DOS boots and you are asked for the date and time—the same as when you boot from a diskette in drive A:. However, the default drive shown in the command prompt is C:, not A:.

When your fixed disk has been set up this way, your diskette drives become supplementary drives. They are used primarily to copy new files into the system, to make copies of files to give to someone else, and to make backup copies of the data on the fixed disk. Most of your daily use is with the fixed disk.

(a) Your fixed disk contains the system files. You place the DOS diskette in drive A: and reboot. From where does the system boot?
(b) In the above example, how can you make the system boot from drive C:?

(a) *Drive A:*
(b) *Remove the diskette from drive A:*

Parking the Fixed Disk Heads

If the fixed disk heads strike the disk surface, major damage can result. To prevent this, many manufacturers recommend that you *park* the fixed disk heads. Some manufacturers want you to park the heads whenever you turn the computer off. Others have you park the heads only when physically moving the computer. In any case, the manufacturer should include with your system software a special program to park the heads. Typical names for this program are PARK, DISKPARK, HEADPARK, SIT, and SHUTDOWN.

For the following questions, check with your system documentation.
(a) Are you supposed to park the disk heads?
(b) If so, how often?
(c) What command are you supposed to use?

The correct answers depend on your system requirements

Exercises

Warning: If your fixed disk has already been used and contains any data at all, do not perform this part of the exercises. Go directly to Part B.

Part A

What You Should Do

1. Decide how you want to partition your fixed disk. If you plan to put more than one operating system on the diskette, decide what percentage of space you

How the Computer Responds

1. Awaits your commands.

will give to DOS partitions and what percentage you will give to other partitions. For the space devoted to DOS, decide how many drives you want to have and what percentages of the total space will be assigned to each drive. *Do this before continuing with this exercise.*

2. If necessary, insert your DOS diskette into drive A: and turn on your system.

2. Boots DOS.

3. Prepare your fixed disk:
   a. At the prompt enter FDISK.
   b. Select Option 1, Create DOS Partition.
   c. Select Option 1, Create DOS Partition.
   d. If you want to devote the maximum size to the primary DOS partition, enter Y and skip to Step 4. If not, enter N.
   e. Decide how many cylinders to assign to the primary DOS partition based on the percentage you determined earlier. Enter the appropriate number of cylinders.
   f. If you want to create an extended DOS partition, select Option 2, Create Extended DOS Partition. (If not, skip to Step m.)
   g. Decide how many cylinders to assign to the extended partition based on the percentage you determined before. Enter the correct number of cylinders.
   h. Enter the desired number of cylinders for each logical drive.
   i. Repeat Steps f through h until you have created all the extended partitions you want.

3.
   a. Displays FDISK Options menu.
   b. Displays the Create DOS Partition menu.
   c. Asks if you want to use the maximum size for the primary partition.
   d. Shows you the total number of cylinders and asks you how many you want to assign to the primary DOS partition.
   e. Returns to the Create DOS Partition menu.
   f. Shows you the number of cylinders available and asks you how many to devote to the extended partition.
   g. Asks you how many cylinders to place in each logical drive for this extended partition.
   h. Shows you the details of each logical drive as it is created.
   i. Continues to carry out your commands.

j. Press Esc to return to the main FDISK Options menu, if necessary.

j. Displays the main FDISK Options menu again.

k. Select Option 2, Change Active Partition.

k. Displays the Change Active Partition menu.

l. Enter the correct number to make the primary DOS partition active.

l. Makes the primary DOS partition active.

m. Press Esc until FDISK terminates.

m. Reboots automatically and displays the DOS command prompt.

4. If you still have space on your disk and want to create extended DOS partitions, restart FDISK and go back to Step 3f. Otherwise, go on to Step 5.

4. Carries out your commands.

5. Format the primary DOS partition.

a. Enter `A>FORMAT C: /S /V`

5.

a. Formats the C: drive and asks for a volume label. (Formatting will take several minutes.)

b. Enter a label for the primary drive.

b. Records the label. Finishes the format and returns the command prompt.

c. Format the other new drives on the hard disk as necessary, using commands similar to this:

```
A>FORMAT D: /V
```

c. Formats the drives as directed.

6. Remove the diskette from drive A: and reboot.

6. Reboots from fixed disk. Displays the new prompt:

```
C>_
```

Note If your computer doesn't boot from the fixed disk, insert the diskette again and reboot from it. Try to switch to the fixed drive. You should go through this part of the exercise again if it doesn't work. Check your documentation first just in case your system is nonstandard.

You should perform Part B of the exercises regardless of whether you created a DOS partition yourself.

Part B

7. Check the directory of the fixed disk.	7.
a. If drive C: isn't active, enter this: `A>C:`	a. Displays: `C>_`
b. Enter DIR.	b. Displays directory.
c. Examine the directory. How much space is available in your primary DOS partition?	c. If you just completed Part A, only COMMAND.COM is listed. The size of your fixed disk or partition depends on how you partitioned the fixed disk.
8. Check the partition status.	8.
a. Insert DOS diskette in drive A:.	a. Waits.
b. Make drive A: the default.	b. Switches active drive. Displays the `A>` prompt.
c. Enter FDISK at the prompt.	c. Displays FDISK Options menu.
d. Select Option 4, Display Partition Information.	d. Displays partition information for the fixed disk.
e. Examine the information. How many cylinders are in the active partition? How many other partitions do you have? What drives do they contain?	e. Waits.
f. End FDISK (press Esc twice).	f. Displays `A>` prompt.

What If It Doesn't Work?

1. If you aren't sure of the status of your fixed disk, start up FDISK and use Option 4, Display Partition Information. This will tell you whether the disk has already been partitioned.

2. If the disk has been partitioned, but you're not sure if it has been formatted, try displaying directories on each of the drives it contains. The message `File not found` tells you that the drive has been formatted but contains no files. The message `Drive not ready` means the drive hasn't been formatted.

3. If you have any trouble preparing your fixed disk with FDISK and FORMAT, get help from your dealer.

Note

Please do not start writing files to your fixed disk until you have completed the next chapter. Planning the layout of your directory tree is an important step, and should precede the placement of any non-operating system files on the disk.

5

Using Directories

If you have high-capacity diskettes or a fixed disk, you can store a very large number of files. DOS lets you organize files using tree-structured directories rather than a single directory. The internal commands MKDIR, CHDIR, RMDIR, and PATH, plus the external command TREE, are used with tree-structured directories.

When you have finished this chapter, you will be able to:

- Use tree-structured directories to handle large numbers of files
- Use the MKDIR command to create new directories
- Use the CHDIR command to change or display the current directory
- Use the RMDIR command to remove a directory
- Use the PATH command to search for programs
- Use the APPEND command to search for nonprogram files
- Use the TREE command to show the structure of a disk's directories
- Specify paths in DOS commands
- Look up the SUBST, JOIN, and ASSIGN commands if needed for particular applications
- Use the FASTOPEN command to speed directory searches

Tree-Structured Directories

You can store hundreds of files on a high-capacity diskette. A fixed disk can hold thousands of files. Dealing with such large directories gets awkward at best and impossible at worst. Try looking through 700 filespecs to find a letter you wrote last July when you can't remember the file's name.

A large directory also slows DOS down. The more names DOS must search to find a particular filespec (especially a global one, where DOS must search the complete directory), the longer it takes.

To assist you in handling a large number of disk files, DOS supports a *tree-structured* directory system. This feature lets you group files into subdirectories. You'll probably want to plan the organization of your fixed disk so that no directory contains more than 50 to 100 files. The files in a directory should be related to each other in some logical way.

Figure 5.1 shows how the directories are related to each other on the disk. The root directory contains a number of entries indicating the location of files on the disk. Some of the entries point to real files, such as COMMAND.COM in the example, while others point to subdirectories. You can see in the example how the SUB1 entry points to the location of the subdirectory named SUB1. SUB1, in turn, includes a list of directory entries pointing to files and subdirectories. In the example, SUB1 points to two subdirectories: SUB11 and SUB12. SUB11 in turn contains files and one subdirectory listing: SUB111.

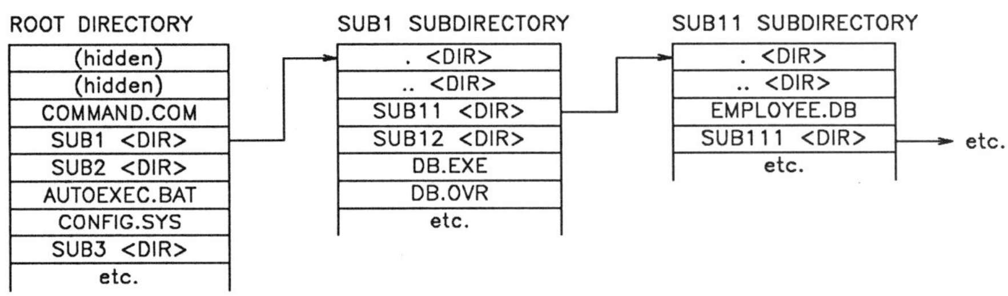

Figure 5.1. Relationship of Directories and Subdirectories on a Disk

A subdirectory is not limited in size, while the size of the root directory is fixed by the FORMAT program. The maximum number of entries in the root directory depends on the disk type. The size of a subdirectory is limited only by the amount of space available on the disk. The size can grow just like a file can grow to meet the needs of the user. Therefore, most users place no files in the root directory except the files needed for booting on drive C:. The rest of the root directory is devoted to subdirectory entries, thus allowing for the maximum number of subdirectories branching off the root directory. Each subdirectory, of course, can contain both files and subdirectory entries.

This book uses the term *directory* to refer to either the root directory or a subdirectory. The term *subdirectory* depicts a relationship between two directories. You might also see the terms *parent directory* and *child directory* to characterize the relationship between a directory and its subdirectories.

(a) Rate these from slowest (1) to fastest (3).
  A. Searching for a specific file in a large directory
  B. Searching for a specific file in a small directory
  C. Searching for a global filespec in a large directory

(b) Select the major difference between a root directory and a subdirectory.
  A. A subdirectory can be much larger than a root directory.
  B. The root directory can contain no file entries, only subdirectory entries.
  C. A subdirectory can contain no subdirectory entries, only file entries.

(a) A—2; B—3; C—1
(b) A

Using Subdirectories

When you first boot DOS, the root directory of the boot drive is current, so you can use any of its files. To use a file on a different drive, you include the drivename in the filespec, as in B:SAMPLE.DAT, or you can make that drive current by entering its name at the prompt. Similarly, if you want to use a file in a subdirectory, you must either specify the file's *path* or change the directory in which you are working. You will learn how to change directories later. First, you will learn how to specify a file's path.

A path specifies the names of all the directories, starting with the current directory, that DOS must go through to get to the desired file.

For example, a disk containing a family accounting system might have two subdirectories in the root directory, named for the two members of the family, George and Martha, and each person might have two subdirectories, one for checks and one for credit cards. Figure 5.2 shows how the tree structure would look.

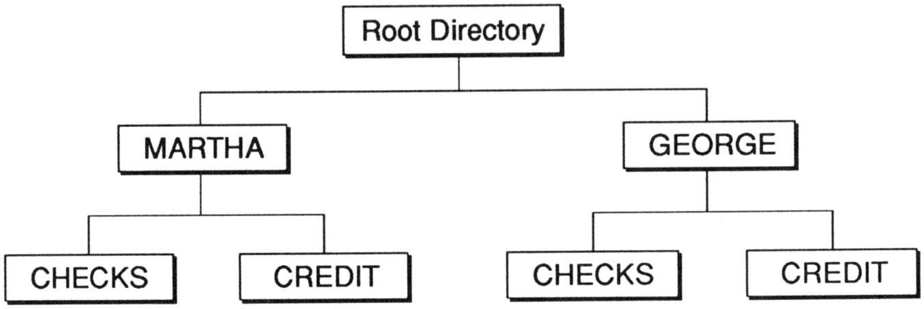

Figure 5.2. Sample Home Directory Structure

Now, George might have a file in his credit subdirectory showing his purchases with his Visa credit card. If the name of this file is VISA.DAT, the filespec including the path from the root directory is:

```
GEORGE\CREDIT\VISA.DAT
```

The backward slash, or backslash (\), is used to separate names in the path. To find the file, DOS will start with the current directory, which is the root directory right now, find the location of the subdirectory GEORGE, look in that subdirectory to find the location of the subdirectory CREDIT, then look in that subdirectory to find the location of the file VISA.DAT. Martha could also have a file named VISA.DAT in her CREDIT subdirectory, but since the path for this duplicate filename is different, DOS finds no confusion between the two files. If a drivename is needed, it precedes the path.

You can have as many subdirectories as you want and need. However, DOS does not permit a full path (from the root directory to the end of the extension) longer than 63 characters, including the backslashes.

Use the diagram in Figure 5.3 to answer the following questions. The filespecs are shown in uppercase letters, while the directory names are in lowercase letters.

(a) How many subdirectories are shown?

For the following questions, assume you're currently working in the root directory.

(b) Write the filespec (including path) for REPAIR.DAT.

(c) Write the filespec for PAYROLL.DAT.

(d) Write the filespec for LEFTOVER.DAT.

(a) Four
(b) INCOME\SERVICES\REPAIR.DAT
(c) OUTGO\PAYROLL.DAT
(d) LEFTOVER.DAT

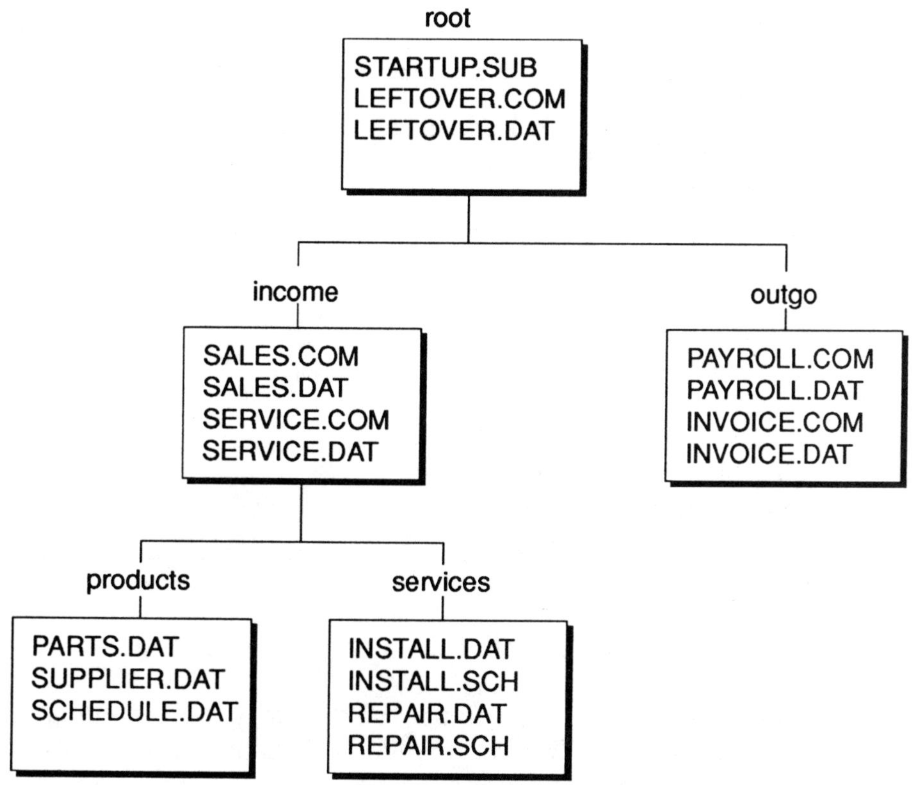

Figure 5.3. Sample Business Directory Structure

Every subdirectory is actually a file; it has a filespec, formed like any other filespec. You can use a file extension (such as .DIR) if you wish. Most people don't use an extension with subdirectory names; this keeps pathnames shorter and allows more subdirectories to be included in a path. The root directory's name is a single backslash.

Suppose you are working in subdirectory MARTHA\CREDIT and you need to access a file in GEORGE\CREDIT. If you specify GEORGE\CREDIT\VISA.DAT, DOS examines the current directory for the subdirectory named GEORGE. Since GEORGE is not a child of the current subdirectory, the path is invalid and you'll get an error message.

You solve this problem by telling DOS to start the path not at the current directory but at the root directory. You do this by starting the path with a backslash. \GEORGE\CREDIT\VISA.DAT will find the file no matter what directory is current. If you don't start the path with a backslash, DOS starts the search in the current directory; this is called a *relative* path. If you do start the path with a backslash, DOS starts at the root directory; this is called an *absolute* path.

Refer back to Figure 5.3. Suppose the INCOME subdirectory is current. Write filespecs for the following:
(a) SALES.DAT
(b) SCHEDULE.DAT
(c) INVOICE.DAT
(d) LEFTOVER.DAT

(a) SALES.DAT
(b) PRODUCTS\SCHEDULE.DAT
(c) \OUTGO\INVOICE.DAT
(d) \LEFTOVER.DAT

DIR with Subdirectories

You learned earlier how to use the directory (DIR) command to list the files on your disk. The DIR command also lists the names of all subdirectories in the current directory. Figure 5.4 shows what the root directory listing of the family accounting disk might look like. The root directory has two subdirectories and one regular file. Since subdirectories are actually special-purpose files, the DIR command counts them in the file total at the bottom.

If you are in the directory GEORGE and enter the DIR command, the response looks like Figure 5.5. The two subdirectories CHECKS and CREDIT and the file TRIAL.BAS are shown. In addition, there are two special directories indicated by "." and "..", which are found in all subdirectories. The first one, shown as a single period, represents the current directory, GEORGE in the example. The other one, shown as a double period, represents the parent of the current directory, the root directory in the example. However, if you were in \GEORGE\CHECKS, then "." would represent CHECKS and ".." would represent GEORGE.

```
B>DIR

 Volume in drive B has no label
 Directory of  B:\

COMMAND  COM     25276   7-24-87  12:00a
GEORGE        <DIR>      2-23-90   6:51p
MARTHA        <DIR>      2-23-90   6:51p
        3 File(s)    330752 bytes free

B>_
```

Figure 5.4. Root Directory of Family Accounting Disk

```
B>DIR

 Volume in drive B has no label
 Directory of  B:\GEORGE

.             <DIR>      2-23-90   6:51p
..            <DIR>      2-23-90   6:51p
CHECKS        <DIR>      2-23-90   6:52p
CREDIT        <DIR>      2-23-90   6:52p
TRIAL    BAS      9819   2-24-90  12:00a
        5 File(s)    320512 bytes free

B>_
```

Figure 5.5. Listing of GEORGE Directory

The symbol ".." can be used as a directory name in paths and commands. For example, if you are in the GEORGE directory and want to display the root directory, you could enter either of these commands:

```
C>DIR \
```

or

```
C>DIR ..
```

If you are in the GEORGE directory and want to view a file in the MARTHA directory, you could use either of these commands:

```
C>TYPE \MARTHA\BUDGET90
```

or

```
C>TYPE ..\MARTHA\BUDGET90
```

You can also use the single period as a directory name in paths and commands, but it is not needed because the current directory is always the default.

(a) True or false? The DIR command will list the names of all subdirectories on the disk.
(b) True or false? The directory ".." is always the root directory.
(c) Write a command to display the files in the current subdirectory.
C>_
(d) Write a command to display the files in the parent directory.
C>_
(e) How can you tell the difference between a file entry and a subdirectory entry in a directory listing?

(a) False: It will show only the subdirectories that are in the current directory
(b) False: ".." is the parent directory of the current directory
(c) C>DIR
(d) C>DIR ..
(e) A subdirectory says <DIR> for the file size

You can display the files in any subdirectory by specifying its path in your DIR command. For example, DIR \GEORGE\CREDIT produces a listing of the named directory no matter what the current directory is.

Refer back to Figure 5.3 to answer these questions. Assume you are working in the root directory.

(a) Write a command to show the root directory.

C>_

(b) Write a command to show the SERVICES directory.

C>_

(c) Write a command to list the OUTGO directory.

C>_

(d) Write a command to list all the files with extension COM in the INCOME directory.

C>_

(a) `C>DIR`
(b) `C>DIR INCOME\SERVICES`
(c) `C>DIR OUTGO`
(d) `C>DIR INCOME\*.COM`

Creating a Subdirectory

The MKDIR command (or its abbreviation MD) is used to create a subdirectory. In the command, you specify the subdirectory's path as necessary. For example, if the root directory is current and you want to create a subdirectory named MARTHA, you could enter

```
C>MKDIR MARTHA
```

To create the subdirectory CHECKS in the subdirectory MARTHA from the root directory, you would enter

```
C>MD MARTHA\CHECKS
```

To create the subdirectory CREDIT in the directory MARTHA from the root directory, you would enter

```
C>MD MARTHA\CREDIT
```

The path you specify starts at the current directory unless it begins with a backslash. From within MARTHA, you could use MD CHECKS to create the subdirectory. From MARTHA you could add a subdirectory for a third family member with the command MD \THOMAS. You could not use MD \DAVIS\CHECKS unless subdirectory DAVIS already exists. If you try to do so you'll get a message `Unable to create directory.`

As indicated earlier, subdirectory names must follow the same rules as filespecs.

(a) Assume the root directory is current. Write a command that will create the subdirectory EXTRA in the subdirectory CREDIT in MARTHA.
C>_

(b) Assume the MARTHA directory is current. Write a command to create the same subdirectory as in Question a.
C>_

(c) Assume the GEORGE directory is current. Write a command to create the same subdirectory as before.
C>_

(d) Assume the GEORGE directory is current. Write the commands needed to create a subdirectory CASH within HOUSING, within the root directory.
C>_

(a) `C>MD MARTHA\CREDIT\EXTRA`
(b) `C>MD CREDIT\EXTRA`
(c) `C>MD \MARTHA\CREDIT\EXTRA`
(d) `C>MD \HOUSING` *followed by* `C>MD \HOUSING\CASH`

Changing the Current Directory

Up to this point, you have not known how to get out of the root directory, although you can reference files and create subdirectories in other directories. You can change directories with the CHDIR command (or its abbreviation CD), making a different one current. The paths are used exactly the same as with the MKDIR command. For example, if you are in the root directory and want to make the directory GEORGE your current directory, you would enter

```
C>CHDIR GEORGE
```

Similarly, if you want to make GEORGE\CHECKS your current directory, you would enter

```
C>CD GEORGE\CHECKS
```

From there, you would make MARTHA\CHECKS current by entering

```
C>CD \MARTHA\CHECKS
```

It's important to start the path with a backslash in this last example. If you don't use the beginning backslash, DOS starts the path with the current directory. If you want to know what directory is current, you would enter

```
C>CD
```

or

```
C>DIR
```

You can return to the root directory by using its name, which is a single backslash. So this command

```
C>CD \
```

returns you to the root directory. If you enter CD from the root directory, the response will be \ to indicate the root directory.

Refer to Figure 5.3 to answer these questions. Consider them as a sequence. After Question a, for example, OUTGO is current.

(a) Write a command to change to OUTGO from wherever you are.

C>_

(b) Now write a command to change to the root directory.

C>_

(c) Write a command to find out which directory is current.

C>_

(d) Write a command to change to the SERVICES subdirectory from the root directory.

C>_

(e) Write a command to show the SERVICES directory.

C>_

(f) Write a command to show the OUTGO directory.

C>_

(g) Write a command to show the root directory.

C>_

(a) `C>CD \OUTGO`
(b) `C>CD \`
(c) `C>CD` *or* `C>DIR` *or* `C>CHDIR`
(d) `C>CD INCOME\SERVICES`
(e) `C>DIR`
(f) `C>DIR \OUTGO`
(g) `C>DIR \`

Removing a Subdirectory

At times you will no longer need a particular directory, and you can use RMDIR (or its abbreviation RD) to remove it. A directory must be empty before DOS will let you remove it. A good idea is to check the directory with the DIR command before you try to remove it. The only entries should be "." and "..", which are always in every subdirectory. If you try to remove a directory that is not empty, DOS will respond with

```
Invalid path, not directory
or directory not empty
```

and the directory will not be removed.

Once you have determined that the directory is empty, you may remove it. For example, to remove the subdirectory GEORGE\CREDIT, you would enter:

```
C>RMDIR \GEORGE\CREDIT
```

This removes the CREDIT subdirectory in GEORGE, but does not remove GEORGE. You can never remove the current directory or the root directory; if you try, you'll get the error message shown earlier.

(a) Suppose \MARTHA\CHECKS\EXTRA is empty and current. Which of these commands, if any, is valid?
  A. `C>RD .`
  B. `C>RD \MARTHA\CHECKS\EXTRA`
  C. `C>RD \`
  D. `C>RD ..`

(b) You want to eliminate \MARTHA\CHECKS\EXTRA. Put these steps in order.
  A. Change to another directory
  B. Erase all files in the EXTRA directory
  C. Enter the RMDIR command

(c) Write a command to remove SALES under INCOME. (Assume SALES is empty.)
  `C>_`

(a) None is valid
(b) B, A, C, or A, B, C
(c) `C>RD \INCOME\SALES`

Setting Up Search Paths

When you enter an external command such as FORMAT, LABEL, or DISKCOPY, DOS looks for an executable file (extension COM, BAT, or EXE) in the current directory only. You can reach the desired program file by switching to the directory it's in with the CHDIR command. Alternatively, you can prefix the command name with a path, as in this example:

```
C>\DOS\FORMAT A:
```

In response to the pathname, DOS will look for the FORMAT.COM file in the C:\DOS directory.

Constantly changing directories and/or prefixing command names with directory paths is time consuming and error prone. You can set up a standard search path in the DOS environment with the PATH command. The path you specify is automatically searched for any external commands (that is, programs or batch files) that are not in the current directory. The path is not used for operands; that is set up in the APPEND command, which we'll cover next. Suppose you have FIXIT.BAT and PARTS.DAT in different directories, and you've specified a path that includes both. This command

```
C>FIXIT PARTS.DAT
```

causes the path to be searched for FIXIT, but only the current directory is searched for PARTS.DAT. If PARTS.DAT is elsewhere, you'll have to include the path in the filespec, set up an APPEND path, or change to that directory before entering the command.

The PATH command sets up a chain of directories to be searched for all future command references. DOS searches for a program file starting with the current directory, then proceeds from directory to directory in the order specified in the search path, until the file is found. For example

```
C>PATH C:\GEORGE\CHECKS;C:\GEORGE\CREDIT;B:\
```

tells DOS to search first the current directory, then directory C:\GEORGE\CHECKS, then C:\GEORGE\CREDIT, and finally B:\ (the root directory on drive B:). Semicolons separate pathnames in the list.

You'll want to work in the directory you use most, and search directories in the order of frequency of use. Put less frequently used directories at the end of the list. We suggest you use only absolute paths in the PATH command and always specify the drivename. That way, it doesn't matter which directory is current when DOS is searching the path for a program file.

Refer back to Figure 5.3.

(a) Write a PATH command so that every directory containing a .COM file will be searched. The programs you use most often are INVOICE.COM and LEFTOVER.COM.

C>_

(b) Suppose the current directory is the root directory and the above path is in effect. You issue the command:

```
C>PAYROLL PAYROLL.DAT
```

Will the PAYROLL program be located?
Will PAYROLL.DAT be located?

(c) Write the command(s) necessary to run the INVOICE program using INVOICE.DAT. The current directory is \INCOME\SERVICES.
C>_

(a) `C>PATH C:\;C:\OUTGO;C:\INCOME`
(b) *PAYROLL.COM will be located but PAYROLL.DAT won't*
(c) `C>INVOICE \OUTGO\INVOICE.DAT` *or* `C>CD \OUTGO` *followed by*
`C>INVOICE INVOICE.DAT`

Each time you use PATH to enter a search path, it replaces the old search path with the new one. To reset the search path so that only the current directory is searched, use the command name followed by a semicolon:

```
C>PATH;
```

To see the current setting for the PATH command, enter PATH with no operands:

```
C>PATH
```

This displays the current search path, but does not change it. The display looks like this:

```
PATH=C:\GEORGE\CHECKS;C:\GEORGE\CREDIT;B:\
```

If you make an error in any of the pathnames in the PATH command, PATH accepts it and DOS ignores it. But when DOS tries to search a path with an invalid drivename, you will see this message:

```
Invalid drive in search path
```

Refer again to Figure 5.3. Suppose you're sitting down to work with these files: LEFTOVER.COM, SALES.COM, and PAYROLL.COM. You'll use SALES.COM ten times as often as the other programs.

(a) Set up a search path for this session.

C>_

(b) Write a command to display the current path.

C>_

(c) Write a command to cancel the current search path.

C>_

(a) Here's what we would do:

```
C>PATH C:\INCOME;C:\;C:\OUTGO
```

This sets up the following search chain:

1. *The current directory*
2. *C:\INCOME*
3. *The root directory*
4. *C:\OUTGO*

Since \INCOME is so heavily used, we might also use CD \INCOME to make it the current directory so that it is searched first

(b) C>PATH

(c) C>PATH;

The PATH command lets DOS access external programs in other directories. If no search path exists, DOS searches only the current directory for an external command. Thus, if you enter

```
C>WORKOUT LOCKFILE.DAT
```

DOS searches the current subdirectory for the WORKOUT program or batch file. It WORKOUT is not there, DOS displays an error message. If a search path exists, however, DOS searches all the directories in the search path for the WORKOUT program.

To summarize the PATH command, here's the format:

Format (internal):

PATH [;] [path[;path...]]

If you use PATH without any options, DOS displays the current search path. If you use PATH with only a semicolon, DOS eliminates the current path. To set up a search path of directories, simply list the complete directory paths, separating them with semicolons. For each program, DOS will search first in the current directory, then in each directory in the PATH command—in the order listed in the command.

The search path in the PATH command has no effect on filespecs used as operands.

Refer again to Figure 5.3.

(a) Suppose you're working in OUTGO and no search path exists. You enter:

```
C>SERVICE \INCOME\SERVICE.DAT
```

What will happen?

(b) How can you use the service program?

A. Enter `C>CD \INCOME`, then reenter the SERVICE command
B. Enter `C>\INCOME\SERVICE \INCOME\SERVICE.DAT`
C. Enter `C>PATH \OUTGO;\INCOME` then enter `C>SERVICE SERVICE.DAT`
D. Enter `C>PATH \OUTGO;\INCOME` then enter `C>SERVICE \INCOME\SERVICE.DAT`
E. Enter `C>CD \INCOME` followed by `C>SERVICE SERVICE.DAT`
F. Any of the above will do

(a) DOS displays an error message
(b) A, B, D, or E; C is wrong because SERVICE.DAT will not be found

---

To create a search path for nonprogram files, use APPEND—in the same way you use PATH. The following command sets up a search path comprised of three directories:

```
C>APPEND C:\GEORGE;C:\GEORGE\CHECKS;C:\GEORGE\CREDIT
```

The path is limited to 127 characters. The following command displays the current nonprogram search path:

```
C>APPEND
```

The following command deletes the nonprogram search path:

```
C>APPEND;
```

There can be only one APPEND search path at a time. A new one overlays the previous one.

The APPEND search path affects reading operations but not writing operations. That is, if you use commands like DIR and TYPE, DOS looks in the APPEND search path to find a file if it isn't in the current directory. But output operations like COPY always place the output in the current directory unless another directory is specified in the command. Be cautious about using APPEND when you work with applications that update files, such as word processors. The application might read the file from somewhere else in the search path, but when it goes to save the updated version, it will save the file in the current directory. Thus, the original version of the file is unchanged in its original directory, and the updated version is on the current directory. If this happens to you, you'll probably spend a lot of time wondering what happened. If you don't use APPEND, you'll have to specify the exact path for a file, but the software then knows exactly where to put updated versions.

(a) Write a command to set up the root directories of drives A:, B:, and C: as the nonprogram search path.
C>_

(b) Write a command to display the current nonprogram search path.
C>_

(c) Write a command to cancel the current nonprogram search path.
C>_

(d) Select the true statements.
- A. A new nonprogram search path overlays the previous nonprogram search path.
- B. You can have only one search path, either program or nonprogram; a new APPEND command overlays the current search path, whether it is an APPEND search path or a PATH search path.
- C. You can have as many program and nonprogram search paths as you need.

(e) Suppose the current directory is C:\GEORGE\CHECKS. The APPEND search path is C:\MARTHA\CHECKS. Your word processor accesses a file named OVERDRAW without specifying a directory. DOS reads it from C:\MARTHA\CHECKS\OVERDRAW, which you revise. Where will the new copy of the OVERDRAW file be written?

(*a*) `C>APPEND A:\;B:\;C:\`
(*b*) `C>APPEND`
(*c*) `C>APPEND ;`
(*d*) *A*
(*e*) *On C:\GEORGE\CHECKS*

The format of the APPEND command is shown below:

Format (external):
APPEND [;] [path[;path...]]

The first time you use APPEND after booting, the program is read into memory like any other external program. Then it stays in memory and acts like an internal program until you boot again. This is called a *Terminate and Stay Resident (TSR)* program. You'll meet two other DOS TSR programs, MODE and PRINT, later in this book. You might also have TSR application programs, such as pop-up alarms, screen capture facilities, and mouse drivers.

(a) What does TSR stand for?
(b) When is the APPEND program loaded into memory?
  A. When the system is booted
  B. The first time you use it
  C. Every time you use it
(c) Why shouldn't you use APPEND if your system is short of memory?
(d) How can you get the APPEND program out of memory again?

(*a*) *Terminate and Stay Resident*
(*b*) *B*
(*c*) *Because the program stays in memory*
(*d*) *Reboot*

Viewing the Tree Structure

After you have created some subdirectories, you can use the external TREE command to provide a list of subdirectories in the same way the DIR provides a list of files in the current directory. Figure 5.6 shows the beginning of the output for a TREE command with no operands or switches. You can see in the figure that DOS is listing each subdirectory on the disk with a list of its subdirectories. Since this listing generally scrolls off the screen, you might want to use echo printing or Ctrl-NumLock to control the display.

The TREE command can also provide you with a list of the files in each directory. To show the filespecs, you should enter

```
C>TREE /F
```

Figure 5.7 shows the beginning of the output. DOS starts with the first entry in the root directory. If it is a file, it is listed. If it is a subdirectory, DOS then follows that path, listing the entries in the subdirectory. Each time TREE encounters a subdirectory, it follows down the path. When it reaches the bottom of the path, TREE moves back up as many levels as necessary to find the next subdirectory to follow. TREE only returns to the root directory when a subdirectory path has been completely traced.

The files in the root directory are listed as they are encountered in the directory between subdirectory entries. Therefore, you might have three subdirectory listings, two root directory files, two more subdirectory listings, three root directory files, and so forth.

The TREE command has only one operand and one switch.

Format (external):
TREE [d:] [/F]

Since it is an external command, TREE.COM must be available on disk. The d: operand lets you check the directory structure on a different disk.

(a) Write a command that will list all files and subdirectories on the current drive.
C>_
(b) True or false? The TREE command can be used instead of the DIR command to find out the names of your files.

```
B>TREE

DIRECTORY PATH LISTING


Path: \GEORGE

Sub-directories:  CHECKS
                  CREDIT


Path: \GEORGE\CHECKS

Sub-directories:  None


Path: \MARTHA

Sub-directories:  CHECKS
                  CREDIT
```

Figure 5.6. TREE Output

```
B>TREE

DIRECTORY PATH LISTING

Files:            COMMAND .COM
                  AUTOEXEC.BAT
                  CONFIG  .SYS
                  DMDRVR  .BIN


Path: \GEORGE

Sub-directories:  CHECKS
                  CREDIT

Files:            TRIAL   .BAS


Path: \GEORGE\CHECKS

Sub-directories:  None

Files:            JAN
```

Figure 5.7. TREE Output with /F Switch

(*a*) `C>TREE /F`
(*b*) *True, but it may give you more information than you need—and it certainly won't fit on one screen*

Default Directories on Nondefault Drives

So far in this book, we have either used the default directory on the default drive, or specified the drivename and/or pathname in the filespec. But every drive has a default directory, even when that drive is not the current drive. For example, suppose you enter this command:

```
C>DIR A:
```

This would produce a listing of the default directory on drive A:, which may or may not be the root directory. If you want a listing of the root directory on drive A:, you might need to enter the command this way:

```
C>DIR A:\
```

When you first boot, the default directory on every drive is the root directory. You can change the default directory on any drive with the CHDIR command. For example, suppose you want to work from drive C: but access some files from D:\WP\ANNREPT. If D:\ is the default directory on drive D:, then each time you want to access a file in D:\WP\ANNREPT, you could include the path name in the command or else add the directory to the APPEND path. Here's how you would use the pathname in the command.

```
C>TYPE C:\WP\ANNREPT\CEOMSG
```

However, if you enter this CHDIR command

```
C>CD D:\WP\ANNREPT
```

then all references to drive D: that don't specify a path will access \WP\ANNREPT. Thus, you can type the same file listed above with this command:

```
C>TYPE D:CEOMSG
```

If you now entered DIR D:, you would get a directory of D:\WP\ANNREPT.

The difference between switching directories and switching drives can be confusing at first. You might think if you enter this command

```
C>CD D:\WP\ANNREPT
```

the result would be to make drive D: current *and* make \WP\ANNREPT current. But that's not true. The command makes \WP\ANNREPT current on drive D:, but it has no effect on the current drive or the current directory on this drive. You must enter the drivename as a command to change drives. When you do, the current directory on the new current drive becomes the default directory.

Suppose C:\GEORGE is the current drive and current directory.

(a) Write a command to make \BANKLIST the current directory on drive A:.

`C>_`

Specify which directory will be accessed by each of the following commands after you enter the above command.

(b) `C>DIR`

(c) `C>DIR A:`

(d) `C>TYPE OUTCHECK`

(e) `C>TYPE A:OUTCHECK`

(a) `C>CD A:\BANKLIST`

(b) C:\GEORGE

(c) A:\BANKLIST

(d) C:\GEORGE

(e) A:\BANKLIST

Organizing Your Fixed Disk

The way you organize your fixed disk directory in the beginning can later make all your work sessions efficient or inefficient. Take some time to make a plan before putting files on your fixed disk. You'll be glad you did.

Each subdirectory should contain related files, ones you want to work on together and erase together when they're not needed.

The root directory should contain as few files as possible. Space for entries is limited in the root directory but unlimited in all subdirectories. However,

COMMAND.COM and two files you will learn about later called AUTOEXEC.BAT and CONFIG.SYS must be in the root directory of the primary DOS partition.

You'll want to create a subdirectory for your DOS external programs. You can call it DOS or UTILITY. If you use a PATH command right after you boot, you can include this directory in the standard search path.

Where do you put your word processor, your spreadsheet, your financial package, and your other application software? Most users establish a separate subdirectory for each one and put related files in the same subdirectory or in its child directories for easy access.

(a) Which is better?
   A. Limit subdirectories; put as many files as possible in the root directory
   B. Keep most files in subdirectories, not in the root directory

(b) Which is better?
   A. Put only related files together in one subdirectory, trying to keep the size under 100 files
   B. Put all your programs in one subdirectory and all your data files in another subdirectory

(c) What subdirectory should be included in a PATH command immediately after you boot?

(a) B
(b) A
(c) The subdirectory containing the DOS external program files

---

Manipulating Directories

Several commands let you manipulate the layout of directories. Ordinarily, PATH and APPEND should serve all your needs. But some applications have special needs. For the most part, these are programs that were released many years ago—before fixed disks, tree-structured directories, and paths were in wide use. DOS has created several commands that let you use drivenames and paths with these programs.

The SUBST command substitutes an imaginary drivename for a path. This facility helps with programs that can handle drivenames but not paths. Here is its format:

Format (external):
SUBST [d: path] [d: /D]

To establish a substitution, specify an imaginary drivename and pathname, as in:

```
C>SUBST E: C:\GEORGE\CHECKS
```

Now you can use E: in filespecs and DOS will substitute C:\GEORGE\CHECKS.

To display all the substitutions currently in effect, enter SUBST with no operands. To delete a substitution, enter the imaginary drivename with the /D switch, as in:

```
C>SUBST E: /D
```

The JOIN command adds one drive's directory tree to another. It accommodates applications that recognize paths but not drivenames. Here is the format of JOIN:

Format (external):
JOIN [d: subdirectory] [d: /D]

To join the entire tree structure on drive C: to the root directory on drive A:, you would enter:

```
C>JOIN C: A:\TEMP
```

Now you can reference any directory on C: from the A:\TEMP path. To list all the joined directories currently in effect, enter JOIN with no operands. To cancel a particular join operation, enter the original drivename with the /D switch, as in:

```
A>JOIN C: /D
```

The ASSIGN command substitutes one drivename for another. It is meant for very old applications that assume the only available drives are A: and B:. The format of ASSIGN is:

Format (external):
ASSIGN [d=d...]

To rename drive C as drive B, you would enter:

```
A>ASSIGN C=B
```

To break an assignment, enter ASSIGN with no operands. This clears all the current assignments.

These three commands are powerful and dangerous. They can cause major problems if used together or in conjunction with APPEND. If you try to use DOS programs such as FORMAT, DISKCOPY, and DISKCOMP on manipulated directories, you could do actual harm to your directories and suffer severe data loss. You'll be learning more commands later that search directories for files to work on: BACKUP, RESTORE, XCOPY, REPLACE, RECOVER, and CHKDSK. Some of these programs will identify and refuse to work with manipulated directories, but some won't. In general, don't use SUBST, JOIN, or ASSIGN.

If you suspect you must use one of these programs to make an application work, read your DOS documentation thoroughly beforehand to learn all the techniques and pitfalls. We haven't spelled them out here. Then enter the command immediately before starting the application and cancel the command or reboot immediately after terminating the application so it doesn't affect any other operations.

(a) What command lets you graft together two drives' directory trees as if they were all one large tree structure?
(b) What command lets you call one drive by another drive's name?
(c) What command lets you call a path by a drivename?
(d) Which commands can cause major problems and should be used with a great deal of caution?
(e) Where can you find more information on how to use, and not use, the directory manipulation commands?

(a) JOIN
(b) ASSIGN
(c) SUBST
(d) All three of them
(e) In your DOS documentation

Speeding Up Directory Access

Accessing a disk is very slow compared to working in memory. Therefore, any time a program must access a file on disk, it is slowed down. The microprocessor sits idle until the disk access is done.

You can speed the process with the FASTOPEN command. FASTOPEN lets DOS store directory entries in memory as it uses them. Then, when DOS needs to access a file again, it doesn't have to search through several levels of directory entries on disk. It can look up the directory entries in memory, find the correct disk location, and access the disk only once, to read or write the data. With some programs, FASTOPEN can make a noticeable difference in the speed of a program.

FASTOPEN can be used only with fixed disks. Why? To prevent you from changing the disk after the directory information has been stored in memory. Otherwise, the results would be disastrous. FASTOPEN has this format:

Format (external):
FASTOPEN d:=nnn...

You must specify the drivename of the drive to which you want to apply FASTOPEN. You can also specify the number of directory entries you want DOS to store in memory. The default is 34, but you might want to change that. If you have more than one fixed disk drive, you can specify several in the command. For example, to specify FASTOPEN with 100 entries for each of three fixed disk drives, you would enter:

```
C>FASTOPEN C:=100 D:=100 E:=100
```

Once FASTOPEN has been specified for a drive, you can't revise or cancel it without rebooting.

(a) Write a command to specify FASTOPEN for drives C: and D:. Use the default number of memory entries for drive C:. Use 20 entries for drive D:.
C>_

(b) Once the above command has been entered, how can you change the number of entries dedicated to drives C: and D:?

(c) What's wrong with this command?

```
C>FASTOPEN A:=20
```

(a) `C>FASTOPEN C: D:=20`
(b) *Reboot*
(c) *You can't use FASTOPEN on a diskette drive*

Determining the correct number of entries to use with FASTOPEN can be tricky. It helps to understand how DOS saves the directory entries. As you access files, DOS saves their directory entries in memory, using one memory slot for each subdirectory entry and one for the file itself. Therefore, if you access C:\GEORGE\CREDIT\VISA.DAT, three slots are used up. Once all the memory slots are used up, DOS overwrites old entries with new ones.

If you use a word processor, it might access a dozen or more files internally in the process of doing its work.

Every time you access a file, DOS searches the memory entries first, looking for the entry that locates the desired file. Only if the entry isn't there does DOS go to the disk directory.

If you specify too few entries in memory, the probability of your next file being recorded in memory will be low, and you won't save much time with FASTOPEN. If you specify too many entries, DOS will spend more time searching the memory entries than it would to access the disk directory. You'll actually slow the system down.

The minimum number of FASTOPEN entries for a drive is ten unless it's possible to have a path longer than that on the drive. Most likely, you won't use the minimum. A number around 100 is more useful.

The maximum number of FASTOPEN entries, counting all the drives, is 999. You'll probably never reach that number unless you have several fixed disk drives. If DOS has to search through more than about 200 entries for one drive, it's wasting time.

Another factor to consider before using FASTOPEN is the amount of memory space you're taking away from other programs. Each memory entry takes up 35 bytes. 100 entries is 3500 bytes. Three drives with 100 entries each means approximately 10K is removed from available memory. If you also have some TSRs in residence, the reserved space could inhibit or slow down some of your applications.

Keeping all the above in mind, you can experiment with FASTOPEN until you reach a comfortable level. Start around 100 entries per drive. For each session, revise the number of entries down a little more until you find a level you like.

Select the true statements.

(a) The more FASTOPEN entries per drive, the faster DOS can open files.
(b) The more FASTOPEN entries per drive, the less memory space for applications.
(c) When all the memory slots are used up, new entries overwrite older ones.
(d) Always specify at least 100 FASTOPEN entries per drive.

b, c

Exercises

These exercises let you practice creating and using subdirectories. If your fixed disk is formatted, use it in this exercise. If not, use a diskette in drive B:.

What You Should Do	*How the Computer Responds*
1. If necessary, boot with your DOS work diskette in drive A:. Place a blank formatted disk in the B: drive or use your fixed disk for this exercise.	1. Boots as usual.
2. Enter a PATH command for your DOS external programs.	2. Stores the path and uses it to find external programs.
3. Switch to your other disk (B: or C:). Turn on Echo Print if you'd like a hardcopy of this exercise.	3. Displays a command prompt for the new default drive.

4. Use the TREE command to check the current directory structure. Don't be surprised if no tree structure shows up, as you have not yet created any subdirectories.	4. Probably displays:
	`DIRECTORY PATH LISTING`
	`No sub-directories exist`

5. Create subdirectories MARTHA and GEORGE as in Figure 5.2. Check with DIR and TREE to see the structure now.	5. Creates and displays the subdirectories as requested.
6. While still in the root directory, create subdirectory CREDIT under GEORGE. Use TREE to verify.	6. Creates and displays the subdirectory as requested.
7. Change directories so that MARTHA is current. Then create CHECKS and CREDIT under MARTHA. Use TREE to verify your structure.	7. Creates and displays the subdirectories as requested.

8. Check the directory of MARTHA to see the listings of the subdirectories.	8. Displays the indicated directory, including:
	`.          <DIR>`
	`..         <DIR>`
	`CHECKS     <DIR>`
	`CREDIT     <DIR>`

9. From within MARTHA, create the \GEORGE\CHECKS subdirectory.	9. Creates the requested subdirectory.
10. Return to the root directory and try DIR and TREE.	10. Displays the requested information.
11. Create a search path that will search the current directory, then the directory of drive A:, then both CREDIT subdirectories. Use PATH to display the path.	11. Creates, then displays, the search path.
12. Use the TREE command without a drive prefix.	12. Displays the directory structure.
13. Delete all subdirectories on the practice disk. Check with TREE to make sure they're gone. Delete the search path as well.	13. Carries out your commands.

14. If your fixed disk doesn't contain subdirectories, create one called DOS. Soon you'll put your DOS external program files in this directory.

14. Creates the DOS subdirectory on the fixed disk.

What If It Doesn't Work?

1. If you have trouble creating subdirectories (MKDIR) or changing directories (CHDIR), remember that a new subdirectory is placed within the current directory unless you prefix the path with \ to start at the root directory.

2. If you have trouble removing directories, remember that you can't remove the current directory. The easiest sequence for removing all these directories is:

```
CHDIR \MARTHA
RMDIR CHECKS
RMDIR CREDIT
CHDIR \GEORGE
RMDIR CHECKS
RMDIR CREDIT
CHDIR \
RMDIR GEORGE
RMDIR MARTHA
```

3. If you have trouble establishing a search path, try again. A simple path like PATH A:\ lets you run the external commands on drive A: from any drive.

Note Take the time now to plan the initial layout of your fixed disk directory. It's wise to plan this in advance because once you put subdirectories on the disk and add files and subdirectories to them, it's very difficult to change them. As you have seen, it's awkward to remove a subdirectory. There are no commands to rename a subdirectory or to move a subdirectory to another position in the tree. In other words, revising the directory structure is difficult. Planning your directory in advance can save you a lot of work later on. You might also want to use MKDIR to create the subdirectories you decide you'll need on the disk. In the next few chapters, you'll learn how to copy files into subdirectories.

6

Copying Files

In this chapter you'll learn about COPY, an internal command used to copy a file from one place to another. You can use it whenever you have the DOS prompt, no matter which drive and directory are active. You might copy a file from one disk to another, from one directory to another, from the keyboard to a disk, from a disk to the printer, and so forth. You can also use COPY to combine two or more files into one file.

When you have finished this chapter, you will be able to:

- Use the COPY command to copy one or more files
- Use the COMP command to compare two files
- Use the COPY command to create a new file on a disk
- Use the COPY command to print one or more files
- Use the COPY command to combine several files into one
- Use the COPY command to change the date and time stamp in the directory
- Interpret DOS messages associated with the COPY and COMP commands

Uses of COPY

One of the most frequent activities you will perform with DOS is to copy files. You might want to copy a file from one disk or directory to another. You can copy from drive A: to B:, from B: to C:, and so forth. Why would you do this?

- Suppose you have just spent a lot of time creating a file. You're going to use the file now, but first you want to make a backup copy for safety's sake. A lot of things can go wrong with disks, as we have mentioned in earlier chapters. It's wise to keep backup copies of all your important files, including any on a fixed disk. (Most computer users ignore this advice until they first lose a disk. Then they develop some type of system for keeping backup copies of all their files.)
- If you have a fixed disk, you will copy all the files from the application program diskettes that you buy to the fixed disk.
- Suppose you want to ship some data files to another person who has a compatible computer. You can use COPY to make up the diskette to be sent.
- If a diskette develops bad sectors, you can copy as many files as possible to another diskette or the hard disk.
- If the files on a disk become fragmented, you can copy them to another disk to bring them together. (You'll learn about this in Chapter 9.) You might also want to make a second copy of a file on the same disk.
- Suppose you have a file containing a letter to your representative. You want to send the same letter to your senator, with some minor changes. Rather than typing out the second letter from scratch, you can copy the first letter and then simply change the copy. Any time you create a file that is similar to an existing file, you can copy the existing file and make changes to the copied version.
- Suppose you are going to make changes to a file that you use frequently. Make a backup copy of the file on the same disk before you begin editing the file, just for safety's sake. If you make the content of the file worse while you are changing it, you can fall back on the backup copy. Once a file has been successfully edited, you can erase the backup copy.
- You may want to transfer a file from one subdirectory to another.

You may also want to copy a file from a disk to another device. For example, one way to print a file is to copy it from the disk to the printer. If you are using some type of auxiliary device, you might use COPY to send a file to that device.

You can also go in the opposite direction. That is, you can copy a file from another device to a disk as long as the source device is capable of input. For example, one way to create a new file is to copy it from the keyboard to a disk. (You will try this at the end of the chapter.) If you have an auxiliary device capable of input, you might want to copy a file from the auxiliary device to a disk. Of course, you can't copy from a printer to a disk.

Finally, you might want to copy a file from one nondisk device to another. For example, you might want to copy from the keyboard to the printer or an output auxiliary unit. All these processes are possible with the COPY command.

(a) Which of the following are possible with the COPY command?

A.	Keyboard to disk	G.	Auxiliary to print
B.	Drive A: to drive C:	H.	Print to disk
C.	Drive B: to drive B:	I.	Keyboard to print
D.	Disk to keyboard	J.	Disk to print
E.	Auxiliary to keyboard	K.	Drive C: to drive A:
F.	Keyboard to auxiliary	L.	Disk to auxiliary

(b) Suppose you spend four hours at the keyboard creating a new file. What should you do before shutting down the computer?

(c) How can you create a new disk file using the COPY command?

(d) Suppose you're going to make some changes to a very important file. What should you do first, for safety's sake?

(a) A, B, C, F, G, I, J, K, L (D and E are not possible because the keyboard is not capable of receiving output data; H is not possible because the printer is not capable of sending data)

(b) Make a backup copy on another disk

(c) Copy from keyboard to disk

(d) Make a backup copy

COPY Format

The format of the COPY command is:

Format (internal):

COPY source destination [/V]

Source indicates the input location—the place the file is to be copied from. The source might be a file or an input device. Destination indicates the location of the new copy; the destination might be a file or an output device.

Both source and destination may be files. Here's an example:

```
C>COPY VISA.DAT CARD.1
```

This command causes the file VISA.DAT in the default directory to be copied and stored in the same directory as CARD.1. The result is two identical files with different names. You can copy the file to a different drive and keep the same name, like this:

```
C>COPY VISA.DAT B:
```

If you don't include a destination filespec, the name is unchanged.

You can copy to or from a specific directory by including the path in the source or destination name.

```
C>COPY VISA.DAT \GEORGE\CREDIT
```

or

```
C>COPY \GEORGE\CREDIT\VISA.DAT A:
```

If you leave out the destination operand, the copy is placed in the default directory.

```
C>COPY A:LOCKFILE
```

This command copies the file named LOCKFILE from the default directory on drive A: to the default directory on drive C:. The copied file also is called LOCKFILE in its new location.

```
C>COPY SOMEDATA
```

This command would result in an error message because you can't have two files with the same name in the same directory. The command implies that C:SOMEDATA should be copied as C:SOMEDATA.

(a) Write a command to copy the file named EXERA from drive C: to drive B:.

C>_

(b) Write a command to make a backup copy of EXERB from drive B:. Call the copy EXERB.BAK and place it on the same drive.
C>_

(c) Write a command to copy EXERC from drive B: to the default drive and directory. Give the file the same name on the default drive.
C>_

(d) What is wrong with this command?

```
C>COPY TWOSONGS
```

(e) Write a command to copy the file NATBANK from subdirectory CHECKS within MARTHA to the A: drive. Name the file NBCHECKS on the A: drive.
C>_

(a) `C>COPY EXERA B:`
(b) `C>COPY B:EXERB B:EXERB.BAK`
(c) `C>COPY B:EXERC`
(d) *You can't copy from C: to C: without changing the filename*
(e) `C>COPY \MARTHA\CHECKS\NATBANK A:NBCHECKS`

Verifying a Copy

You can add /V to the COPY command to cause data to be verified as it is copied. When you use /V, DOS compares each destination sector, as soon as it is written, to its source sector. If a mistake is found, it is corrected immediately. If you use the /V option, you can put it anywhere after the word COPY in the command. All of the following are valid:

```
C>COPY/V TOUCAN B:
C>COPY /V TOUCAN B:
C>COPY TOUCAN/V B:
C>COPY TOUCAN /V B:
C>COPY TOUCAN B:/V
C>COPY TOUCAN B: /V
```

Write a command to copy a file named EXERA from drive C: to drive B: and verify the copy.

```
C>_
```

`C>COPY /V EXERA B:` *(you could put the /V anywhere after the word COPY)*

The COMP command compares two files. If you've forgotten to use /V with COPY, you might use COMP to verify that the copied file is identical to the original. Or you might want to check if a file has been changed since it was copied. If a program starts misbehaving, for example, you could compare the copy on your fixed disk with the original copy on the diskette from the vendor. You could do this by running COMP on files that were once identical. The format is:

Format (external):
COMP source destination

Figure 6.1 shows a complete COMP dialog for a successful comparison. If you

```
C>COMP AUTOEXEC.BAT A:

C:AUTOEXEC.BAT and A:AUTOEXEC.BAT

Files compare ok

Compare more files (Y/N)? N

C>_
```

Figure 6.1. Successful COMP Comparison

```
C>COMP


Enter primary file name
AUTOEXEC.BAT

Enter 2nd file name or drive id
A:

C:AUTOEXEC.BAT and A:AUTOEXEC.BAT

Files compare ok

Compare more files (Y/N)? N

C>_
```

Figure 6.2. COMP Asks for Filespecs

answer Y to the last question or enter only COMP with no operands, DOS asks for the filespecs, as shown in Figure 6.2.

Just as in COPY, you can omit the second filename if it's the same as the first. You can specify drivenames and pathnames as needed.

You can compare groups of files by specifying global filenames. If you specify a global source and only a drivename or path for the destination, as in

```
C>COMP *.COM A:
```

DOS compares matching files with the same name from both locations. If you specify both a global source and a global destination, as in

```
C>COMP *.DAT *.BAK
```

DOS matches files that have the same characters in the global parts of their filespecs. In the above example, DOS would compare GOLD.DAT with GOLD.BAK, AT.DAT with AT.BAK, and so forth.

(a) Write a command to compare LONG and SHORT. Both files are on drive A:.

```
C>_
```

(b) Write a command to compare all files with extension .DAT on drive A: with files of the same name on drive B:.

```
C>_
```

(c) Which command is not valid?

A. `C>COMP`

B. `C>COMP A:FORESURE`

C. `C>COMP QUIZ2`

(a) `C>COMP A:LONG A:SHORT`

(b) `C>COMP A:*.DAT B:`

(c) C—since the default directory is the same for both the source and the destination, you're trying to compare C:QUIZ2 with C:QUIZ2

You've seen what happens in a successful comparison. An unsuccessful comparison can result in various messages. Suppose the comparison identifies one or more mistakes:

```
C>COMP TEACT.A TEACT.B
C:TEACT.A and C:TEACT.B
Compare error at OFFSET 4
File 1 = 72
File 2 = 6C
Compare more files (Y/N)?_
```

The meanings of "OFFSET 4," "72," and "6C" are not crucial (unless you're trying to fix the disks and you can interpret these codes). The point is that a mismatch was found and the files are not the same.

If the two files have different sizes in their directory entries, DOS won't even try to compare them:

```
C>COMP TEACT.A TEACT.C
C:TEACT.A C:TEACT.C
Files are different sizes
Compare more files (Y/N)?_
```

If the two files being compared are very different, COMP gives up after ten errors:

```
C>COMP TEACT.A TEACT.B
C:TEACT.A C:TEACT.B
Compare error at OFFSET 0
File 1 = 74
File 2 = 6E

Compare error at OFFSET 1
File 1 = 68
File 2 = 6F

Compare error at OFFSET 2
File 1 = 69
File 2 = 77
    .
    .
    .
Compare error at OFFSET 8
File 1 = 74
File 2 = 6C

Compare error at OFFSET 9
File 1 = 68
File 2 = 20

10 Mismatches - ending compare

Compare more files (Y/N)?_
```

The above messages show mismatches in the first ten bytes of the two files, enough to show that the files don't match.

You might also encounter a message saying `Eof mark not found`. An Eof (end of file) mark signifies the end of some text files but not program files. COMP displays this message whenever it doesn't find an Eof mark. If the files being compared are program files, the Eof mark doesn't matter. If the files being compared are text files, then don't worry about the message unless a lot of errors show up. Then you might examine the files to see if they are actually different. Most of the time, you can ignore this message.

The message `File xxxx empty` means that the indicated file contains no data. Something must have gone wrong during the copy process. Try it again.

Which statement is true?

(a) `Eof mark not found` means something is wrong with one or both of the files
(b) COMP gives up after one mismatch
(c) COMP won't even try to compare two files with different sizes

c is true; a is false—it is not an error in program files; b is false—COMP doesn't quit until ten errors are found

Nondisk Copies

The COPY command can be used to copy to and from peripheral devices attached to your computer. Figure 6.3 shows the devicenames that can be used for the destination. All except LPTn and PRN can also be used as the source. Other than NUL:, which has no effect with COPY but is useful in other commands, you might find occasion to use all these devices at one time or another. In Figure 6.3, the device names are shown with colons, just like drivenames. However, the colons are optional. For this reason, you cannot use devicename words for filenames.

CON:	This stands for "console." As source, it's the keyboard; as destination, it's the monitor.
COMn:	The nth serial port (n can be 1 through 4).
AUX:	The same as COM1:.
LPTn:	The nth parallel port (n can be 1 through 3).
PRN:	The same as LPT1:.
NUL:	A nonexistent device. Data sent to NUL goes nowhere.

Figure 6.3. DOS Devicenames

```
C>COPY CON KEYFILE
```

This command copies a file from the keyboard to drive C:, where it is called KEYFILE.

```
C>COPY B:KEYFILE LPT1:
```

This command sends the file named KEYFILE from drive B: to the first parallel port; in effect, it prints the file. The colon after LPT1 is optional.

(a) Write a command to copy a file from the auxiliary device to the monitor.
    C>_
(b) Which of the following cannot be used as filespecs?
    A. COPY
    B. CON
    C. KBD
    D. LPT1
    E. AUX
    F. MON
(c) Write a command to copy file VISA.DAT in subdirectory CREDIT within GEORGE on drive C: to the printer connected to the first parallel port.
    C>_

(a) `C>COPY AUX CON`
(b) B, D, E
(c) `C>COPY \GEORGE\CREDIT\VISA.DAT LPT1` *(you also could have used PRN for the destination)*

Keyboard to Disk

You can use the COPY command to create a new disk file in standard American Standard Code for Information Interchange (ASCII). Suppose you want to create a file named ADDRESES on drive C:. This command copies from the keyboard (CON) to a file named ADDRESES on the default drive:

```
C>COPY CON ADDRESES
```

COPY responds by moving the cursor to the next line and then waiting for you to enter data for the file. You can type as many lines as you want, ending each with Enter. Figure 6.4 shows what a complete interaction might look like. COPY stores each line in memory until the F6 key is pressed (this shows up as ^Z in the figure). When F6 is pressed, all lines are copied to the disk.

```
C>COPY CON: ADDRESES
ADAMS 216 CAROB COURT
ANSON 3451 LOUISA DR
BECHT 15E CELERON ST
BUSH 1600 PENNSYLVANIA AV
COUSINS 2121 RIDGEFIELD AV
DREW 195 BROADWAY RD
EGGARS 616 STONEHENGE WAY
ENGELS 7795 PRESTON BLVD
EPHRON 489 COMMERCE AV
FINGAL 56 HAGSTROM RD
FOCHMEIER 100 A STREET
^Z

        1 File(s) copied
C>_
```

Figure 6.4. Making a Disk File from the Keyboard

As you type, you can correct a line by using the Backspace key, just as in typing a command. Once you press Enter, however, the line is saved in memory, but it is not yet written to the disk.

To end a file and cause it to be written on the disk, you must enter an end-of-file mark, which is Ctrl-Z. It displays on the screen as ^Z. There are two ways to type it. You can depress Ctrl and Z at the same time, or you can press the F6 key. Do this only at the beginning of a new line; if you put ^Z somewhere else, DOS won't recognize it as an end-of-file mark.

When you copy a file using the keyboard as the source, DOS accepts all input until you enter an end-of-file mark. You won't get any special messages, no matter what you type.

Once COPY writes the file on disk, the copy function has been completed. If you check the directory, you'll see the new filespec. If you used the specifier of an existing file, your new file destroys (overwrites) the existing one. You won't even get a warning message.

Note

Copying from the console is an awkward way to create a new file. If you have a line editor such as EDLIN or a word processor, you won't ever have to use COPY for this purpose. However, if you want to create an ASCII text file containing just a couple of lines that aren't too difficult to type, you might find it quicker to use COPY CON than starting up your word processor and saving a file in ASCII mode.

(a) Write a command to create a new file named TALENTS on the B: drive.
C>_
(b) Write a command to create a new file named DINARO on the C: drive.
C>_
(c) Write a command to create a new file named NATBANK.DAT in C:\MARTHA\CHECKS.
C>_
(d) How do you end a file that you create this way?
(e) Which function key generates an end-of-file mark?

(a) `C>COPY CON: B:TALENTS` *(You could omit the colon after CON)*
(b) `C>COPY CON: DINARO`
(c) `COPY CON: C:\MARTHA\CHECKS\NATBANK.DAT`
(d) Enter an end-of-file mark by pressing Ctrl-Z or F6
(e) F6

Disk to Printer

You can also use COPY to print a text file from disk; the files you create with COPY CON are always printable as text files. For example:

```
C>COPY ADDRESES LPT1
```

The command prints lines until it reaches the end-of-file mark. If you entered Ctrl-Z somewhere other than the beginning of a line, the last line might not print properly.

If your computer has additional printers, you may be able to use the devicenames LPT2 and LPT3 also. If you have a serial printer, you can use COM1 or COM2, but only if you have entered the correct MODE command to tell DOS the communication characteristics (baud rate and so forth) of the printer. The MODE command is covered in Chapter 11.

(a) Write a command to print the file named DINARO from drive A:.
C>_
(b) Write a command to print the file named NATBANK.DAT in C:\MARTHA\CHECKS.
C>_

(*a*) `C>COPY A:DINARO LPT1`
(*b*) `C>COPY C:\MARTHA\CHECKS\NATBANK.DAT LPT1`

COPY Messages

The COPY command might generate several possible messages, depending on its progress.

If the copy is performed successfully, you'll see this message: `1 File(s) copied`. Later in this chapter, you'll see how to copy more than one file with a single COPY command.

If the destination drive already contains a file with the specified name, *that file will be overlaid,* with no warning. You'll see this message: `1 Files(s) copied`. It's wise to check your destination disk before entering the COPY command unless you specifically want to overlay a file on the destination drive.

Even though DOS lets you overlay a file by using the same name, it won't let a file overlay itself. If you accidentally enter a command that would lead to such a copy, as in C>COPY FAULTS, you'll see this message:

```
File cannot be copied onto itself
         0 File(s) copied
```

Any time a copy cannot be completed, you'll see an explanatory message and the `0 File(s) copied` message. For example, you will see `0 File(s) copied` after `File not found` and `Insufficient disk space.`

Some disks and files can't be copied because they are copy protected. You'll get some sort of message, depending on the nature of the copy-protect technique, if you try to copy files from a protected disk.

(a) Suppose you have this interaction:

```
C>COPY COMMAND.COM
File cannot be copied onto itself
         0 File(s) copied
C>_
```

What's wrong?

(b) Suppose you have this interaction:

```
C>COPY EXB B:
EXB File not found
          0 File(s) copied
C>_
```

What's wrong?

(c) Suppose you have this interaction:

```
C>COPY EXB B:EXB.NEW
Insufficient disk space
          0 File(s) copied
C>_
```

What's wrong?

(a) You need to specify a destination other than C:COMMAND.COM
(b) C:EXB couldn't be found
(c) The file won't fit on the disk in drive B:

Single-Drive Copies

If you have only one disk drive, you can still copy files from one diskette to another. DOS assigns the names A: and B: to the same diskette drive if the system has only one diskette drive. Here is an example of an interaction between you and DOS for a single-drive, diskette-to-diskette copy:

```
C>COPY A:PRZAP B:
```

(COPY locates C:PRZAP and copies it into memory)

```
Insert diskette for drive B:
and strike any key when ready...
```

(you remove the source diskette, insert the destination diskette, and press a key; COPY copies the file from memory onto the B: diskette)

```
     1 File(s) copied
C>_
```

At this point, DOS knows that the destination diskette is still in drive B:. The next command involving drive A: results in this message: `Insert diskette for drive A: and strike any key.` Here's an example:

```
C>DIR A:
Insert diskette for drive A:
and strike any key...
```

When you press a character key (regardless of whether you actually changed the diskette), DOS assumes the correct diskette is now installed and lists the directory.

Suppose you have a very basic computer system with just a single diskette drive and 256K memory. How can you copy a file too large to fit in memory? The COPY command brings as much of the file as possible into memory, then asks for the destination diskette and writes that part. Then COPY asks you to reinsert the source diskette to copy more of the file. You insert the source and destination diskettes as directed until the copy is complete.

Write a command to copy BELLOWS from the installed diskette to another diskette on a single-drive system.

```
A>_
```

```
A>COPY BELLOWS B:
```

Global Filespecs

COPY commands can reference global filespecs. Figure 6.5 shows a typical interaction. You can see that each file that matches the filespec is listed on the monitor as it is copied. The message at the bottom tells you how many files were copied.

This command tells DOS to copy from the B: drive all files whose names start with STAR and have no extension.

```
C>COPY B:STAR*
```

Notice that this is different from the DIR command that ends a global filename with an asterisk. With DIR, the filespec matches all files that start with STAR and have *any* extension. With COPY (and most commands), the filespec matches files that start with STAR and have *no* extension; it's the same as STAR*. (where the period is included).

You can also use a command such as COPY BE??.* to cause all matching files to be copied. You can use COPY A:*.* B: to copy all files on drive A: to drive B:. It's not the same as DISKCOPY, however. With COPY *.*, files may be rearranged on the disk, hidden files aren't copied, the directories and FAT aren't copied, and the existing files on B: are retained unless overwritten with other files of the same name.

Here's another example:

```
C>COPY *.* LPT1
        1 File(s) copied
C>_
```

This command says to copy all files from the default directory to the line printer. The system puts all the files together end to end and copies them as one file, which is why the message indicates only one file is copied. No spaces or filespecs appear between printed files. Don't try this approach unless every file that matches the specification is printable. Files with extension COM or EXE, as well as files prepared by word processors, graphics programs, spreadsheets, desktop publishers, database programs, and the like, are generally not printable.

```
C>COPY *.BK* B:
CHAP01.BKS
CHAP00.BK
CHAP02.BK!
CHAP04.BKS
CHAP03.BK!
CHAP05.BK
        6 File(s) copied

C>_
```

Figure 6.5. Copying with a Global Filespec

(a) Write a command to copy all files from drive B: to drive A:.

```
C>_
```

(b) Write a command to copy all the files with no extension from drive A: to drive C:.

```
C>_
```

(c) Write a command to copy all the files with extension DOC to the printer attached to LPT2.

```
C>_
```

(a) `C>COPY B:*.* A:`

(b) `C>COPY A:*` *or* `C>COPY A:*.`

(c) `C>COPY *.DOC LPT2`

Concatenation

You can use the COPY command to *concatenate* files. This means you copy two or more files together to create one file. Concatenation happens automatically if you use a global filespec when copying to the printer, as you saw in the previous frame. Other times, use a plus sign (+) to indicate the source files you want to combine or concatenate. You may put spaces around the + symbol or not, as you wish. Here's an example:

```
C>COPY LEFT + RIGHT WHOLE
LEFT
RIGHT
       1 File(s) copied
```

The new WHOLE file contains first LEFT and then RIGHT. The original LEFT and RIGHT are unchanged. You can concatenate as many files as you want this way, as long as the destination disk has room for the new file. To concatenate five files, CHAP1 through CHAP5, you could enter:

```
C>COPY CHAP1 + CHAP2 + CHAP3 + CHAP4 + CHAP5 REPORT
```

If you don't specify a destination for the concatenated files, DOS uses the first file in the list as the destination. It doesn't create a new target file unless one is specified at the end of the command.

When DOS encounters this command:

```
C>COPY OLD.DAT + NEW.DAT
```

it adds the contents of NEW.DAT to the file OLD.DAT. NEW.DAT doesn't change, but OLD.DAT is now different.

This command results in all five files, in order, in CHAP1. The other files aren't changed.

```
C>COPY CHAP1 + CHAP2 + CHAP3 + CHAP4 + CHAP5
```

(a) Write a command to concatenate TRUE and FALSE into a new file named LOGIC.
C>_

(b) Write a command to concatenate PARTS from drive A: and PARTS from drive B: into a new file called TOTPARTS on the default drive.
C>_

(c) Change your command above to put TOTPARTS on the B: drive.
C>_

(d) Write a command to add the contents of MID.USA and WEST.USA to the existing file EAST.USA.
C>_

(a) C>COPY TRUE + FALSE LOGIC
(b) C>COPY A:PARTS + B:PARTS TOTPARTS
(c) C>COPY A:PARTS + B:PARTS B:TOTPARTS
(d) C>COPY EAST.USA + MID.USA + WEST.USA

Note Files concatenated according to this method must have end-of-file marks. If for any reason you want to concatenate program files or any other files without end-of-file marks, then you must use some special switches. Most of the time, you would have no need to do this. If you need to know how, see your DOS reference manual for details.

When you copy a file without concatenation, the date and time stamp in the directory entry are also copied. That is, the copy does not receive the current date and time. That's because you have not changed the file.

Concatenation is different. When you use COPY to create a new file by concatenating two or more files, the new file receives the current date and time stamp. Thus, if you merge BFILE and CFILE into AFILE, the date and time associated with AFILE are updated.

If you want to copy a file and force the copy to have a new date and time, you can "pretend" to concatenate it, as in:

```
C>COPY B:WORDWRAP+
```

This will copy WORDWRAP from drive B: to the default drive; the current date and time are associated with C:WORDWRAP. You can use this method to update the date and time of any file, without actually making a copy of it.

If you want to specify a name (or drive) for the destination file and use the current date and time, code two commas after the plus sign so that DOS doesn't read the destination file as part of the concatenation. The commas signal DOS that there are no more files to concatenate. Here's an example:

```
C>COPY WORDWRAP+,, B:NEWWRAP
```

This makes a copy of WORDWRAP called NEWWRAP on drive B:, which is associated with the current date and time. If the two commas are omitted here, DOS tries to concatenate NEWWRAP into WORDWRAP instead.

(a) In which case does DOS assign the current date and time to a file?
   A. Whenever you make a change to a file
   B. Whenever you copy a file
   C. Whenever you concatenate a file

(b) Write a command to copy FORCEFLD from drive A: to drive B:. The new copy should have the current date and time.
   C>_

(c) Write a command to copy QUASARS from drive B: to drive C:. The new copy should have the current date and time.
   C>_

(d) Write a command to update the date and time associated with PLANTERS on drive C:.
   C>_

(a) *A, C*

(b) `C>COPY A:FORCEFLD+,, B:`

(c) `C>COPY B:QUASARS+`
(d) `C>COPY PLANTERS+`

If any source file cannot be found during concatenation, DOS just skips that file and goes on. No warning message is displayed unless DOS can't find any source files.

When no destination is specified, DOS concatenates into the first source file *that it can find*. Look at this command:

```
C>COPY FILEALL + FILEA + FILEB + FILEC
```

If FILEALL is missing but FILEA is present, DOS uses FILEA as the destination file. No warning message is displayed.

Suppose you have this interaction:

```
C>COPY BIGFILE + AFILE + BFILE
          1 File(s) copied
C>_
```

(a) Do you know that all three files were found and copied?
(b) True or false? If BIGFILE is missing, DOS will create it from AFILE + BFILE.

(a) No (DOS doesn't warn you unless it can't find any of the files)
(b) False (It will use the first source file it can find)

You can use global filespecs to concatenate files. If you specify a global source and a single destination, all the matching source files are concatenated to create the destination file. Here is an example:

```
C>COPY *.DAT ALL.DAT
```

This concatenates all the files in the current directory with extension DAT. The result is called ALL.DAT. The concatenation is made in the order in which DAT files are found in the directory. If the source directory already contains an ALL.DAT, the other DAT files are concatenated into it. In such a case, you may see this message `Contents of destination lost before copy`. Don't panic. What it means is this: ALL.DAT was set up as the destination file. The first DAT file was added to it; the next DAT file was added to that; and so forth. Then, DOS found ALL.DAT in the directory as a source file because ALL.DAT matches the filespec *.DAT. DOS has trouble using ALL.DAT as both the source and the destination in a concatenation, so it issues the above (somewhat cryptic) message, skips over ALL.DAT as a source file, and goes on to the next source file. No harm has been done, since the original ALL.DAT remains as the first part of the new file.

You can also do a parallel concatenation using global identifiers. In a parallel concatenation, files with identical filenames but different extensions are concatenated together. In the following example, we're concatenating DAT files with CAT files to create FAT files:

LOST.DAT + LOST.CAT = LOST.FAT
FOUND.DAT + FOUND.CAT = FOUND.FAT
TRUE.DAT + TRUE.CAT = TRUE.FAT
FALSE.DAT + FALSE.CAT = FALSE.FAT

The command C>COPY *.DAT + *.CAT *.FAT accomplishes the parallel concatenation. This is the only instance where it is appropriate to use a global filespec as a destination in a COPY command.

(a) Write a command to concatenate all the files with filename PARTS and send the new file to the line printer. (Don't store the concatenated version on disk.)
C>_
(b) Write a command to concatenate all the files that start with P3. Name the new file PROJECT3.
C>_
(c) Write a command to do a parallel concatenation. Matching files with extensions B1, B2, and B3 should be concatenated together and placed in files with extension ALL.
C>_
(d) What does the message `Content of destination lost before copy` mean?
A. The destination file has been accidentally destroyed and the copy is not good

B. The destination file has been changed through concatenation
C. There is something wrong with the destination file and you should erase it immediately

(e) When can you use a global destination filespec?
A. Never
B. Anytime you want
C. Only when doing parallel concatenation

(a) `C>COPY PARTS.* LPT1`
(b) `C>COPY P3*.* PROJECTS`
(c) `C>COPY *.B1 + *.B2 + *.B3 *.ALL`
(d) *B*
(e) *C*

Exercises

These exercises let you practice using COPY on your system. You'll create files from the keyboard, print files, and concatenate them. You'll also practice copying files from one place to another.

What You Should Do	*How the Computer Responds*
1. Boot with your system diskette in drive A: if necessary.	1. Boots and displays the command prompt.
2. **Fixed disk only**	2.
a. If your DOS external programs have not been copied to your fixed disk, copy them to the subdirectory you created in Chapter 5: `A>COPY *.* C:\DOS`	a. Lists the DOS files as it copies them to the subdirectory.
b. Create another subdirectory for practice programs and make it current.	b. Creates a subdirectory and makes it current.

3. **Diskette systems only** a. Place the diskette you formatted earlier in drive B:. b. Make drive B: current.	3. Makes the diskette in drive B: current.
4. Create a file on the current drive. a. Type COPY CON FILEA.X. b. Type THIS IS FILE A. c. Press Enter, then F6, then Enter again. d. Type DIR to see the filespec.	4. a. Moves the cursor to the next line and waits for you to enter data. b. Stores the line in memory. c. Copies file from memory to disk. Displays `1 File(s) copied`. d. Displays the directory with FILEA.X.
5. Create three more files named FILEB.X, FILEA.Y, and FILEB.Y. Put one or two lines (your choice) in each one.	5. Accepts the data and stores it on the disk.
6. Check the directory. Note the dates and times of your new files.	6. Displays directory containing files.
7. Use COPY to PRN to print one or two files.	7. Prints files as requested.
8. Combine the FILEA files into a new file called ALLA. `C>COPY FILEA.* ALLA` Copy ALLA to the console to see the result.	8. Combines the files, then displays the result on the console.
9. Create a file PRESDENT containing a list of the years presidents took office along with the last name of each president. (You'll use this file in later chapters to practice sorting, finding specified lines, and displaying one screenful at a time (paging). For the paging exercise, you'll need at least 25 lines in the file. So if you don't want to enter all 41 lines, enter at least 25.)	9. Creates the file as requested.

Here's the list:
1789 Washington
1797 Adams
1801 Jefferson
1809 Madison
1817 Monroe
1825 Adams
1829 Jackson
1837 Van Buren
1841 Harrison
1841 Tyler
1845 Polk
1849 Taylor
1850 Fillmore
1853 Pierce
1857 Buchanan
1861 Lincoln
1865 Johnson
1869 Grant
1877 Hayes
1881 Garfield
1885 Cleveland
1889 Harrison
1893 Cleveland
1897 McKinley
1901 Roosevelt
1909 Taft
1913 Wilson
1921 Harding
1923 Coolidge
1929 Hoover
1933 Roosevelt
1945 Truman
1953 Eisenhower
1961 Kennedy
1963 Johnson
1969 Nixon
1974 Ford
1977 Carter
1981 Reagan
1989 Bush

Enter Ctrl-Z or press F6 on the last line and press Enter.

10. Print the list with COPY.

10. Prints the file as requested.

11. Copy the file to the same directory but name it PRESCOPY. Then compare the two files. You might need to enter a drive or path for the COMP command since it is no longer on the default drive:

```
B>A:COMP PRESDENT PRESCOPY
```

or

```
C>\DOS\COMP PRESDENT PRESCOPY
```

11. Copies the file, then shows that the two files are identical. (May display the `Eof mark not found` message.)

12. If you want, create and copy more files.

12. Follows your instructions.

What If It Doesn't Work?

1. If you have trouble copying, remember to put the source first, then the destination.

2. If you have trouble with COMP, try making the copy with /V. Then try COMP again. Don't worry about "Eof mark" messages. COMP is an external program, so you may have to include the drivename or the pathname with the programname.

7

Managing Files

In this chapter, you'll learn to use several internal and external commands to manage files. With these commands, you can change a file's name, display a file on the console, erase it from the directory, or print it on a printer. You can also protect a file from change or erasure. You'll find all these file management commands necessary when working with DOS.

When you complete this chapter, you will be able to:

- Use the RENAME command to change the name of a file
- Use the TYPE command to display the contents of a file on the monitor
- Use the DEL command to remove files from a directory
- Use the ATTRIB command to protect a file from being changed or erased
- Use the PRINT command to print files
- Use the FIND command to display data from a file
- Use the FC command to compare two files

Changing a Filespec

You have already learned to copy a file and give the copy a new name. Sometimes you'll want to change the name without making a new copy. The RENAME internal command (or its abbreviation REN) lets you do this by specifying the old name followed by the desired new one.

Format (internal):
RENAME current-filespec new-filespec

You can change the name of SAMPLE in the default directory to FULLTASK.DAT with this command:

```
C>REN SAMPLE FULLTASK.DAT
```

Since RENAME is an internal command, you can't use a drivename or path with it; RENAME is always available in memory when DOS is running. However, you may need a drivename or path as part of the current-filespec to indicate which file's specifier is to be changed. You won't need a drivename or path with the new-filespec since RENAME doesn't relocate the file. If you include a drivename or path with the new-filespec, DOS gives you an error message.

Suppose your diskettes contain these files:

Drive A:	**Drive B:**
VENDORS.DAT	PAYROLL.COM
CUSTOMER.DAT	BILLING.COM
LETTER.WH	WS.COM
	WSMGS.OVR
	WSOVLY.OVR

(a) Which commands are correct?
A. `C>RENAME PAYROLL.COM B:SAVEPAY.COM`
B. `C>RENAME B:BILLING.COM PAYABLE.COM`
C. `C>RENAME B:BILLING.COM PAYABLE.COM`
D. `C>RENAME A:VENDORS.DAT A:SELLERS`

(b) Write a command to change the name of CUSTOMER.DAT to RECEIVE.DAT.
C>_

(c) Write a command to change the name of B:BILLING.COM to INVOICE.COM.
C>_

(d) Write a command to create a copy of LETTER.WH on drive B: and rename the copy as ORDER6.

(a) B, C

(*b*) C>REN CUSTOMER.DAT RECEIVE.DAT *(You could use RENAME instead of REN)*

(*c*) C>REN B:BILLING.COM INVOICE.COM

(*d*) C>COPY LETTER.WH B:ORDER6 *(You can't use RENAME to copy a file)*

RENAME requires two filespecs. If you forget to include either of them, you'll see the message `Invalid number of parameters.` Another error message you might see is `Duplicate file name or file not found.` This message means one of two things—either no file matches the current-filespec or there is already a file with the new-filespec. You have to figure out which problem you're facing and change the command accordingly. For example, suppose you are working with a disk that contains only these files:

JONES585
SANDS585
APRET585
BIANC685

You want to change the name of last file to RUN685. Here is the interaction:

```
C>REN RUN685 BIANC685
Duplicate file name or file not found
C>_
```

The problem is that the current-filespec and the new-filespec are reversed. So RENAME couldn't find a file named RUN685 and there is already a file named BIANC685.

If the file is renamed successfully, DOS won't provide a message. Figure 7.1 shows what the screen looks like when a renaming operation is successful.

The absence of an error message means the file was renamed as requested. You can verify this by checking the directory.

```
C>REN A:CONFIG.SYS CONFIG.BAK

C>_
```

Figure 7.1. Successful RENAME Command

(a) What is wrong with this command?

```
C>REN STALER B:SAVE
```

(b) Look at this interaction:

```
C>REN CHAPTER3
Invalid number of parameters
C>_
```

What went wrong?

(c) Look at this interaction:

```
C>REN CHAPTER3 CHAPTER5
Duplicate file name or file not found
C>_
```

What could be wrong?

A. There is already a CHAPTER5 in the directory
B. There is no CHAPTER3 in the directory
C. You have to spell out RENAME
D. RENAME can't find a file called CHAPTER5

(a) You can't change the drivename with the RENAME command—you'll see the message `Invalid parameter`
(b) One filespec is missing from the command
(c) A and B

Displaying File Contents

The TYPE command displays the contents of a text file. You can use TYPE to check the contents of a file at the console or, with echo printing, to print the file contents. TYPE works only with ASCII files. It doesn't work with binary program files or graphic files and can give strange results with files created by word processors, spreadsheets, desktop publishers, and the like. You won't do any damage if you TYPE a non-ASCII file, but the displayed data will look like nonsense and the console may beep a few times. Also, if echo printing is on, some form feeds (signals that start a new page) may be sent to the printer, causing paper to be wasted. You can stop the TYPE output with Ctrl-Break.

Format (internal):
TYPE filespec

Since TYPE is an internal command, you won't need a drivename or path before it. The filespec can, of course, have a drivename and/or path. To type a file on the default drive named SORTED, you would enter:

```
C>TYPE SORTED
```

The contents of the file are displayed on the monitor. To type the file named PRESENT.DOC from drive B:, you would enter:

```
C>TYPE B:PRESENT.DOC
```

To display the file named LETTER.WH in a nondefault subdirectory on drive C:, you would enter:

```
C>TYPE \CORRESP\LETTER.WH
```

The most common error message with TYPE is `File not found`. By now, you know what this error message means.

(a) Write a command to display the file named CHAPTER1.TEX.
C>_
(b) Write a command to display the file named FIRESIDE on the B: drive.
C>_
(c) What type of file types successfully with TYPE?
(d) Suppose you have the following interaction:

```
C>TYPE EXERCISE.D
File not found
C>_
```

What went wrong?

(a) `C>TYPE CHAPTER1.TEX`
(b) `C>TYPE B:FIRESIDE`
(c) ASCII
(d) There is no file named EXERCISE.D on the default directory

The TYPE command can also be used to print the contents of a file. You can print a file that fits on the screen by displaying it, then pressing Shift-PrtSc to print the screen. You can also use echo printing (Ctrl-PrtSc or Ctrl-P) to cause the file to be printed as the contents are displayed on the console.

A file that contains more than 22 lines will scroll off the top of the console before it is finished. To read the entire contents at the console, you can use Ctrl-NumLock (or Ctrl-S) to suspend the TYPE display. When you press any character, the display continues. If you press Ctrl-Break (or Ctrl-C) at any time before TYPE is completed, the command is interrupted and you'll see the default drive prompt again.

You can't use global filespecs with TYPE, since DOS can display only one file at a time. If you try, you'll see the message `Invalid file name or file not found.`

(a) Suppose you want to print the file named B:FIRESIDE as it is typed. What control function would you use before entering the TYPE command? What keys are used to activate this function?
(b) Suppose you start to type a file and change your mind. What control function could you use to discontinue the output without waiting until the end of the file? What keys are used to activate this function?
(c) Suppose the typed file starts scrolling off the top of the screen before you can read it. What control function could you use to stop scrolling? What keys are used to activate this function? What keys are used to let the display continue?
(d) What is wrong with this command?

```
C>TYPE LETTER.*
```

(a) Echo Print; Ctrl-PrtSc (or Ctrl-P)
(b) Break; Ctrl-Break (or Ctrl-C)
(c) Pause; Ctrl-NumLock (or Ctrl-S); any character key
(d) You can't use a global filespec with TYPE

Removing a File from a Disk

If you want to erase a file from a disk, use the DEL command, which has a format much like TYPE.

Format (internal):
DEL filespec

To erase the file named INVENTY.DAT, you enter the command `C>DEL INVENTY.DAT`. To erase a file on drive B: named SORTED.TMP, you enter `C>DEL B:SORTED.TMP`. Since DEL is an internal command, you never use a drivename or path before it, although you can use them as part of the filespec as needed. You can use ERASE instead of DEL if you prefer; it has the same rules and works the same way.

You can use global filespecs in the DEL command to erase several files at once. DEL *.COM erases all files on the default disk or directory that have extension COM. The entry DEL B:SAMPLE??.* erases all files on drive B: whose filespecs begin with the six characters SAMPLE. The instruction DEL B:*.* erases all files in the current directory on drive B:. So does DEL B: (with no filespec).

If you try to erase all files in a directory, DOS gives you one chance to change your mind. Figure 7.2 shows an example. If you type N and press Enter, no files are erased. If you enter Y, the files are gone for good.

Be especially careful with global deletions. DOS does not list the names of the files it deletes. To be safe, use DIR with the same global filespec first to see what files match the filespec. Then enter the DEL command if the listed file names are, in fact, the files you want to delete.

```
C>DEL *.*
Are you sure (Y/N)?Y

C>_
```

Figure 7.2. Erasing All Files in a Directory

Suppose you are working with these two disks:

Drive C:	**Drive B:**
TABLE.DAT	EXTRA
TABLE.COM	EXTRA.A
TABLE.DOC	NEW.ONE
	NEW.TWO

(a) Write a command to erase the file named TABLE.DAT.
`C>_`
(b) Write a command to erase the file named EXTRA.
`C>_`
(c) Write a command to erase NEW.ONE and NEW.TWO.
`C>_`
(d) What command should precede the above command, for safety's sake?
`C>_`
(e) Write a command to erase all files from drive B:.
`C>_`

(You could use ERASE instead of DEL in any of these.)
(a) `C>DEL TABLE.DAT`
(b) `C>DEL B:EXTRA`
(c) `C>DEL B:NEW.*`
(d) `C>DIR B:NEW.*`
(e) `C>DEL B:*.*` *or* `C>DEL B:`

If DEL can't find the file(s) you specify, you will see the standard `File not found` message. If you forget to specify a filespec, you will see the `Invalid number of parameters` message.

Another error situation occurs if the disk is write-protected. Here's the message:

```
Write protect error writing drive d
Abort, Retry, Fail?_
```

A file cannot be erased from a write-protected disk. Either remove the write protection and try again or give up trying to erase the file. Similarly, you can't erase a file that is individually write-protected. You'll learn in the next frame how to protect a file from deletion and to unprotect it again.

Be very careful when you use the DEL command. Once you have entered the command, the file is virtually gone. You don't get a second chance. (However, you can buy external programs that can recover erased files under certain circumstances.)

(a) Suppose you have this interaction:

```
C>DEL TABLE.D
File not found
C>_
```

What went wrong?

(b) Suppose you have this interaction:

```
C>DEL
Invalid number of parameters
C>_
```

What went wrong?

(c) Suppose you have this interaction:

```
C>DEL B:SAMPLE2
Write protect error writing drive B
Abort, Retry, Fail?_
```

What do you enter to cancel the DEL command?
How can you erase the file?

(a) There is no file named TABLE.D on the default drive
(b) You forgot to include a filespec
(c) A for Abort; remove the write-protection and enter the DEL command again

---

Protecting a File

You already know how to use write protection to protect a complete diskette from any change. Sometimes you may want to protect individual files on a diskette or fixed disk. For example, you may want to make sure no one erases the customer file accidentally. Or you may want to keep anyone from making changes in a report. You can use the ATTRIB command to set a protection attribute to Read/Only for a file. The file can still be displayed and printed, but it can't be erased and its contents can't be changed. It can be renamed, but the contents remain Read/Only. Suppose you want to protect WASHTRIP.RPT.

```
C>ATTRIB +R WASHTRIP.RPT
```

The switch (+R) sets the specified file to Read/Only, which write protects the file.

Suppose you try to create a new file with the same name. You'll see an error message as in this interaction:

```
C>COPY CON WASHTRIP.RPT
12/17 PSA flight 273 to DC
12/28 PSA flight 181 to LA
^Z
File creation error
             0 File(s) copied
C>_
```

DOS won't let the protected file be overwritten. (It would be nice if DOS told you this *before* you typed the file.)

If you try to erase the file, you might see this interaction:

```
C>DEL WASHTRIP.RPT
Access denied
C>_
```

DOS won't erase a file with a Read/Only attribute.

Figure 7.3 shows what happens when you try to erase all files on the diskette when one file is protected. You don't get any warning message, but DOS does not erase any protected files. The directory shows that FILEA, FILEF, and FILEG remain in the directory.

You can copy or type a protected file. If you copy the file, the protection is not copied. That is, the new copy is not protected unless you specifically enter an ATTRIB command to protect it.

```
C>DEL *.*
Are you sure (Y/N)?Y

C>DIR

 Volume in drive C is FIXED DISK
 Directory of  C:\STYLES

.            <DIR>       5-25-89   5:10p
..           <DIR>       5-25-89   5:10p
FILEA              41    5-25-89   3:48p
FILEF              40    6-05-89   9:00a
FILEG              40    6-05-89   9:00a
        5 File(s)   5134336 bytes free

C>_
```

These files did not get deleted.

Figure 7.3. Effect of Global Deletion on Protected Files

Suppose you have entered this command: `ATTRIB +R LETTER.WH`.

(a) Which of these commands will work correctly?

A. `COPY LETTER.WH B:`

B. `DEL LETTER.WH`

C. `COPY CON LETTER.WH`

D. `TYPE LETTER.WH`

E. `DEL *.*`

(b) What will happen if you enter DEL LETTER.*?

A. You'll see the message `Access denied`.

B. All files with filename LETTER will be erased—regardless of whether they are protected.

C. All unprotected files with filename LETTER are erased.

D. No files are erased.

(c) Suppose you enter this command:

```
C>COPY LETTER.WH B:
```

What will appear next?
A. `Access denied`
B. `1 File(s) copied`
C. `File creation error`

(a) A, D (E will work but the protected file won't be erased)
(b) C
(c) B (the copy is not protected)

The ATTRIB command can also be used to check the protection status of a file or to turn Read/Only protection off.

Format (external):
ATTRIB [+R | -R] filespec

Since ATTRIB is an external command, you may use a drivename and a path if ATTRIB.EXE isn't in the default directory or search path. As you've seen, +R turns the Read/Only attribute on. You can use -R to turn it off again. If you don't use either switch, DOS displays the status of the specified file. As you can see in Figure 7.4, you can use a global filename to check several files at once. Protected files have an R to the left of the filespec, while unprotected files don't.

If you happen to enter a filespec that doesn't exist, you'll see the message `Invalid path or File not found`. If you neglect to use a + or - before R, you'll see `Syntax error`.

The Read/Only file status does not appear in the directory; you must use ATTRIB to check the status of a file.

ATTRIB is not the best file protection available to you. It won't stop a prankster, coworker, or computer virus from damaging your files. Keeping good, up-to-date backup copies is your best protection. But ATTRIB is better than nothing, especially for preventing careless mistakes. It's so easy to enter `C>DEL *.*` when you meant to say `C>DEL B:*.*`. Especially on your fixed disk (where you can't use a write-protect tab) use ATTRIB to make copies of your crucial files Read/Only.

```
C>ATTRIB *.*
       R  C:\STYLES\FILEA
          C:\STYLES\FILEB
          C:\STYLES\FILEC
          C:\STYLES\FILED
          C:\STYLES\FILEE
          C:\STYLES\FILEF
       R  C:\STYLES\FILEG
          C:\STYLES\FILEH
          C:\STYLES\FILEI
       R  C:\STYLES\FILEJ
          C:\STYLES\FILEK
          C:\STYLES\FILEL

C>_
```

Figure 7.4. Attribute Listing

(a) Write a command to give BILLINGS on drive B: a Read/Only attribute.
C>_
(b) Write a command to check the status of BILLINGS on drive B:.
C>_
(c) Write a command to allow you to erase BILLINGS.
C>_

(a) C>ATTRIB +R B:BILLINGS
(b) C>ATTRIB B:BILLINGS
(c) C>ATTRIB -R B:BILLINGS

Note || You will learn another function for the ATTRIB command in Chapter 9.

Printing a File

You have learned several ways to print a file so far in this book. You can screen print a short file, copy a file to the printer, or echo print while typing a file. The most convenient way, however, is with the PRINT command. It lets you print one or more files and *continue doing other work* at the same time. As with the other methods, PRINT prints only ASCII files.

To print a single file, simply enter PRINT followed by the filespec, as in:

```
C>PRINT WORKDATA.DAT
```

PRINT is an external command, so you can use a drivename and path as part of the command name. PRINT is also partially a TSR (terminate and stay resident) program. The first time you use it after booting, DOS will ask:

```
Name of list device [PRN]:_
```

DOS wants to know the name of the device on which to print. If you don't say otherwise, it uses PRN, which is your default or only printer. To print on that device, simply press Enter. To select a different device, type the appropriate devicename and press Enter. (Refer back to Figure 6.3 for a list of the names you could use if you have other devices.) For the remainder of the session, until you boot again, all PRINT commands are directed to the device you select with this first PRINT command.

The next message you see is:

```
Resident part of PRINT installed
```

This reminds you that part of PRINT stays in memory until you boot again.

Here's the next message you see, assuming the WORKDATA.DAT file is found:

```
C:\WORKDATA.DAT is currently being printed
```

Now DOS has given the order for the file to be printed. In a few seconds, you will hear the printer functioning. While the file is printing, you can go right on using DOS. You don't have to wait for the print job to finish before you use the system for other work. This gives PRINT a distinct advantage over TYPE and COPY.

(a) True or false? You can PRINT files while doing other work using DOS.

(b) Which statement is true?

A. Every time you use PRINT, DOS asks you for the name of the print device

B. DOS asks for the name of the print device only the first time you use PRINT after booting

(c) True or false? Once the PRINT program has been installed, it stays in memory until you boot again.

(d) Write a command to print the file named TURNOUT.315.

C>_

(a) *True*

(b) *B*

(c) *True*

(d) `C>PRINT TURNOUT.315`

To print more than one file, you can list all the filespecs (up to 10) with the PRINT command or use several print commands. Figure 7.5 shows an interaction in which four files are *queued* up to print. A queue (pronounced "cue") is a waiting line; the print queue is a line of files waiting to be printed. DOS queues the files in the same order you list them in your command; they are printed in that order. The printer advances to a new page after each file is printed.

You can also use a global filespec with PRINT. Figure 7.6 shows an example. The global filespec B:*.BAT matched three filespecs. The files are queued in the order they were found in the directory.

```
C>PRINT FILEA FILEB FILEC FILED
Name of list device [PRN]:
Resident part of PRINT installed

    C:\STYLES\FILEA is currently being printed
    C:\STYLES\FILEB is in queue
    C:\STYLES\FILEC is in queue
    C:\STYLES\FILED is in queue

C>_
```

Figure 7.5. Printing Multiple Files

```
C>PRINT B:*.BAT

    B:\AUTOEXEC.BAT is currently being printed
    B:\LIST.BAT is in queue
    B:\SEND.BAT is in queue

C>_
```

Figure 7.6. Global Filespec in PRINT Command

(a) What is a queue?
   A. A waiting line
   B. A disk directory
   C. The cable between the system unit and the printer
(b) Write a command to print two files, GRADE8 and GRADE9, in that order.
   C>_
(c) Write a command to print all the files starting with the letters PC.
   C>_

(a) *A*
(b) `C>PRINT GRADE8 GRADE9`
(c) `PRINT PC*`

Once you have started printing files, you can add more files to the end of the print queue by entering more PRINT commands. Up to ten files can be queued at once. When you add files to the end of the queue, DOS displays the status of the entire queue. Figure 7.7 shows an example. If your queue is full when you try to add files, you'll see this message: `PRINT queue is full.` The PRINT queue is also displayed, as shown in Figure 7.8.

```
C>PRINT FILEA

    C:\DOSBOOK\TEXT05 is currently being printed
    C:\STYLES\FILEA is in queue

C>_
```

Figure 7.7. Adding Files to the PRINT Queue

```
C>PRINT FILEJ
PRINT queue is full

    C:\DOSBOOK\TEXT05 is currently being printed
    C:\STYLES\FILEA is in queue
    C:\STYLES\FILEB is in queue
    C:\STYLES\FILEC is in queue
    C:\STYLES\FILED is in queue
    C:\STYLES\FILEE is in queue
    C:\STYLES\FILEF is in queue
    C:\STYLES\FILEG is in queue
    C:\STYLES\FILEH is in queue
    C:\STYLES\FILEI is in queue

C>_
```

Figure 7.8. Full PRINT Queue

(a) How many files can be queued for printing?
(b) When you add files to the print queue, do they go to the beginning or the end of the queue?
(c) Write a command to add SURGERY.LST to the print queue.

```
C>_
```

(a) Up to ten
(b) End
(c) `C>PRINT SURGERY.LST`

If you want to view the print queue without adding files to it, simply enter the command PRINT with no operands, as in:

```
C>PRINT
         C:BIRTHDAY.LST is currently being printed
         C:TESTINSP.LST is in queue
         C:C4SECT3 .LST is in queue
C>_
```

To remove a file from the print queue, use the PRINT command again with /C (cancel), as in:

```
C>PRINT C:TESTINSP.LST /C
         C:BIRTHDAY.LST is currently being printed
         C:C4SECT3 .LST is in queue
C>_
```

To erase the entire print queue, use /T (terminate), as in:

```
C>PRINT /T
PRINT queue is empty
C>_
```

DOS displays a message if a file is currently being printed. You may have to turn off the printer to empty its memory if you want to stop printing immediately.

(a) Write a command to remove all files with extension DAT from the print queue.
C>_
(b) Write a command to empty the print queue.
C>_
(c) Write a command to find out what's in the print queue.
C>_
(d) How do you erase the print queue and stop printing immediately?

(a) C>PRINT /C *.DAT *or* C>PRINT *.DAT /C
(b) C>PRINT /T
(c) C>PRINT
(d) *Enter* PRINT /T, *then turn off the printer*

Here's the PRINT format:

Format (external):
PRINT [filespec] [/P] [/C] [/T]

The /C (cancel) switch deletes one or more files from the queue. The /P (print) control operand adds one or more files to the queue; this switch is assumed if you don't specify any control operand. The /T (terminate) control operand empties the queue.
You can specify more than one operation in one command. The command

```
C>PRINT NAMES /C ADDRESS PHONES BIRTHDAYS /P HOLIDAYS
```

cancels three files (NAMES, ADDRESS, and PHONES) from the queue and adds two files (BIRTHDAYS and HOLIDAYS) to the queue. Each switch applies to the filespec to its left and all those to the right until another switch overrides it. Thus, the /P switch controls BIRTHDAYS, because that's the file to the left of the switch.
PRINT has several additional switches you can use to increase the efficiency of printing. For example, you can increase the size of the PRINT queue. Since these switches change your computer's environment, they are covered in a later chapter. The default operands are in effect until you change them. They are fine for general use.

(a) What file(s) are canceled from the queue as a result of this command?

```
C>PRINT B:BILLINGS C:PAYROLL /C B:MEMO.BAK
```

(b) What file(s) are added to the queue as a result of the command in Question (a)?

(c) Write a command to add QUESC1 and QUESC2 to the print queue and to remove ANSB1.

C>_

(d) Write a command to remove EXERA, EXERB.BAT, and EXERC from the print queue and to add NEWFILEA and NEWFILEB to the queue.

C>_

(a) B:PAYROLL.DAT and B:MEMO.BAK

(b) B:BILLINGS

(c) `C>PRINT QUESC1 QUESC2 ANSB1 /C` *or*
`C>PRINT QUESC1 /P QUESC2 ANSB1 /C` *or*
`C>PRINT ANSB1 /C QUESC1 /P QUESC2`

(d) `C>PRINT EXERA /C EXERB.BAT EXERC NEWFILEA /P NEWFILEB,` *or*
`C>PRINT NEWFILEA NEWFILEB EXERA /C EXERA.BAT EXERC,` *or you could have /C or /P after each filespec*

Using the PRINT command can create some problems. If the printer isn't ready to print—because it's not turned on, not online, or out of paper—DOS may simply wait until the printer is ready, or you may see a message like this:

```
Errors on list device indicate that it
may be off-line. Please check it.
```

Other messages might also appear, depending on your printer and the problem. Adjust your printer, enter the command again, and the problem should be gone.

A printer can print only one thing at a time. If PRINT is printing a file on LPT1 and you request a screen print, the screen print is started when the file is finished. If you enter PRINT while a screen print is being done, DOS finishes the screen print before printing from the PRINT queue. If you enter PRINT during echo printing, PRINT takes over and turns off echo printing. You'll have to press Ctrl-PrtSc again to start echo printing again after PRINT is finished. If you press PrtSc during echo printing, the screen is printed, but echo print isn't turned off.

Assume you have a single printer on LPT1: for these questions.

(a) True or false? You can print the screen and PRINT a file at the same time.
(b) Suppose PRINT is in effect. You press Shift-PrtSc. What happens?
(c) Suppose echo printing is on and you enter a PRINT command. What happens?

(a) False
(b) When PRINT is finished, the screen is printed
(c) Echo printing is automatically turned off

Finding Data in a File

Suppose you have 500 letters on a disk. You know one of them refers to the new NEPTUNE converter, but you don't remember which one. How can you find out? You could TYPE each one to the screen, scan the contents, and locate the right one eventually. You could PRINT the files and scan them until you find the right one. Or you could use the FIND command to search the files automatically. If you're pretty sure the file you want is TEXT05, you could use this command:

```
C>FIND "NEPTUNE" TEXT05
```

Figure 7.9 shows what the output looks like when the file does not contain the word NEPTUNE. Figure 7.10 shows what the output looks like when NEPTUNE is found. Each line containing NEPTUNE is displayed on the screen.

You can ask DOS to search in several files if you like, but you can't use global filespecs. You'll find all the lines containing the string if you list the filespecs as in:

```
C>FIND "Trantor" CHAP1 CHAP2 CHAP3 CHAP4 CHAP5
```

The string you use must be enclosed in quotes. The FIND command will locate exact matches only. For example, the FIND command above won't find TRANTOR (in all uppercase letters).

```
C>FIND "NEPTUNE" TEXT05

---------- TEXT05

C>_
```

Figure 7.9. Negative FIND Output

```
C>FIND "NEPTUNE" TEXT05

---------- TEXT05
   When used at the city or county level, the NEPTUNE converter can realize
installation costs can be recovered in less than five years' time if NEPTUNE is
a demonstration of the NEPTUNE converter can be arranged at either the

C>_
```

Figure 7.10. FIND Output with Matching Lines Displayed

(a) Write a command to locate the phrase IBM in file SAMPLE2.
C>_
(b) Write a command to locate the phrase PC DOS in NEWFILEA and NEWFILEB.
C>_
(c) Write a command to locate "DuoTech, Inc." in DAVIS.LET or CARSON.LET.
C>_

(a) `C>FIND "IBM" SAMPLE2`
(b) `C>FIND "PC DOS" NEWFILEA NEWFILEB`
(c) `C>FIND "DuoTech, Inc." DAVIS.LET CARSON.LET`

The FIND command has additional parameters you can use as well.

Format (external):
FIND [/V] [/C] [/N] "string" filespec

The /V switch reverses the FIND effect; it lists all lines that do not contain the string. The /C switch gives you a count; it displays the number of lines that contain the string, but does not display the actual lines. The /N switch shows the file line number before each line that contains the string. Unlike most commands, the position of the switches is important in FIND. Switches must precede the operands.

In the interaction in Figure 7.11, the first command shows the basic FIND. The second uses the /C switch. Only the number of matches (3) is displayed. The last FIND command uses the /N parameter. Each displayed line containing the string is preceded by a number indicating the line in the file. When /V is used, lines not containing the string are found. You can use /V /C or /V /N to get a count or itemized listing of the lines that don't contain the string.

If the FIND command lists several files, switches are applied to all. You can't use the same command to get a listing from one file and a count from another.

Both /C and /N won't apply in a single command. /C overrides /N if both are used.

```
C>FIND "NEPTUNE" TEXT05

---------- TEXT05
   When used at the city or county level, the NEPTUNE converter can realize
installation costs can be recovered in less than five years' time if NEPTUNE is
a demonstration of the NEPTUNE converter can be arranged at either the

C>FIND /C "NEPTUNE" TEXT05

---------- TEXT05: 3

C>FIND /N "NEPTUNE" TEXT05

---------- TEXT05
[26]   When used at the city or county level, the NEPTUNE converter can realize
[45]installation costs can be recovered in less than five years' time if NEPTUNE
 is
[59]a demonstration of the NEPTUNE converter can be arranged at either the

C>_
```

Figure 7.11. Examples of FIND

(a) Write a command to search the files BUDGET83.DAT and BUDGET84.DAT for account number "79051" and then to display each matching line.

C>_

(b) Write a command to count the number of matching occurrences of the string DISKETTE in the files named DESCRIP1.DAT and DESCRIP2.DAT.

C>_

(c) Write a command to list all the lines in CUSTOMER that do not contain the value San Diego and give the line number of each.

C>_

(a) `C>FIND "79051" BUDGET83.DAT BUDGET84.DAT`

(b) `C>FIND /C "DISKETTE" DESCRIP1.DAT DESCRIP2.DAT`

(c) `C>FIND /N /V "San Diego" CUSTOMER`

Comparing Files

You read in Chapter 6 how COMP compares files. You can also compare files using the FC (File Compare) command. FC gives you more useful messages than COMP when differences are found in ASCII files. FC also offers a number of options that COMP doesn't allow.

Figure 7.12 shows a basic FC interaction. Two files are compared and no differences are found. The command simply names two files as operands.

Figure 7.13 shows what happens when differences are found. For ASCII files, FC identifies sections or areas that are different. The display shows the last line that is identical before the different section starts. Then all the lines in the different section are displayed. Finally, it shows the first line that is identical again. Therefore, in the example in Figure 7.13, you see three lines from HOME.DB and three lines from HOMEDB.BAK. The first and last lines are identical. The middle line is different. You can also see at the bottom of the display that HOME.DB contains a line that is missing from HOMEDB.BAK. For text file users who don't understand hexadecimal code, FC provides more useful information than COMP.

FC offers several switches. You will probably find /C and /N to be the most useful. The /C switch causes FC to ignore case, while /N includes line numbers in the display.

```
C>FC CHAP00.ASC CHAP00.BAK
fc: no differences encountered

C>_
```

Figure 7.12. Basic FC Comparison

```
C>FC HOME.DB HOMEDB.BAK
***** HOME.DB
LOVESEAT, BROWN PLAID $399 9/1/87
RUG, PERSIAN 4' X 6' $199 1/26/88
COFFEE TABLE, LIGHT OAK $189 2/28/89
***** HOMEDB.BAK
LOVESEAT, BROWN PLAID $399 9/1/87
RUG, PERSIAN 4" X 6" $199 1/26/88
COFFEE TABLE, LIGHT OAK $189 2/28/89
*****

***** HOME.DB
CHEST, CEDAR $499 6/15/89
***** HOMEDB.BAK
*****


C>_
```

Figure 7.13. File Comparison with Differences

If FC finds more than 100 lines in a row that are different, it terminates the job with the message `Resync failed. Files are too different.` After finding mismatched lines, FC must find at least two matching lines in a row before it considers the mismatching sections to be ended. Therefore, you might find single matching lines in the middle of a mismatched section.

FC will also compare non-ASCII files on a byte-by-byte basis rather than a line-by-line basis. The output shows you (in hexadecimal) each byte that differs, much as COMP does.

(a) Write a command to perform a line-by-line comparison of A:CHAP1 and B:CHAP1.

C>_

(b) Adapt your command in Question (a) to ignore case.

C>_

(c) Adapt your command in Question (b) to list line numbers.

C>_

(a) `C>FC A:CHAP1 B:CHAP1`
(b) `C>FC A:CHAP1 B:CHAP1 /C`
(c) `C>FC A:CHAP1 B:CHAP1 /C /N`

Exercises

In these exercises, you will use the RENAME, DEL, TYPE, and PRINT commands on your sample files. You'll see what happens when you set a Read/Only attribute. And you'll practice using FIND to locate data.

What You Should Do	*How the Computer Responds*
1. Boot your system if necessary. Make the diskette or directory containing your practice files current.	1. Follows your instructions.
2. Rename files.	2.
a. Get a directory of your practice files.	a. Displays the requested directory.
b. Change the filespec of FILEA.Y to NEXT.	b. Makes the change, but no message is displayed.
c. Change the filespec of FILEA.X to FIRST.A.	c. Makes the change, but no message is displayed.
d. Check the directory again.	d. Displays the changed directory.
3. Type files.	3.
a. Type FILEA.ALL.	a. Displays the contents of FILEA.ALL.
b. Use Echo Print and TYPE to print a copy of PRESDENT.	b. Displays and prints PRESDENT.
c. Type the other files if you wish.	c. Follows your instructions.
4. Check attributes.	4.
a. Check the attribute of NEXT.	a. Displays filespec with no R. (Ignore the A in the listing for now. You'll learn about it in Chapter 9.)
b. Set NEXT to Read/Only.	b. Records the file's attribute, but displays no message.
c. Check the attributes of all files in the directory.	c. Displays the filespec of NEXT with R. No other files have R.

5. Erase files.	5.
a. Erase FIRST.A.	a. Erases the file, but displays no message.
b. Erase NEXT.	b. Refuses to erase the file.
c. Turn off the Read/Only attribute and erase NEXT.	c. Erases the file after the attribute is changed.
6. Print files.	6.
a. Use PRINT to print the file PRESDENT.	a. Asks for name of list device. Then displays `Resident part of PRINT installed`. Displays print queue information. Then starts printing PRESDENT.
b. While that file is printing, print FILEA.ALL.	b. Shows FILEA.ALL in your print queue.
c. Practice using PRINT with other files as desired.	c. Follows your instructions.
7. Find data in files.	7.
a. Use FIND to locate the string Adams in PRESDENT.	a. Displays two lines containing "Adams."
b. Use FIND to count the presidents' names that contain "and."	b. Our file contains two.
c. Use FIND to identify the line numbers and list all presidents' names containing "son."	c. Our list contains seven lines.
8. Practice using the commands more if you like. Take care not to erase your copy of the PRESDENT file.	8. Follows your instructions.

What If It Doesn't Work?

1. If you have trouble with RENAME, TYPE, or DEL, check the filespec first. These internal commands shouldn't give you any trouble if the filespec is correct.

2. If you have trouble with ATTRIB, make sure the ATTRIB.EXE file is available on the default drive or in the program search path. Then check

your filespec. Don't forget to put a + or - before the R to turn Read/Only on or off.

3. PRINT and FIND are external commands. Make sure the program files are on the default drive or in the program search path. If the program files are available, make sure your filespecs are correct. Since both of these commands have complex formats, you might have trouble at first getting the command syntax correct. Use the format statements in this chapter and keep trying until the commands work correctly.

8

Entering Commands—Advanced Techniques

By now, you know the basics of entering DOS commands; you've been practicing commands since Chapter 1. But DOS also offers several advanced features for entering commands. Some are time-savers: for example, pressing F3 recalls your previous command to the screen. Some give you extra power; for example, you can redirect output that normally appears on your screen to a disk file or some other place. This chapter will teach you to use advanced features for entering commands.

When you have completed this chapter, you will be able to:

- Use the function keys, Insert, and Delete to recall and edit the previous command
- Redirect input and output from the standard devices
- Use SORT to rearrange a file or other input
- Use MORE to display output in screen-sized pages
- Pipe data from one command to another

Recalling and Changing a Command

DOS remembers the previous command you entered. You can use the function keys to recall that command and change it. For example, suppose you entered DIR A: to get a directory of a diskette. This diskette doesn't contain the file you want so you change diskettes. Instead of retyping the command, you can press F3. DIR A: is recalled from memory and displayed at the command prompt. All you have to do is press Enter. If you change your mind, you can press Esc to cancel the command.

Suppose instead, you want to next get a directory of the B: diskette. You can use F3 to display the DIR A: command, then backspace and change the A: to B:.

Suppose you entered the command 4YPE JOHNSON.LET (with a typo in the first character). Naturally, DOS rejects your command. But it remembers it just the same. You can type T, then F3. The T overlays the first character in the saved command (the 4), and F3 recalls the rest of the command. Now you can press Enter and invoke the correct command.

Suppose you entered the command as TYP4 JOHNSON.LET. You can use F1 to display a single letter. After pressing F1 three times you have C>TYP. Now press E, then F3. The command is correct and can be entered.

(a) What key displays the next character in command memory?
(b) What key displays all remaining characters in command memory?
(c) Suppose you want to enter this command:

```
C>COPY B:TRACK A:
```

Instead you type:

```
C>COPY B;TRACK A:
```

How can you correct this after DOS rejects it? (More than one answer might be correct.)

A. Press F3, backspace to ;, change it to :, press F3 again
B. Press F1 six times, type :, press F3
C. Press F1 six times, type :, press F1 eight times
D. Type COPY B:TRACK A:

(a) F1
(b) F3
(c) All would make the correction

The Insert and Delete keys can be used when recalling commands from memory. Suppose you type:

```
C>DEL JJOHNSON.LET
```

When DOS rejects it, you can't just use F3 to restore it. Instead use F1 four times to display DEL and the space or five times to display the first J. Then press Delete to erase the next character from command memory. Next press F3 to recall the remainder of the command. The Del key deletes the next character in the stored command. You don't see its effect on the screen until more characters are displayed.

Now suppose you deleted too many characters, so the line looks like this:

```
C>DEL OHNSON.LET
```

Press Escape to cancel the command, then press F1 four times. When DEL followed by a space is displayed, press Insert, then J. Now press F3 to display the rest of the command. Ins inserts the next characters you type into the stored command. When you press another control key (F1, F3, or Del, for example), Insert stops.

(a) Suppose you intended to type this command:

```
C>COPY B:TRACK A:
```

Instead you typed:

```
C>CPY B:TRACK A:
```

How can you correct this after DOS rejects it? (More than one answer may be correct.)

A. Press F1, the Ins, then F3
B. Press F1, then O, then F3
C. Press F1, then Ins, then O, then F3
D. Type COPY B:TRACK A:

(b) Here is our most common error—forgetting a drivename in a filespec.

```
C>COPY TRACK A:
```

How could you modify this to insert the drivename?

(c) Suppose you type:

```
C>COPY B:TRRACK A:
```

How could you correct the name?

(a) C and D
(b) Press F1 five times, press Ins, type B:, press F3
(c) Press F1 eight or nine times, press Del once, press F3

You have seen how F1, F3, Ins, and Del can be used to modify a command stored in keyboard memory. The F2 and F4 keys can also be useful. The F2 key copies the remaining characters up to a specified character. The F4 key skips over the remaining characters up to a specified character. To use either F2 or F4, you first press the function key, then type the specified character. For example, suppose you type:

```
C>TYPE JJOHNSON.LET
```

You could, of course, press F1 five times, then delete the extra J. It's quicker to press F2, then J. The display will look like this:

```
C>TYPE _
```

Now you can press Del, then F3, to correct the command. Suppose you type:

```
C>DEL \GEORGE\CHECKS\MC.DAT
```

Then you find out that the desired file is in the default directory, not in \GEORGE\CHECKS. To fix this, you could press F2 then G to display the first four characters, resulting in this display:

```
C>DEL _
```

Then press F4 followed by M to delete \GEORGE\CHECKS\ (all the characters up to the next M). The screen still looks like this:

```
C>DEL _
```

The display doesn't change because all you did was delete characters from the saved command. Now you can press F3 to recall the remainder of the command.

```
C>DEL MC.DAT_
```

Which key is used to accomplish each of the following to change the stored command?

(a) Display the remaining characters in the command
(b) Display the remaining characters up to a specified character
(c) Display the next character
(d) Insert one or more characters at the cursor
(e) Delete one character at the cursor
(f) Delete the remaining characters up to a specified character
(g) Suppose you intended to enter this command:

```
C>COPY B:TRACK A:
```

Instead you entered:

```
C>COPY B;TRACK A:
```

How could you correct it using F2 or F4?

(h) Suppose you entered

```
C>COPY B:TRACKLK A:
```

How could you correct it using F2 and F4?

(a) F3
(b) F2
(c) F1
(d) Ins, followed by the character(s)
(e) Del
(f) F4
(g) Press F2, then ;, then :, then F3
(h) Press F2, then L, then F4, then space, then F3

Redirection of Standard Input and Output

You can redirect a command's input and output from the standard devices. For example, the DIR command automatically displays the directory on the screen. You can redirect that output to the printer or even a disk file. Here's how this is done.

The command to redirect output is > followed by a devicename or filespec. To redirect DIR output to the printer, enter:

```
C>DIR >PRN:
```

To redirect DIR output to a file named DIRECTRY, enter:

```
C>DIR >DIRECTRY
```

Refer back to Figure 6.3 for a list of the devicenames you can use.

When you redirect output to an existing file, the contents of the file are overwritten with the new output. To add to the end of the existing file instead, use >> in place of >. If the file doesn't exist, DOS creates it. If it does exist, the new data is appended to the file. For example, to add the disk directory for drive B: to the data already in DIRECTRY, enter:

```
C>DIR B: >>DIRECTRY
```

The command to redirect input is < followed by an input device or filespec. You'll see how this works a bit later.

(a) Write a command to TYPE the file named RCENTER.DAT. Redirect the output to the second parallel printer port.
C>_

(b) Write a command to check the directory of the diskette on drive B: and print the result.
C>_

(c) Write a command to add the directory of drive A: to the file named VOLUME.DAT.
C>_

(a) `C>TYPE RCENTER.DAT >LPT2:`

(*b*) `C>DIR B: >PRN` (*or* `>LPT1`)
(*c*) `C>DIR >>VOLUME.DAT`

Redirection works well with FIND. For example, suppose your CUSTLIST file lists all your customers' names and addresses, and you want to extract a second file containing only customers with ZIP code 90403. You could enter:

```
C>FIND "90403" CUSTLIST >NEARLIST
```

The new file (NEARLIST) will start with a row of dashes and the name CUSTLIST to indicate the source of the data. You could add suppliers to your list from your SUPPLIST file this way:

```
C>FIND "90403" SUPPLIST >>NEARLIST
```

Write a command to extract all lines containing PARTTIME from the file EMPLOYES and to redirect the lines to a new file called PARTEMPS.

```
C>FIND "PARTTIME" EMPLOYES >PARTEMPS
```

Filters

IBM defines a *filter* as a program that reads data from the standard input device (the keyboard), manipulates (filters) it some way, then writes the data to the standard output device (the monitor). Figure 8.1 shows the filter as a piece of hardware, but in fact it is software.

IBM's definition is somewhat deceptive because you can redirect the input and output easily. So the data can come from a disk file, be filtered, and go to another disk file or the printer.

Whatever the definition, DOS includes three filters:

- SORT rearranges the order of the lines in a file
- MORE breaks output into screen-sized chunks so you can page through a long set of data
- FIND searches a file for a specific string and counts or lists all lines containing that string, as you learned earlier

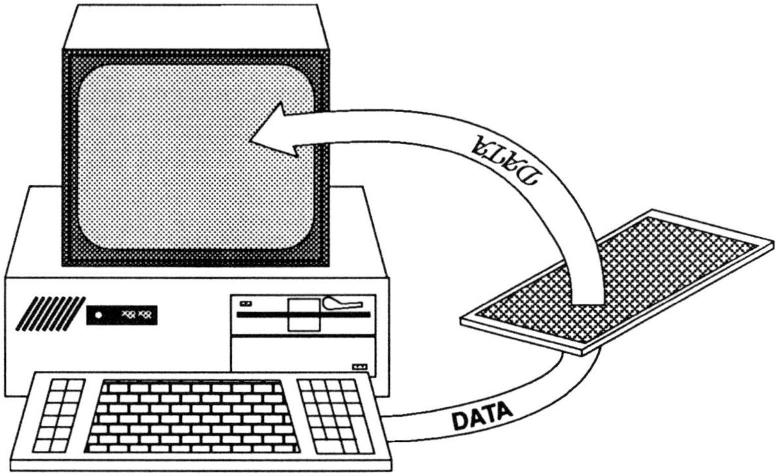

Figure 8.1. Filtering Process

(a) True or false? All DOS external programs are filters.
(b) Are filters hardware or software?

(a) False
(b) Software

Sorting a File

Sometimes you'll want to use data in a specific sequence. For example, you might want to look at a disk directory in alphabetical order or print a list of accounts in account-number sequence. The command to read data from the standard input device, sort the data, then write it to the standard output device is:

Format (external):
SORT [/R] [/+n]

Combined with I/O (for Input/Output) redirection, this is a convenient way to sort ASCII files. The largest file you can sort is 63K.

In the following example, we use input redirection (<) to sort the BUDGET.DAT file and to show the result on the monitor (the standard output device):

```
C>SORT <BUDGET.DAT
```

DOS uses BUDGET.DAT as the input instead of the keyboard. To send the sorted output to a file instead of the monitor, you could use:

```
C>SORT <BUDGET.DAT >BUDGET.SRT
```

The sort order is numbers 0 through 9, letters A through Z (case is ignored), and then special symbols. You can reverse the order with the /R switch.

Suppose you want to view the current directory in alphabetical order. You could use these two commands:

```
C>DIR >SAVEDIR
C>SORT <SAVEDIR
```

The first command saves the directory in a disk file. The second command sorts that file and displays the results on the monitor. You'll see how to do this with one command later in this chapter.

Unless you specify otherwise, the program sorts the data starting in column 1 of each line. If you want to start somewhere else, use the /+n switch, where n is a column number. For example, to sort the RECEIVBL file by account number, which starts in column 4, enter:

```
C>SORT /+4 <RECEIVBL >DUELIST
```

This command says to sort starting in column 4 from the file named RECEIVBL and to put the sorted output in a file named DUELIST. Notice that both the input and output are redirected here.

If you sort input from the keyboard, use F6 (or Ctrl-Z) to terminate the input file, just as you do when creating a new file with COPY CON:.

(a) Write a command to sort input from the keyboard and write it to the file called OUTPUT.DAT.

C>_

(b) Write a command to sort data from the keyboard in reverse order starting in position 12.

C>_

(c) Write a command to sort data from the PURCHASE.DAT file and write it to the SORTED.DAT file. The sort should start in position 1.

```
C>_
```

(a) `C>SORT >OUTPUT.DAT`
(b) `C>SORT /R /+12`
(c) `C>SORT <PURCHASE.DAT >SORTED.DAT`

Displaying Pages

Scanning a file on your monitor screen with TYPE can be a challenge. The lines usually scroll by too fast to read. Pausing with Ctrl-NumLock gives you some haphazard control. The MORE command solves the problem by writing only one screenful of data and pausing with the message:

```
- - More - -
```

To cause the command to continue processing, you press any character on your keyboard.

MORE assumes the standard input and output devices unless you redirect them. Most of the time, you will redirect the input to a disk file (ASCII format). Redirecting the output to a disk file or other device makes no sense, since the purpose is reading the screen.

If you want to see the file named PAYABLE.DAT, you would enter:

```
C>MORE <PAYABLE.DAT
```

Be very careful to type <, not >. If you type >, which is the *output* redirection symbol, DOS will quietly erase the indicated file, if it isn't Read/Only, and wait for you to enter new data from the keyboard. So you'll lose your file, even if you don't enter any data.

Write a command to display the file named RECEIVE.DAT one page at a time.

```
C>_
```

```
C>MORE <RECEIVE.DAT
```

Piping

You can chain two or more commands together. The output of the first command becomes the input to the second command. This technique is called *piping* because you can think of the data traveling down a pipeline from the first to the second command. You don't see the data traveling between commands. You see only the output from the final command.

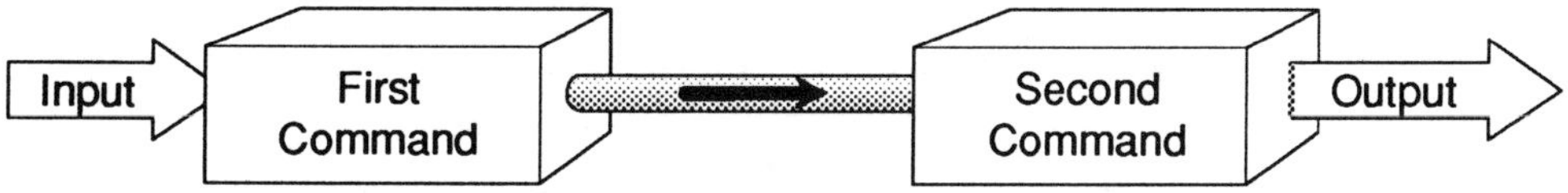

Figure 8.2. Piping Process

The most common example of piping is the sorted directory. You pipe the output from DIR to SORT. The result is a disk directory displayed in alphabetical order. Figure 8.3 shows an example of the command to sort a directory listing along with the output of the command. The command is DIR | SORT. The vertical bar is the piping symbol. You may omit the spaces if you like. You can see that the heading and footing lines also get sorted along with the file entries, making the output somewhat awkward.

```
C>DIR | SORT


       16 File(s)  17461248 bytes free
 Directory of  C:\RUTH
 Volume in drive C has no label
.            <DIR>      5-15-90   8:16a
..           <DIR>      5-15-90   8:16a
AWARD1   CHP       752  5-24-90  12:36p
AWARD1   CIF       128  5-24-90  12:36p
AWARD1   DOC     26496  5-24-90  12:36p
JOBAID            4352  5-20-90  10:54a
JOBAID   BAK      4352  5-20-90  10:51a
JOBAID   EVG      6400  5-19-90   5:27p
PANELLET GEN      3200  5-22-90   3:16p
PREPACK          20480  5-22-90   3:35p
PREPACK  BAK     20096  5-22-90   1:05p
ROGER    522      2304  5-22-90   4:07p
ROGER    BAK      2304  5-22-90   3:48p
SCHEDULE          1664  5-22-90   4:05p
SCHEDULE BAK      1664  5-22-90   4:04p
SIDENOTE          1792  5-22-90  12:42p

C>_
```

Figure 8.3. A Sorted Directory

How about breaking that sorted directory into screen-sized chunks?

```
C>DIR | SORT | MORE
```

The DIR output is piped to SORT, where it is rearranged. Then the SORT output is piped to MORE, which sends it to the screen in pages.

Other commands pipe as well. Suppose you want to display all the records from PRODUCTS.DAT that contain both SILVER and GOLD.

```
C>FIND "SILVER" PRODUCTS.DAT | FIND "GOLD"
```

Since the output from the first command becomes the input to the second command, the second command cannot specify an input filespec. If you want to store the output on disk, just add output redirection at the end of the command.

Here's a command to display all the directory items containing the two-letter string WS.

```
C>DIR | FIND "WS"
```

How is this different from DIR WS*.*? The piped command picks up WS anywhere in the filespec. Thus it selects WS.COM, NEWS.5ID, and ACTION.JWS. The DIR WS*.* command finds only those filespecs that *start* with WS.

As you can see, the use of DOS filters combined with piping gives you the flexibility to create some real powerhouse commands. Your imagination and creativity provide the only limits.

(a) Write a command to display all directory entries for files last modified on 5-10-89.
C>_

(b) Adapt your above command to display the results in alphabetical order.
C>_

(c) Write a command to select all lines from PRODUCTS.DAT containing J29 and send the output to SAVEIT in alphabetical order.
C>_

(d) Adapt your above command to send the output to the monitor, broken into screen-sized pages.
C>_

```
(a) C>DIR | FIND "5-10-89"
(b) C>DIR | FIND "5-10-89" | SORT
(c) C>FIND "J29" PRODUCTS.DAT | SORT >SAVEIT
(d) C>FIND "J29" PRODUCTS.DAT | SORT | MORE
```

Piped commands can use all the normal operands and switches. For example, this command would make up a directory of all the COM files in the current directory of drive C:, sort it in reverse order starting in column 24 (the date), and display the results on the monitor:

```
C>DIR C:*.COM | SORT /R /+24
```

You can use redirection with piping if you apply some common sense. For example, you can redirect the input of the first command, but redirecting the output makes no sense since the output is piped to the second command. Likewise, you can redirect the output of the final command, but not the input.

(a) Write a command to get a directory of drive D:, alphabetize it, and store the result on drive D: as DIRD.
C>_
(b) Write a command to select all records from OVERDUE containing the string BUSHNELL, sort them in reverse order starting in column 60, and print the result.
C>_

```
(a) C>DIR D: | SORT >D:DIRD
(b) C>FIND "BUSHNELL" <OVERDUE | SORT /R /+60 >PRN:
```

Piping works this way: DOS makes a temporary file of the first command's output and redirects the second command's input to that file. When the second command terminates, the temporary disk file is automatically erased. You should never see it in your directory unless DIR is one of the piped commands. (However, if you happen to see a file named %PIPEx.$$$ in your directory, that's a temporary piping file that hasn't been erased yet.)

DOS puts the temporary file on the default drive, no matter what other drives are involved in the commands themselves. So, you can't pipe if your default drive is write-protected or doesn't have any space left.

Suppose you have no fixed disk. Your write-protected DOS diskette is in drive A:. Drive B: contains your inventory files but no DOS files; it is not write-protected. Write commands to get a directory of drive B:, sort the directory in alphabetical order, and store it on drive B: as FILEDIR.

```
A>_
```

`A>B:`

`B>DIR | A:SORT >FILEDIR` *(Since A: is write-protected, you must make B: the default drive or DOS can't store its temporary piping file. Once B: is the default drive, you must attach a drivename to the external SORT command, since SORT.COM is on A:, not B:. However, you couldn't attach a drivename to the DIR command since it is an internal command.)*

Now you've learned a number of DOS "tricks" to make your life easier. You can practice them on-line in the following exercises.

Exercises

These exercises let you practice the DOS features you have learned in this chapter.

What You Should Do	*How the Computer Will Respond*
1. Boot your system if necessary. Make your disk or directory containing the PRESDENT file the default directory.	1. Boots and displays the command prompt, then carries out your commands.
2. Enter a PATH command to make all your DOS external programs available. If they are on drive A:, enter `PATH A:`. If they are on drive C: in the DOS subdirectory, enter `PATH C:\DOS`.	2. Stores whatever PATH command you enter and uses it to find external program files.

3. Make a copy of PRESDENT called PRESBACK, in case you accidentally overwrite PRESDENT during this exercise.

3. Copies the files as instructed.

4. Get a directory of the default drive by entering `DIR`.

4. Displays the requested directory.

5. Now get the same directory again using F3. (Press F3 followed by Enter.)

5. Recalls the DIR command from memory and executes it again.

6. Now get a different directory.
   a. Press F3.
   b. Type a space followed by B: or C:.
   c. Press Enter.

6.
   a. Displays `DIR`.
   b. Adds what you type to the command.
   c. Displays the requested directory.

7. Enter this command *including the typos*:

```
TYPER PRESIDENT
```

7. Shows `Bad command or filename` message.

8. Now correct the first typo:
   a. Press F1 four times.
   b. Press Del once.
   c. Press F3.
   d. Press Enter.

8.
   a. Displays `TYPE_`.
   b. Deletes the R from memory. (Nothing shows on the screen.)
   c. Displays `PRESIDENTS`.
   d. Says `File not found`.

9. Now correct the remaining typo:
   a. Press F2.
   b. Type I.
   c. Press Delete.
   d. Press F3.

9.
   a. Waits for the next character.
   b. Displays `C>TYPE PRES_`.
   c. Deletes the I from memory. (Nothing shows on the screen.)
   d. Displays `C>TYPE PRESDENT_`.

10. Now look at the PRESDENT file one page at a time.
   a. Type MORE followed by a space.
   b. Press Ins.
   c. Type <.

10.
   a. Displays what you type.
   b. Gets ready to insert characters.
   c. Inserts and displays <.

d. Press F3.

d. Displays `PRESDENT`. (The whole command is now `MORE <PRESDENT`.)

e. Press Enter.

e. Displays the first page of PRESDENT and waits for you to press a key.

f. Press any character key.

f. Displays the second page of PRESDENT.

11. Now sort the presidents in alphabetical order, creating a file called PRESSORT:

a. Enter:

```
SORT /+5 <PRESDENT >PRESSORT
```

a. Sorts the old file to create the new file.

b. Display the sorted file:

```
MORE <PRESSORT
```

b. Displays the sorted file one page at a time.

12. Select all presidents who took office in the 20th century, sort them in descending order of year, and print the results. Here's the command:

```
FIND "19" PRESDENT | SORT /R >PRN:
```

12. Prints a list of all the selected presidents starting with Bush and ending with Roosevelt (Teddy).

13. Since it's the classic example of piping, try this one:

```
DIR | SORT | MORE
```

13. Displays a sorted directory, one page at a time.

What If It Doesn't Work?

1. If at first you have trouble using the function keys, Insert, and Delete, keep trying. It can take a while to get used to these keys. Remember, press Delete only once per character, and *don't hold it down* or it will start repeating. Press Insert only once to turn it on. A second time turns it off. Function keys F1 through F4 and Delete turn it off as well.

2. If MORE gets no response, be sure you used <, not >. If you used >, you erased the PRESDENT file; make new copy from PRESBACK. Press Ctrl-Break to restore the DOS prompt.
3. If the SORT command gives you trouble, you probably typed the command incorrectly. Press F3 to see what command you entered, fix it, and try again. Make a new copy of PRESDENT if necessary (see 2 above).
4. If piping gives you trouble, make sure the default disk is not write-protected and has some room. Then make sure you're using the correct piping symbol, the vertical bar.

9

Advanced Disk Management

This chapter covers several techniques you may need to use occasionally. You'll learn to check the integrity of a disk to see if it needs restructuring for better efficiency. You'll learn to recover most of a file when a sector on a disk goes bad. You'll also learn some methods for backing up files. The process of restoring backed up files after a disk crash is also covered here. You'll also learn two more ways of copying groups of files. These copying techniques come in handy for backing up as well as upgrading software.

When you have finished this chapter you will be able to:

- Check the status of a disk and memory with the CHKDSK command
- Use RECOVER to rescue most of a file damaged by bad sectors on a disk
- Use BACKUP to back up all or a selected subset of the files in a directory
- Use RESTORE to make backup files usable again
- Use XCOPY to copy selected files from an entire subtree
- Use REPLACE to copy matching files from an entire subtree
- Use REPLACE to copy missing files in an entire subtree

Checking a Disk

The CHKDSK command, in its simplest form, provides you with a status report of the specified disk and of memory. Figure 9.1 shows an example. If the volume has no label, the top line of the display is omitted. The largest section of the status report concerns the disk itself. These lines give the disk capacity (1.2MB in Figure 9.1), the amount of space used by the hidden files, user files, directories, and bad sectors, and the amount of space available on the disk. The bad sectors reported here are the ones that were originally identified and blocked out when the disk was formatted. CHKDSK does not analyze the disk for new bad sectors. That is done by RECOVER, discussed later in this chapter.

The last section of the status report gives you the total memory size (640K in the figure) and the amount available for use. The amount available for use reflects the amount taken up by DOS, any TSRs, FASTOPEN directory space, and other factors that you'll learn about in Chapter 12. Since CHKDSK is always in memory when this report is prepared, you'll have about 9K more bytes available when CHKDSK isn't running.

CHKDSK is an external program, so it must be available on disk. If you have your DOS external programs on a fixed disk and have entered the appropriate PATH command so they can be found, there won't be a problem. If you have your DOS external programs on drive A: and you want to check another diskette using the same drive, you have a problem. The best solution is to move the CHKDSK program to another drive and run the command from that drive, as in:

```
B>CHKDSK A:
```

```
C>CHKDSK A:
Volume BAND NEWS   created May 23, 1990 1:35p

  1213952 bytes total disk space
    52736 bytes in 2 hidden files
     3048 bytes in 6 directories
     1024 bytes in bad sectors
  1060352 bytes in 48 user files
    96792 bytes available on disk

   655360 bytes total memory
   555328 bytes free

C>_
```

Figure 9.1. CHKDSK Disk Status Report

(a) Write a command to display the amount of memory in your personal computer.

C>_

(b) Write a command to check the status of the diskette in drive B:.

C>_

(c) Select the true statements about the CHKDSK display in Figure 9.1.

A. CHKDSK found new bad sectors and the diskette needs to be reformatted
B. The bad sectors reported by CHKDSK are the ones blocked out by FORMAT
C. The diskette in the figure is bootable
D. The diskette has about 95K of available space
E. The diskette has about 104K of available space
F. Memory has about 554K of available space
G. Memory has about 563K of available space

(a) `C>CHKDSK`
(b) `C>CHKDSK B:`
(c) *B, C, D, G*

The main function of CHKDSK is to check the directories and FAT (file allocation table) on a disk for possible problems. If something unexpected happens while DOS is writing in a directory or the FAT, such as a power loss or a sudden blow to the disk unit, the directory or FAT could be damaged. When the disk drive hardware starts to go bad, as they all do eventually, it might enter mistakes into the directories and FAT. You might notice that you've lost part of a text file, or garbage appears in a text file, or a program begins malfunctioning. That's usually because DOS can no longer identify all the sectors belonging to the file. They're still on the disk, but they are no longer associated with the file through the directory and FAT. On the other hand, the FAT might show incorrect sectors belonging to the file or allocate the same sectors to two different files.

CHKDSK can identify many of these problems. A number of messages are possible, describing various problems with directories and FATs. If you specify the /F switch with CHKDSK, it attempts to fix the problems. Sometimes the fix solves the problem, sometimes it solves part of the problem (perhaps rescuing 75 percent of a file), and sometimes it doesn't help at all. But if the file is already damaged, /F probably won't make it any worse.

The most common FAT problem is lost clusters, parts of files that have lost their links to the rest of the file. This might be where your missing data is. Even if you haven't used /F, CHKDSK displays this message when it identifies lost clusters on a disk:

```
xxx lost clusters found in xxx chains
Convert lost chains to files (Y/N)?_
```

A chain is a series of clusters that come from the same file. What CHKDSK does with them depends on your answer to this question and whether you have specified the /F switch. With /F, if you answer N, CHKDSK frees the clusters, making them available for new data. This is one way to free up more space on an old disk. If you answer Y with /F, CHKDSK converts each chain into a file named FILExxxx.CHK in the root directory, starting with FILE0001.CHK. You can then examine each file and decide what to do with it. You might find your lost data. You'll probably find some unreadable files (perhaps part of a program file) and some old data that you thought you erased a long time ago. In this case, you can erase the files now. Without /F, if you answer N, CHKDSK ignores the lost clusters. If you answer Y, CHKDSK reports how many files would have been created if /F had been specified. (DOS expects you to redo the CHKDSK with the /F switch.)

If you are having trouble with a diskette, the easiest solution is to eliminate the troubled diskette and return to your backup files. If it's crucial to rescue the data from a troubled disk, then run CHKDSK on it without /F to see what messages you get. If problems appear, try copying all the files to a clean disk (with COPY *.* not DISKCOPY), to save as much data as possible. Then run CHKDSK again with the /F switch on the troubled diskette. Answer Y to the lost clusters question.

You can also buy some utility programs that let you examine data sector-by-sector on a disk and rescue individual sectors into files. You might be able to find lost data this way.

You can sometimes rescue a text file with CHKDSK, but it's almost impossible to piece a program file back together from lost sectors. Always make backup copies of programs as soon as you receive them. Store the originals and work with the backups. Then if the copy develops problems, you can restore it from the original.

If it's your fixed disk that's giving you problems and you don't have good, up-to-date backups of all the files on the disk, you might ask your dealer or repair technician to help you rescue the data from the disk. Frequent disk errors can be a sign that the drive hardware is malfunctioning.

(a) Suppose you have a diskette containing a program and associated data files that you use almost every day. Suddenly the program is giving you problems and one of the data files has lost a large chunk of data from the middle. What should you do? Put these in order from most preferable (1) to least preferable (3).

A. Run CHKDSK with the /F switch to rescue as much of the disk as possible

B. Make a new diskette from backup copies of the program and data files; throw the troubled diskette away

C. Ask your dealer for help

(b) What does this message mean?

```
 7 lost clusters found in 3 chains.
Convert lost chains to files (Y/N)?_
```

A. Some data on the disk is not associated with any file

B. Some files on the disk contain no data

C. Some files have been accidentally combined and should be separated

(c) What does the /F switch do?

A. Tries to fix the disk

B. Completely fixes the disk

C. Rescues lost clusters into files if you enter Y

D. Deletes lost clusters if you enter N

E. Ignores lost clusters if you enter N

(a) A—2; B—1; C—3
(b) A
(c) A, C, D

CHKDSK can also check how individual files are stored. As a disk gets used, some files are erased, some new ones are added, and existing ones are expanded. Eventually, the available space on the disk is not in one contiguous chunk at the end of the disk, but broken into small areas located here and there around the disk. For example, a diskette might have 400K available, but it might be in six separate pieces. If you then add a 300K file to the diskette, that file gets spread over several blocks. The file is said to occupy noncontiguous blocks. When a file occupies noncontiguous blocks, DOS takes longer to read and write it.

You can check a file's storage status by including a filespec with the CHKDSK command. Figure 9.2 shows an example in which we check all the files on drive A:. You can see that three files occupy noncontiguous blocks.

You can use global or individual filespecs to check files. The names of any matching files that contain noncontiguous blocks are listed. If all the specified files are contiguous, DOS reports:

```
All specified file(s) are contiguous
```

DOS stores files in contiguous space if possible, since that makes for more efficient processing. So how can you rearrange files on a disk to make them all contiguous? You have to copy all the files to a blank disk using a command similar to this:

```
C>COPY A:*.* B:
```

COPY reorganizes the files as it copies them, and the resulting disk is more efficient than the original one.

```
C>CHKDSK A:*.*

  1213952 bytes total disk space
    52736 bytes in 2 hidden files
  1060352 bytes in 48 user files
   100864 bytes available on disk

   655360 bytes total memory
   555328 bytes free

A:\CHAP09
   Contains 8 non-contiguous blocks.
A:\CHAP01
   Contains 4 non-contiguous blocks.
A:\WPHELP2.FIL
   Contains 2 non-contiguous blocks.

C>_
```

Figure 9.2. CHKDSK File Status Report

(a) Which of these commands will identify all noncontiguous files on a disk?
   A. `CHKDSK B:`
   B. `CHKDSK B:COMMAND.COM`
   C. `CHKDSK B:*.*`

(b) Write a command to determine if any COM files on the disk in drive C: are noncontiguous.
   `C>_`

(c) What is the primary disadvantage of files that contain noncontiguous blocks?
   A. Creates a messy directory
   B. File processing is less efficient
   C. CHKDSK can't be used on the disk

(d) Suppose the diskette in drive A: contains several files with noncontiguous blocks. There is a blank, formatted diskette in drive B:. Write a command to reorganize the files so they all occupy contiguous blocks.
   `C>_`

(a) C
(b) `C>CHKDSK *.COM`
(c) B
(d) `C>COPY A:*.* B:`

You can also use CHKDSK to provide a list of all files and paths on a drive—somewhat like TREE, but in a different format. (A CHKDSK listing is much more compact.) Use the /V switch to accomplish this. Figure 9.3 shows an example. Each directory is listed, followed by the files contained in it. Unfortunately, CHKDSK follows down the paths of subdirectories as it encounters them, so if a directory contains a mixture of files and subdirectories, the files will not all be listed together. You'll have to search the listing to find all the files belonging to one directory. In spite of this, the CHKDSK path listing is very useful for locating files and providing compact documentation of a disk.

CHKDSK does something that neither TREE nor DIR do—it lists hidden files. Notice in Figure 9.3 that the files named IO.SYS and MSDOS.SYS are the first two files in the list because these must always be the first two files in the root directory of a bootable disk.

```
C>CHKDSK A: /V
Directory A:\
      A:\IO.SYS
      A:\MSDOS.SYS
      A:\ANSI.SYS
      A:\DRIVER.SYS
      A:\RAMDRIVE.SYS
      A:\COUNTRY.SYS
      A:\DISPLAY.SYS
      A:\KEYBOARD.SYS
      A:\PRINTER.SYS

  1213952 bytes total disk space
    52736 bytes in 2 hidden files
    68608 bytes in 7 user files
  1092608 bytes available on disk

   655360 bytes total memory
   555328 bytes free

C>_
```

Figure 9.3. CHKDSK File Listing

Write a command to produce a compact listing of the directories and files on fixed disk C:.

C>_

C>CHKDSK /V

Here's the complete format of CHKDSK.

Format (external):
CHKDSK [d:] [filespec] [/V] [/F]

CHKDSK always produces a status report of the indicated drive and memory, including an analysis of any problems in the directories and FAT. Notice that you can request a nondefault drive (d:). CHKDSK provides additional information if you use any other operands or switches.

A specific or global filespec results in a report of noncontiguous blocks for the indicated files. The /V switch results in a listing of all directories and files (with complete paths) on the disk. The /F switch causes CHKDSK to attempt to fix any directory problems it finds.

(a) Write a command to find out if any files with filename PAYROLL on the B: drive are noncontiguous.
C>_
(b) Modify the command to cause it to display a listing of all directories and files on the B: drive as well.
C>_
(c) Write a command to find out if any files on the C: drive are noncontiguous.
C>_
(d) Write a command to find out if there are any bad sectors on the disk in drive A: and how much memory is available in the computer.
C>_
(e) Write a command to check the disk in drive A: for problems with the directory and FAT and to fix any problems encountered.
C>_
(f) Suppose CHKDSK finds some noncontiguous files. What's the best way to clean them up?
A. Rerun CHKDSK with the /F operand
B. Copy all the files to another disk
C. Erase unnecessary files to free up more space

(a) `C>CHKDSK B:PAYROLL.*`
(b) `C>CHKDSK B:PAYROLL.* /V`
(c) `C>CHKDSK C:*.*`
(d) `C>CHKDSK A:`
(e) `C>CHKDSK A: /F`
(f) B

Recovering Files on Disk

When you format a disk, any bad sectors are marked so they won't be used for files. Occasionally, a disk develops bad sectors after it already contains data. The RECOVER command can be of some use in rescuing the file. RECOVER can also be dangerous, however. It's wiser to be sure to make regular backup copies so that a bad sector is no crisis.

You'll know when a file has developed bad sectors. When you try to access the file, you'll get a `Sector not found error reading drive d:` message or perhaps a `Data error reading drive d:` message. Once this happens, test the file by trying to copy it. If you can't copy it (and it hasn't been copy protected by the manufacturer), then only one DOS command can access it—RECOVER. You can use this format of RECOVER:

Format (external):
RECOVER filespec

RECOVER gathers as much data as possible from the named file and writes it into a new version of the file. This is done sector by sector, bypassing bad sectors. The resulting file may have some extra data, especially if it was in noncontiguous blocks. Once you have recovered the file, re-edit it with the same program that created it in the first place. Then you can delete extra data and re-enter missing data. There is no point in recovering a file that you won't be able to edit. The best files to recover are nonprogram files that you have created with your word processor, spreadsheet, database program, and so forth.

RECOVER can also be used to recover a complete disk. Just enter RECOVER without a filespec. This would be appropriate if the directory is damaged (evidenced by data errors when you try to get a directory). The problem with using RECOVER on an entire disk is that it changes every filename to FILExxxx.REC. You must then try to figure out what each file is. This means looking at each one with your word processor, then your spreadsheet, then your database manager, then your graphics program, and so forth. You might have to change the extension of each file to an acceptable extension in order to examine the file with these application packages. You might also have to change the extension to COM to try to run the file as a program, then possibly EXE to try to run the file again as a program. It could take you all day or longer to figure out what each file is after recovering an entire disk. It's better to recover individual files whenever possible. But if the directory is trashed, you can't do that.

Other solutions that avoid recovering the entire directory are available for recovering data from a damaged diskette. The best solution, of course, is to retrieve data from your backup copy. There are also utility programs you can buy that let you rescue data from a disk sector-by-sector.

(a) What is the best solution for recovering bad sectors in a file?
   A. Have backup copies ready to use
   B. Use CHKDSK to identify the problem
   C. Use RECOVER to rescue as many sectors as possible

(b) Suppose you know there is a bad sector in LINCOLN.C1 on the B: disk. Write a command to salvage most of the file.
   `C>_`

(c) Why should you avoid entering the RECOVER command without a filespec?
   A. Because RECOVER requires a filespec
   B. Because it renames all files on the disk and you won't know what kind of files they are
   C. Because it deletes all files on the disk and reformats the disk

---

(a) A
(b) `A>RECOVER B:LINCOLN.C1`
(c) B

Backing Up Data

The first part of this chapter should have convinced you to back up your files regularly. You already know how to back up individual files with COPY. Every time you change a file, you can COPY it to another disk for backup purposes. (If the file's on the fixed disk, copy it to a diskette. That way a head crash won't wipe out both copies.) And you know how to use DISKCOPY to back up every application diskette as soon as you buy it—if it's not copy protected—so you never take the chance of losing expensive software.

You also have to decide where to store your backup diskettes. If you keep them in the same room with your computer, you risk losing everything in a fire. It's better to take your diskettes regularly to another location where they are also protected from disaster, theft, vandalism, and the like.

Sometimes it's not convenient to back up every file as soon as you change it. Many people prefer to back up all changed files at the end of the day. Some users wait a few days between backups.

The best solution is to devise a regular backup system. Decide how often you will back up files, what diskettes you will use, whether you will always overlay older backup versions with newer backup versions, how you will label the diskettes, how you will document them, where you will store them, and how long you will keep them before recycling them.

Figure 9.4 shows a system based on a weekly cycle. Once each week you back up the entire fixed disk. You might want to omit program files since you still have the originals, but you might find it easier to just include all files with the global filespec *.*. You then take the backup diskettes to a safe place, away from the computer location. While you're there, you get last week's diskettes, which are now out of date.

On a daily basis you back up modified files only. You put this diskette away in a safe place. Do you take it to the alternate location? That depends on how rigorous you want to be and how crucial the data is. If you keep the diskette near your computer, you stand the chance of losing the diskette in the same fire or flood that kills your computer. Then you could lose up to six days of revisions and new files. You recycle these daily diskettes when you back up the entire fixed disk again.

To restore an individual file, determine which backup diskette contains the latest version and restore it from that diskette. (You could even fall back to an earlier version by selecting the appropriate diskette.) If the fixed disk crashes, you can restore all the files (after repair) this way:

1. Get the complete backup set of files from the alternate location and copy all files to the fixed disk. This will restore everything except the latest versions of files that were modified after the complete backup was made.
2. Copy the week's modified files to the disk *in chronological order*. That way, if a file was modified more than once, the latest version is copied to the disk last, overwriting previous versions.

If a disaster wipes out your system and your daily backup diskettes, you have to fall back to last week's versions of your files and lose several days of work.

The weekly system described here is just one approach to a backup system. You might want to take a more rigorous approach, perhaps backing up the entire fixed disk daily and backing up modified files hourly. You might want to make several copies of the backup diskettes, storing them in various locations. Or you might want to be more relaxed, perhaps backing up the entire disk only once a month and backing up modified files every few days. That depends on your system security needs. The point is to have some system and stick to it.

Once a Week	Back up fixed disk completely. Take the backup diskettes to a storage location away from the computer. Return all last week's backup diskettes for reuse.
Daily	Back up modified files only. Put these backup diskettes in a safe place. Save until next week's complete backup operation.

Figure 9.4. A Weekly Backup Routine

(a) Rate the security needs of your system on a scale of 1 (desperately vital) to 10 (not very important).
(b) Based on that rating, how often do you think you should back up your entire fixed disk (or all your working diskettes if you don't have a fixed disk)?
(c) How often do you think you should back up modified files?
(d) Where will you keep your backup diskettes to avoid losing them in the same disaster that wipes out your computer?
(e) True or false? Good quality disk drives won't fail.
(f) What should you do with application diskettes as soon as you buy them?

(a) through (d) The answers depend on your system
(e) False; all disk drives fail eventually
(f) DISKCOPY them (if you can)

The BACKUP and RESTORE commands can help you establish and maintain a regular backup system. BACKUP can copy files from the current directory and from all its subdirectories and their subdirectories, making it much more convenient than COPY, which can access only one directory at a time. Furthermore, BACKUP can select all files that have been modified since the previous time BACKUP was run. Or it can select all files that have been modified after a specified date and time. COPY can select files only by name.

The BACKUP command format is shown below:

Format (external):
BACKUP source target [/F] [/S] [/M] [/A] [/D:date] [/T:time] [/L[:filespec]]

You must specify both source and target drivenames. You can also specify a path and/or a filespec for the source. The target must be a specific drivename.

Here are two legitimate BACKUP commands.

```
C>BACKUP C: A:
C>BACKUP C:*.* A:
```

Both commands have the same effect. They back up all files in the current directory of drive C: to drive A:.

This command backs up all the files in the root directory of drive C: to drive B:.

```
C>BACKUP C:\ B:
```

This command backs up all files with extension DAT in directory C:\INVOICES to drive B:.

```
C>BACKUP C:\INVOICES\*.DAT B:
```

Figure 9.5 shows a complete BACKUP interaction. The `Insert` message doesn't appear if the target isn't removable. A similar message appears if the source is removable. Notice that the target diskette is numbered. That's in case more than one target diskette is required to complete the BACKUP, which often is the case when you are backing up a fixed disk. After the BACKUP is finished, put that sequence number on the diskette label along with the date of the backup. If you need to restore the files, the RESTORE program will ask for the backup diskettes by number. If you save several sets of backup diskettes, you will need the date to know which set of diskettes to use. You can also see which files were selected for backup by the command. The entire filespec is shown for each file selected.

To back up an entire fixed disk, you might need 30 or more target diskettes, depending on how much data is on the fixed disk. But you don't generally have to back up the entire fixed disk. Any purchased software will be safe on its original diskettes in storage. You'll only have to regularly back up data files on a regular basis.

```
C>BACKUP C:F*. A:

Insert backup diskette 01 in drive A:

Warning! Files in the target drive
A:\ root directory will be erased
Strike any key when ready

*** Backing up files to drive A: ***
Diskette Number: 01

\DOSBOOK\F6DEVICE
\DOSBOOK\F2NOMSG
\DOSBOOK\F2FILES
\DOSBOOK\F2SPEC
\DOSBOOK\F3SAMDIR
\DOSBOOK\F6DEVS

C>_
```

Figure 9.5. A BACKUP Interaction

Assume BACKUP.COM is in the current directory path.

(a) Write a command to back up all files in the current directory.

C>_

(b) Write a command to back up all .FW files from the FRAME directory of drive C: to the diskette in drive A:.

C>_

(c) Write a command to back up A:NSPI.SD onto the diskette in drive B:.

C>_

(d) Write a command to back up the file named DAILYIN.DAT in the C:\WATSON\RECORDS directory.

C>_

(e) Suppose you have this interaction:

```
C>BACKUP *.* A:
Invalid drive specification
C>_
```

What's wrong?

(a) `C>BACKUP C: A:`
(b) `C>BACKUP \FRAME\*.FW A:`
(c) `C>BACKUP A:NSPI.SD B:`
(d) `C>BACKUP \WATSON\RECORDS\DAILYIN.DAT A:`
(e) *You must specify a source drivename*

When backing up a complete fixed disk, you might need many target diskettes. All target disks must be formatted in advance unless you specify the /F switch in the BACKUP command. The /F switch tells BACKUP to format any unformatted diskettes. Even though the switch is optional, you should make a habit of including it, especially when backing up your fixed disk. If you run out of formatted diskettes in the middle of a backup operation and have not specified /F, you have to cancel the BACKUP command with Ctrl-Break and start over. You could waste half an hour or more this way. If you have specified /F in the first place, you can insert unformatted diskettes and BACKUP will format and use them. Since the /F switch can prevent lost time, the examples from here on include it in all BACKUP commands.

The /S switch includes all subdirectories of the source directory in the backup. The command `BACKUP C:\ B: /S /F` causes all files in the root directory of the fixed disk, and all levels of subdirectories beneath it, to be backed up to drive B:. In other words, all files on drive C: will be backed up. The command `BACKUP C:\GEORGE A: /S /F` causes only the subtree starting at C:\GEORGE to be backed up.

(a) Write a command to back up all files in directory C:\FRAME and its subdirectories to drive A:.
`C>_`

(b) Write a command to back up all files in all directories on drive A: to drive B:.
`C>_`

(a) `C>BACKUP C:\FRAME A: /S /F`
(b) `C>BACKUP A: B: /S /F`

BACKUP can be used to back up all the files you have been working with lately. You might not remember which files you have changed since the previous BACKUP. You can use the /M switch to back up all files that have been modified since the last BACKUP. Using /M lets you keep backup copies of your latest files without having to keep track of all the files that you modify and without having to back up all your files every time you use backup.

How does DOS know which files have been modified since the last time BACKUP was run? By the *archive* attribute in the directory entry. Whenever you modify a file, which includes creating a new file, DOS turns on that file's archive attribute. BACKUP turns off the archive attributes as it backs up a file. After a backing up a complete directory or subtree, all the archive attributes are off. Then as you create and modify files, the archive attributes are turned on one by one. The next BACKUP operation with the /M switch selects only those files with the archive attributes turned on.

DOS manipulates archive attributes automatically, but you can also view and change them with the ATTRIB command. Figure 9.6 shows how the attributes appear in the ATTRIB listing. The files with an A in the left column have their archive attributes on. In other words, they have been modified since the last BACKUP operation. You can use a listing like this to decide whether it's time to do another BACKUP run if you don't do them on a regular basis.

```
C>ATTRIB A:*.*
  A        A:\ANSI.SYS
           A:\DRIVER.SYS
           A:\RAMDRIVE.SYS
  A        A:\COUNTRY.SYS
           A:\DISPLAY.SYS
  A        A:\KEYBOARD.SYS
  A        A:\PRINTER.SYS

C>_
```

Figure 9.6. ATTRIB Listing Showing Archive Attributes

You can also force files to be backed up by turning on their archive attribute with the +A switch. For example, suppose you want to include VENTURA.EXE in the next BACKUP run, even though it hasn't been changed. You could enter this command:

```
C>ATTRIB VENTURA.EXE +A
```

More commonly, you can avoid backing up files by turning off their archive attributes with the -A switch. For example, you might want to turn off the archive attributes of all EXE and COM files. There's no sense in backing up program files that already have complete diskette backups. Here's the command you could use:

```
C>ATTRIB *.EXE -A
```

followed by:

```
C>ATTRIB *.COM -A
```

The archive attribute also interacts with XCOPY, which you will learn later in this chapter.

The archive attribute is not the only way to select files for backup. You can also select them by the date and time they were last modified. If you want to back up all files that were modified on or after some date, you use the /D:date switch. The date format is the same as when you boot. If you want to back up all files in the current directory that were modified on or after April 17, 1990, you could enter:

```
C>BACKUP C: A: /D:04-17-90 /F
```

You can also specify a time with the date using the /T:time switch. For example, if you want to back up all files in the default directory that were modified on or after April 17, 1990 on or after 3:30 P.M., you could enter:

```
C>BACKUP C: A: /D:04-17-90 /T:15:30 /F
```

Regardless of which method you use to select files, BACKUP turns off the archive attribute of every file it copies.

(a) Write a command to back up all files modified on or after July 10, 1990 on the entire disk.
C>_

(b) Change the above command so that only files modified at or after 9:00 A.M. on July 10 will be backed up.
C>_

(c) Write a command to back up all files in the root directory that were modified since the last backup.
C>_

(d) Write a command to view the archive attributes of all files in the current directory.
C>_

(e) Write a command to turn on the archive attribute of all .DAT files in the current directory.
C>_

(f) Write a command to turn off the archive attribute of all .COM files in the current directory.
C>_

(a) `C>BACKUP C:\ A: /D:7-10-90 /F /S`
(b) `C>BACKUP C:\ A: /D:7-10-90 /F /S /T:9`
(c) `C>BACKUP C:\ A: /M /F`
(d) `C>ATTRIB *.*`
(e) `C>ATTRIB +A *.DAT`
(f) `C>ATTRIB -A *.COM`

Backing up a complete fixed disk might take 30 or more diskettes. BACKUP does not simply copy files to the backup diskettes. It organizes them in a special fashion that only BACKUP and RESTORE can handle. All you see in the diskette directory is CONTROL.xxx and BACKUP.xxx. CONTROL.xxx contains the control information (for example, the directory) and BACKUP.xxx contains the concatenated files. These two files are Read/Only so that you can't erase them accidentally. In addition, BACKUP changes the label of the backup diskette to read BACKUP xxx.

How can you find out when a particular file was backed up and what diskette it is on? You can keep your own list, or you can ask BACKUP to keep a log. Figure 9.7 shows an example of a short backup log. You can see the date the backup was made on the first line. For each file that was backed up, you can see its full filespec and the number of its backup diskette; in the example, they were all placed on diskette 001.

To make a backup log, specify the /L switch. If you don't include a filespec, the log is named BACKUP.LOG and is placed in the root directory of the source drive, no matter which directories you backed up. You can override the default filespec by including a filespec with the /L switch, as in

```
C>BACKUP C:\TYPESET\*.STY A: /F /M /L:C:\TYPESET\STYLES.LOG
```

This command places the log on the same directory that is being backed up and names it STYLES.LOG. You cannot put the backup log on the backup diskette.

If BACKUP finds a log file of the same name in the same location, it adds to the log file instead of overwriting the file. This helps you keep a running log of which files were backed up when—and where they are. You also can then edit the backup log to erase entries that are no longer valid because you eliminated the backup diskette(s).

Because the backup log is so vital to finding the correct backup diskette from which to restore files, from here on we include the /L switch on all BACKUP commands.

```
C>TYPE C:\BACKUP.LOG

6-10-1989  18:8:41
001  \STYLES\FILEA
001  \STYLES\FILEB
001  \STYLES\FILEC
001  \STYLES\FILED
001  \STYLES\FILEE
001  \STYLES\FILEF
001  \STYLES\FILEG
001  \STYLES\FILEH
001  \STYLES\FILEI
001  \STYLES\FILEJ
001  \STYLES\FILEK
001  \STYLES\FILEL
C>_
```

Figure 9.7. Sample Backup Log

(a) Suppose you need to restore JOHN-V1 from your backup diskettes. How can you find which diskette it's on?
   A. Look at the directory of each backup diskette
   B. Look in the backup log

(b) Write a command to back up the entire fixed disk to diskettes in drive A:. Keep a backup log.
   C>_

(c) Suppose you want to print the backup log created by the above command. Write the correct command.
   C>_

(d) Suppose the backup log runs to several pages and you want to find all entries for JOHN-V1. Write a command to find and display just those lines from the backup log. (Hint: Use the FIND command.)
   C>_

(a) *B*

(b) `C>BACKUP C:\ A: /S /F /L`

(c) `C>PRINT C:\BACKUP.LOG` *(You could also use TYPE or COPY with the output directed to the printer. If you specified a nondefault log file in (b), use that name in this command as well.)*

(d) `C>FIND "JOHN-V1" C:\BACKUP.LOG`

BACKUP erases any existing files in the root directory of the target diskettes unless you specify the /A switch. You can let BACKUP erase the old files to replace old backup files with new ones when you are backing up the entire disk or subtree. But if you are backing up modified files, the situation is different.

Suppose on Tuesday you modify and back up FILEA, FILEB, and FILEC. On Wednesday you modify and back up FILEA, FILEB, and FILED. If you erase Tuesday's backups, you now have no backup of the latest version of FILEC.

The /A switch causes BACKUP to *append* the new backup files to the old. If you used the /A switch on Wednesday, you would have six files on the backup log: two versions of FILEA, two of FILEB, one of FILEC, and one of FILED. The multiple versions don't hurt. The RESTORE program can handle them, as you'll see shortly.

(a) It's Monday morning. Write a command to back up the entire fixed disk. Overwrite whatever files are in the root directories of the target diskettes in drive A:.

`C>_`

(b) It's Monday evening. Write a command to back up whatever files you have created and modified today. Overwrite whatever files are in the root directories of the target diskettes in drive A:.

`C>_`

(c) It's Tuesday evening. Write a command to back up all files you have created and modified today. Add these files to the diskette in drive A:, which already contains the files backed up on Monday evening.

`C>_`

(d) Suppose you modified JOHN-V1 on Monday and Tuesday. How many versions of JOHN-V1 will exist on the backup diskettes created by Questions (b) and (c) above?

(a) `C>BACKUP C: A: /F /S /L`
(b) `C>BACKUP C: A: /F /S /L /M`
(c) `C>BACKUP C: A: /F /S /L /M /A`
(d) Two

Restoring Backup Files

If you have a good backup system, it is easy to recover from file loss. If your fixed disk crashes, you can restore files from your backup diskettes after the disk has been repaired. If a diskette develops bad sectors or gets damaged, you can restore the lost files from their backups. If you accidentally erase a file, you can replace it. Even if you edit a file and then decide you don't like the editing, you can restore the unedited version.

The only way to retrieve a file from a disk created by BACKUP is with the RESTORE command. Throughout this discussion of RESTORE, we assume that valid backup copies of the desired files have been made on diskettes by BACKUP.

Suppose you accidentally erased CHAP15 from your fixed disk. You can restore the file with this command:

```
C>RESTORE A: CHAP15
```

The first operand specifies the drive containing the backup diskette. CHAP15 specifies the file to be restored. Since no drivename or path are included, the file will be copied to the default directory. Matching files in the target directory are overwritten. Files that don't match are added to the directory.

Figure 9.8 shows a sample RESTORE interaction. First, RESTORE asks for any removable diskettes. Then it reads the diskette and displays the date of the backup. Read the date; it can warn you if you don't have the latest backup version in the drive. Then the diskette number is displayed, followed by a list of the files that were restored from that diskette.

When BACKUP saves a file, it saves the full pathname for the file. Therefore, RESTORE knows which directory each backup file belongs to. RESTORE will not restore a file to a different directory than the one the file came from. If the backup diskette contains files from C:\NOVEL and you try to restore them to C:\HIST101, you will see this interaction:

```
C>RESTORE A: C:\HIST101\*.*
*** Files were backed up 5-19-90 ***
*** Restoring files from drive A: ***
Diskette: 01
Warning! No files were found to restore
C>_
```

```
C>RESTORE A: *.*

Insert backup diskette 01 in drive A:
Strike any key when ready


*** Files were backed up 08-02-1989 ***

*** Restoring files from drive A: ***
Diskette: 01
\STYLES\FILEA
\STYLES\FILEJ
\STYLES\SYMBOLS.DAT
\STYLES\TESTCR.DAT
\STYLES\TESTCR.HLP
\STYLES\TESTCR.DOC
\STYLES\FILEG
\STYLES\WILLOW.TMP
\STYLES\ICONS.DAT
\STYLES\REFORM

C>_
```

Figure 9.8. Sample RESTORE Interaction

(a) Suppose you accidentally erased ANNUAL.REP. Write the command to restore it to the current drive and directory.

C>_

(b) Suppose you edited C:\ADMIN\PERSONEL\EMPLOYEE.DB incorrectly. You want to recover yesterday's version so you can redo the editing. Write a command to restore EMPLOYEE.DB to the correct directory.

C>_

(c) If the desired file already exists in the target directory, will RESTORE overwrite the file with the backup version?

(d) If the desired file is missing from the target directory, will RESTORE add the file?

(a) `C>RESTORE A: ANNUAL.REP`

(b) `C>RESTORE A: D:\ADMIN\PERSONEL\EMPLOYEE.DB`

(c) Yes

(d) Yes

If you create your backup diskette with the /A (append) switch, several versions of the desired file might exist on the backup diskettes. RESTORE finds and restores the first version, then overwrites it with the second version, and so on. The final result is the last version of the file that was found on the source diskette, which is the last one you backed up. Figure 9.9 shows a sample interaction. You can see that four versions of FILEA. were found on the backup diskette. The last version, which should be the most recent version, is the one that remains in the target directory.

As you can see, you don't have to worry about finding the most recent version when you create your backup diskettes with the /A switch. This switch automatically restores all versions, resulting in the most recent version at the end.

Suppose your backup diskette contains two versions of CHAP16—one modified on 4-21-90 at 9:17 A.M. and one modified on 4-23-90 at 3:06 P.M.

(a) Write a command to restore CHAP16 to the current directory.

C>_

(b) Which version will end up on your fixed disk?

(*a*) C>RESTORE A: CHAP16
(*b*) *The one modified on 4-23-90 at 3:06* P.M.

```
C>RESTORE A: FILEA

Insert backup diskette 01 in drive A:
Strike any key when ready


*** Files were backed up 08-02-1989 ***

*** Restoring files from drive A: ***
Diskette: 01
\STYLES\FILEA
\STYLES\FILEA
\STYLES\FILEA
\STYLES\FILEA

C>_
```

Figure 9.9. RESTORE with Several Versions of a File

If you back up many files or very large files, you'll accumulate several backup diskettes numbered 01, 02, etc. For example, if you back up 30MB of data onto 1.2MB diskettes, you'll end up with 25+ backup diskettes.

When you enter a RESTORE command, RESTORE begins by asking you for diskette number 01. It searches that diskette for the desired file(s), then asks for diskette 02, and so on. If you don't override it, RESTORE will search the entire set of diskettes looking for all versions of the backup file.

If you want to restore only one file or a small group of files, your backup log tells you which diskette(s) they're on. If you haven't put the diskette numbers on the external labels, you can examine the directories to find the desired diskettes. Figure 9.10 shows what the directory of a backup diskette looks like. You can see the 003 in the label and in the filespecs. And you can see on what date the files were last added.

```
C>DIR A:

 Volume in drive A is BACKUP  003
 Directory of  A:\

BACKUP   003     7128   8-02-89   2:30a
CONTROL  003      555   8-02-89   2:30a
        2 File(s)   1205760 bytes free

C>_
```

Figure 9.10. Directory of a Backup Diskette

Suppose you want to restore a file that you know is on diskette number 03. When RESTORE asks for diskette number 01, insert diskette number 03. When RESTORE displays this message

```
Warning! Diskette is out of sequence
Replace diskette or continue if okay
Strike any key when ready_
```

simply press any character key to force RESTORE to accept diskette 03. In the same manner, you could then skip to diskettes 07, 13, 28, and so on.

There is one condition under which RESTORE will not let you skip a diskette. When BACKUP saves files, it fills each diskette completely before starting another. It even splits a file over two diskettes if necessary. In fact, a very large file might occupy several diskettes. RESTORE knows when it needs to finish a split file it has partially restored. In that case, RESTORE will insist on the next diskette in sequence. If you try to give it another diskette, RESTORE terminates with this message:

```
*** Not able to restore file ***
```

(a) Suppose you want to restore CHAP15, which is somewhere in a 40-diskette set. Which commands could help you figure out which diskette CHAP15 is on?

A. `C>MORE <C:\BACKUP.LOG`
B. `C>PRINT C:\BACKUP.LOG`
C. `C>FIND "CHAP15" C:\BACKUP.LOG`
D. `C>SORT <C:\BACKUP.LOG`

(b) Now you know that CHAP15 is on diskette 22. But your diskettes have no external labels. You count down 22 diskettes in the stack and place that diskette in drive A:. Which command(s) will tell you whether it's the right diskette?

A. `C>VOL A:`
B. `C>LABEL A:`
C. `C>DIR A:`
D. `C>CHKDSK A:`

(c) Now you have diskette 22 in drive A:. Write the command to restore CHAP15.

`C>_`

(d) How do you respond to this message?

```
Insert backup diskette 01 in drive A:
Strike any key when ready
```

(e) How do you respond to this message?

```
Warning! Diskette is out of sequence
Replace diskette or continue if okay
Strike any key when ready_
```

(f) Now RESTORE says:

```
*** Files were backed up on 05-17-90 ***
*** Restoring files from drive A: ***
Diskette: 22
\CHAP15

Insert backup diskette 23 in drive A:
Strike any key when ready_
```

What should you do now?

A. Jump to the last diskette in the set
B. Continue giving RESTORE the diskettes it asks for
C. Go back to diskette number 01

(g) Why should you avoid terminating RESTORE with Ctrl-Break or rebooting when RESTORE asks for another diskette?
A. Because it won't go back to the command prompt
B. Because it might have restored only part of a split file
C. Because it might not have restored the latest version of the file
D. Because it might damage the target

(h) Suppose your CUSTOMER.DB file is 2MB long. You can't COPY it to diskette because COPY can't fit it on one diskette. What is the only DOS command that will save this file on diskette?

```
C>_
```

(a) All of them
(b) All of them
(c) `C>RESTORE A: CHAP16`
(d) Strike any key
(e) Strike any key
(f) A or B
(g) B, C
(h) `C>BACKUP C:CUSTOMER.DB A: /F`

So far, we've restored individual files only. But you can do a global restore, much as you do a global backup. For example, suppose you accidentally entered this command:

```
C>DEL *.DAT
```

To restore the .DAT files to the current directory, you could enter this command:

```
C>RESTORE A: *.DAT
```

RESTORE searches the backup diskette(s) on the source drive for all files that match the global filespec, including the specified or implied directory, and restores these files. As usual, later versions overwrite earlier versions.

Figure 9.11 shows a complete interaction using the filespec CHAP*.*. RESTORE lists the files as it finds and restores them.

```
C>RESTORE A: CHAP*.*

Insert backup diskette 01 in drive A:
Strike any key when ready


*** Files were backed up 08-02-1989 ***

*** Restoring files from drive A: ***
Diskette: 01
\DOSBOOK\CHAP01
\DOSBOOK\CHAP02
\DOSBOOK\CHAP03
\DOSBOOK\CHAP04
\DOSBOOK\CHAP05
\DOSBOOK\CHAP06
\DOSBOOK\CHAP07
\DOSBOOK\CHAP08
\DOSBOOK\CHAP09

C>_
```

Figure 9.11. Restoring with a Global Filespec

RESTORE overwrites matching files in the target directory, even if they're Read/Only. But what if the version on the target drive is a *newer* version, not yet backed up? You've just lost some data. The /P (prompt) switch can help to prevent this. It identifies files with a positive archive attribute and displays this message:

```
Warning! File CHAP01
was changed after it was backed up
Replace the file (Y/N)?_
```

For Read/Only files it displays this message:

```
Warning! File CHAP01
is a read only file
Replace the file (Y/N)?_
```

You can then decide whether to overwrite each file individually.

The /P switch is a "safety valve" when doing global restores. We will show it in all RESTORE commands from here on.

(a) Write a command to restore all files from drive A: to the current directory. Use the prompt feature.

```
C>_
```

(b) Write a command to restore all files starting with CHAP to D:\PROJSTAR. Use the prompt feature.

```
C>_
```

(c) What files are prompted by /P?

A. All files selected to be restored
B. All files that will overwrite source files
C. All files that will overwrite source files that have a positive archive attribute
D. All files that will overwrite source files that are marked Read/Only
E. All files that will not overwrite source files

(a) `C>RESTORE A: *.* /P`
(b) `C>RESTORE A: D:\PROJSTAR\CHAP*.* /P`
(c) *C, D*

You can restore files to a single directory or to an entire subtree. The /S switch causes an entire subtree to be restored. DOS will create subdirectories as necessary.

Figure 9.12 shows an example. Before the RESTORE, drive C: has just been formatted and contains only a root directory and the system files. The backup diskette contains 13 files; their filenames indicate which directories they belong in. After the restore, all the necessary subdirectories have been created. The RESTORE command for this particular example is:

```
C>RESTORE A: C: /S /P
```

Suppose you removed the entire subtree starting at C:\INB from the fixed disk. Now you decide you want to restore it. The correct backup diskette is in drive A:. Write the necessary command.

```
C>_
```

```
C>RESTORE A: C:\INB /S /P
```

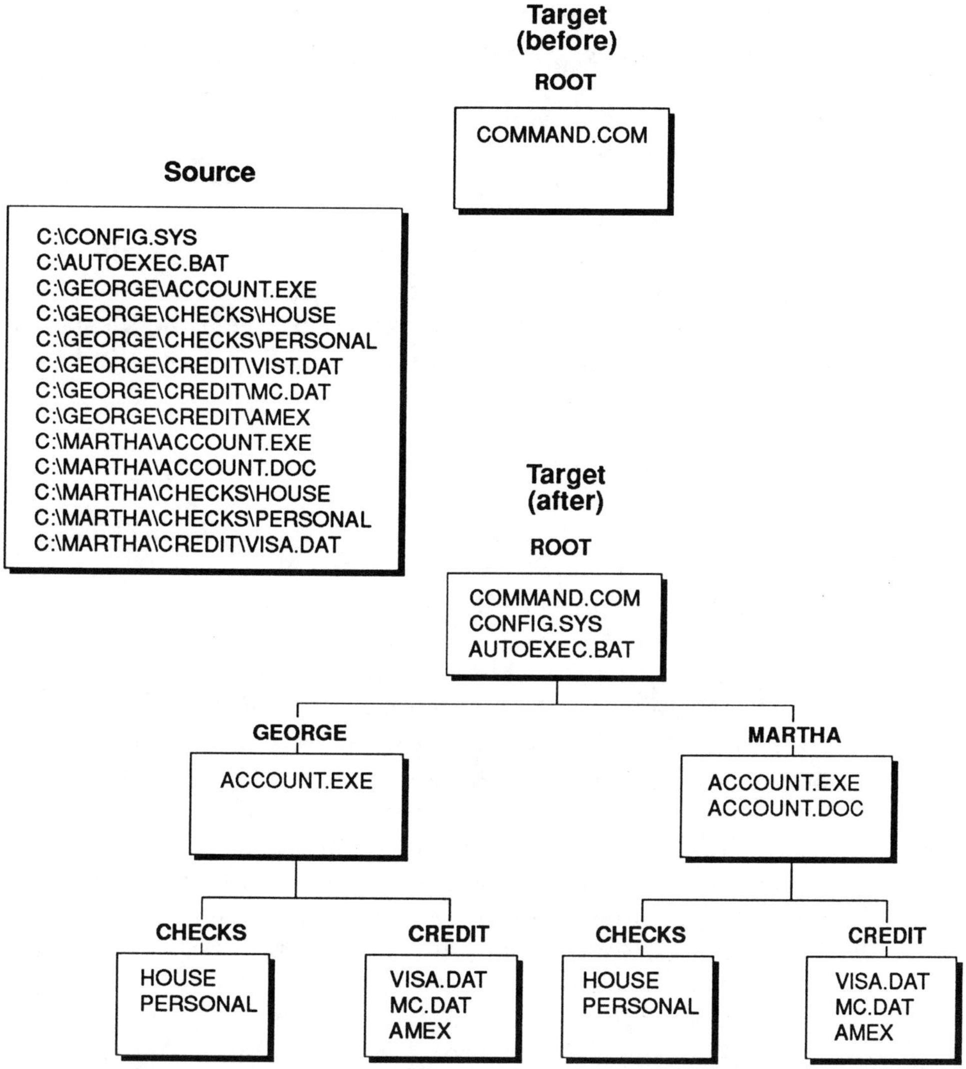

Figure 9.12. Restoring an Entire Subtree

Here's the complete RESTORE format:

Format (external):

RESTORE source [target] [/P] [/S] [/M] [/N]
[/B:date] [/A:date] [/L:time] [/E:time]

The source must be a drivename; neither a pathname nor a filespec can be specified for the source. If you don't specify a target, RESTORE selects all the files from the backup diskette(s) that belong in the current directory. If you specify a target drivename, then RESTORE selects all files from the backup diskette(s) that belong in the current directory on that drive.

If you specify a target pathname, you must also specify a filespec. RESTORE does not assume *.* when you give a target pathname but not the filename. It finds no files to restore. When you specify a target filespec, RESTORE selects all the files from the backup diskette(s) that belong in the designated or implied directory and that match the filespec. For example, suppose the backup diskette contains the files shown in Figure 9.12. What would this command do?

```
C>RESTORE A: C:\GEORGE\CREDIT\*.DAT /P
```

It would restore the files named C:\GEORGE\CREDIT\VISA.DAT and C:\GEORGE\CREDIT\MC.DAT, but not C:\GEORGE\CREDIT\AMEX, since that file doesn't match the target filespec.

The /P switch causes RESTORE to warn you when it will overwrite a newer version with an older version or overwrite a Read/Only file.

The /S switch causes RESTORE to select files for restoration from an entire subtree headed by the target directory. Subdirectories on the target diskette are created as necessary to receive files from the source diskette.

The other switches all select files to be restored. The /M switch causes RESTORE to compare the source and target directories. Any files in the target that have been modified since the previous backup (as indicated by a positive archive switch in the target directory entry) are restored, thus eliminating the modifications. Any missing files are also restored. The intention of the /M switch is to undo modifications. Suppose on Tuesday you modify three files in C:\BAND\NEWS. In addition, you delete two files. Then you realize that all the work you did was wrong and you want to return to Monday night's position. You put Monday night's backup diskette in drive A: and enter this command:

```
C>RESTORE A: C:\BAND\NEWS\*.* /M /P
```

The /N switch restores only missing files to the target directory. Suppose in the previous example you don't want to restore the modified files, only the deleted ones. Then you could enter this command:

```
C>RESTORE A: C:\BAND\NEWS\*.* /N
```

The /B:date, /A:date, /E:time, and /L:time switches let you select files for restoration based on their date/time stamps in the *target* directory. The /B:date switch selects files to be overwritten with a time stamp on or before the specified date. The /E:time switch selects files to be overwritten with a time stamp at or *earlier* than the specified time. The /A:date switch selects files to be overwritten with a date stamp on or *after* the specified date. The /L:time switch selects files to be overwritten with a time stamp at or *later* than the specified time.

No matter which time/date switches you use, missing files are restored. That is, if C:\NOVEL\CHAP15 exists in the source directory but not the target directory, it is restored to the target directory.

(a) Write a command to undo today's modifications and deletions. Yesterday's backup diskette is in drive A:. Restore the entire fixed disk, but let each selected file be prompted.
C>_

(b) Revise the above command to restore deletions only.
C>_

(c) Suppose your current directory contains a group of files previously modified on 7-01-90 and another group previously modified on 7-05-90. Write a command to restore the first group but not the second.
C>_

(a) `C>RESTORE A: C:\*.* /S /M /P`
(b) `C>RESTORE A: C:\*.*  /S /N /P`
(c) `C>RESTORE A: C:*.* /B:7-01-90`

You can restore your entire fixed disk after a crash. It has been repaired, repartitioned with FDISK, and reformatted with the /S switch. It contains only the root directory with the hidden files and COMMAND.COM.

You also have a set of 25 diskettes with files backed up the previous Monday morning, backing up the entire disk. In addition, you have one diskette containing all the daily modified files.

(a) Write a command to restore the entire disk—all files and all subdirectories—from the weekly complete backup diskettes.

C>_

(b) Now write a command to restore all the modified files from the daily backup diskette.

C>_

(a) `C>RESTORE A: C:\*.* /S`

(b) `C>RESTORE A: C:\*.* /S`

Note

BACKUP and RESTORE have changed considerably from earlier DOS versions. If your version of DOS is older than DOS 3.3, BACKUP and RESTORE work differently. You cannot use the new RESTORE to restore files backed up by an earlier version of BACKUP. Nor can your earlier version of RESTORE restore files backed up by the new BACKUP. If you need to restore files backed up by an earlier version of DOS, you'll need to boot that version of DOS in order to use the matching RESTORE command.

Extended Copy Functions

Wouldn't it be nice if COPY had some of BACKUP's features? Or if BACKUP made usable files? The XCOPY (extended copy) command combines some of the best features of BACKUP and COPY. It makes usable copies like COPY, and it selects modified files like BACKUP. It also copies from an entire subtree like BACKUP. The basic command has the same format as COPY:

XCOPY source [target] [/V]

For example, to copy all .DAT files from the current directory to drive A:, you could enter:

```
C>XCOPY *.DAT A: /V
```

XCOPY outperforms COPY even in this basic form because it is much faster. Instead of copying one file at a time, XCOPY copies as much data at once as memory can hold. Unlike COPY, XCOPY cannot handle devices other than disk drives. Also, XCOPY cannot concatenate files.

Use XCOPY in answering Questions (a), (b), and (c).

(a) Write a command to copy all files from B: to the current directory. Verify the copies.
    C>_

(b) Write a command to copy all .COM files from A: to B:. Verify the copies.
    C>_

(c) Write a command to copy all .DOC files from the current directory to drive A:. Rename them as .TXT files. Verify the copies.
    C>_

(d) Indicate whether COPY (C) or XCOPY (X) does it better:
    A. Concatenate files
    B. Copy a group of files from one drive to another
    C. Make a new file by copying from keyboard to disk
    D. Select modified files to copy
    E. Select files from an entire tree
    F. Copy to a printer or communications port

(a) `C>XCOPY B: /V` *or* `XCOPY B:*.* /V` *(You could also include a target drive-name)*

(b) `C>XCOPY A:*.COM B: /V`

(c) `C>XCOPY *.DOC A:*.TXT /V`

(d) A—C; B—X; C—C; D—X; E—X; F—C

XCOPY can select modified files in several ways. The /M switch acts just like the BACKUP and RESTORE /M switches. It selects all archive files in the source directory. The /M switch also turns off the archive attribute when it copies the file. The /A switch does the same thing, but doesn't turn off the archive attribute. The /D:date switch selects files that were created or modified on or after the specified date. This switch does not use or affect the archive attribute.

How do you choose between /M, /A, and /D:date? That depends on your regular backup system. Suppose your backup routine is built around BACKUP with the /M switch. Every day before you shut down, you use BACKUP with /M to back up modified files. In this case, you don't want XCOPY to turn off archive attributes. Use /A or /D:date whenever you want to select modified files with XCOPY.

When would you use the /M switch? Many users prefer to build their backup system around XCOPY instead of BACKUP. XCOPY offers several advantages. The backup copies are usable "as is." You don't need a special program like RESTORE to read the files. Furthermore, you can read the directory of the backup diskette directly; you don't need a backup log. Suppose your fixed disk crashes and is out of use for several days. You can continue to access your backup files on diskette if they have been made by XCOPY instead of BACKUP. Furthermore, XCOPY doesn't create several versions of the same file on the backup diskette. If XCOPY backs up a file named POPULATE.DAT on Monday, then backs up a newer version of the same file on Tuesday, Tuesday's version overwrites Monday's version. Only one version of the file exists on the XCOPY backup diskette—the latest version.

You can see that XCOPY has several advantages over BACKUP and RESTORE. Its major disadvantage is in handling full disks. XCOPY, like COPY, gives up when the target disk is full. It displays a `Disk full` message and terminates itself, even if there are more files to copy. You have to insert another diskette and reenter the command. (If the /M switch is used, the files already copied won't be selected again because their archive attributes are now off.) Furthermore, XCOPY cannot back up a file that is larger than a diskette. Only BACKUP can span a file over two or more diskettes.

(a) Write a command to copy all archive files from the current directory to A:. Turn off the archive attribute of every copied file. Verify the copies.
C>_

(b) Adapt your above command to leave the archive attributes alone.
C>_

(c) Adapt your above command to select files created or modified on or after 5-10-90.
C>_

(d) Does the command you wrote for Question (c) turn off the archive attributes of the copied files?

(e) Identify each of the following as an advantage of XCOPY (X) or BACKUP (B).
A. Target diskettes are usable as is
B. New files overwrite earlier versions
C. Can span a file across two or more diskettes
D. Resulting diskette directory is readable

(a) `C>XCOPY *.* A: /M /V`

(b) `C>XCOPY *.* A: /A /V`
(c) `C>XCOPY *.* A: /D:5-10-90 /V`
(d) *No*
(e) *A—X; B—X; C—B; D—X*

One XCOPY feature that would work nicely with every copy command—as well as with the delete command—is the /P (prompt) switch. This switch causes XCOPY to ask you about every file it selects for copying. Figure 9.13 shows a sample interaction. You can see that five files matched the CHAP*.* global filespec and the /A switch. We said "Yes" to four of them but chose not to copy the CHAP01.BAK file.

You frequently create or modify files that don't need to be backed up: letters, notes to yourself, temporary scratch pads, WordStar .BAK files, WordPerfect .BK! files, and so forth. The /P switch lets you reject them when backing up modified files.

You'll also find /P handy when a global filename includes files you want to exclude. For example, suppose you want to copy CHAP01 through CHAP17, but not CHAP18. Rather than enter 17 separate COPY or XCOPY commands, you could enter this command:

```
C>XCOPY CHAP* A: /V /P
```

The /P switch slows XCOPY down, and you have to stay at the keyboard for the entire copy operation, but sometimes it's the most convenient way to get a job done.

```
C>XCOPY CHAP*.* A: /A /P
CHAP01 (Y/N)? Y
CHAP02 (Y/N)? Y
CHAP03 (Y/N)? Y
CHAP04 (Y/N)? Y
CHAP01.BAK (Y/N)? N
        4 File(s) copied

C>_
```

Figure 9.13. Sample Prompted XCOPY Interaction

(a) Write a command to copy all files from drive A: to the current directory. Use the prompt feature.
C>_

(b) Identify each statement as describing the /P switch for RESTORE (R) or for XCOPY (X).

A. Prompts for every selected file

B. Prompts only if a newer version or a Read/Only file will be overwritten

(a) C>XCOPY A:*.* /P

(b) A—X; B—R

XCOPY lets you copy selected files from an entire tree or subtree to a corresponding tree somewhere else. Figure 9.14 shows how this process works. The command for the XCOPY in the figure is:

```
C>XCOPY \EMAIL A:\ /S /V
```

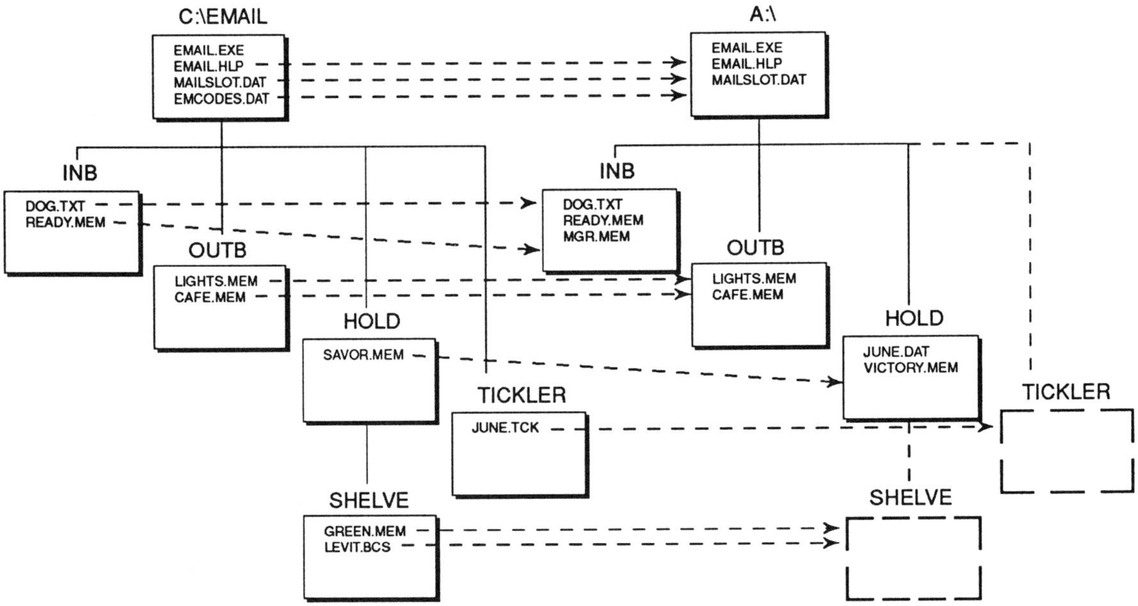

Figure 9.14. Using XCOPY with a Complete Subtree

The source tree starts at C:\EMAIL. The target tree starts at A:\. XCOPY treats the top source directory and the top target directory as parallel directories, even if their names don't match. Thus in the example, all the files from C:\EMAIL are copied to A:\. Three of the files overwrite existing files; a fourth file was added to the directory.

For each subdirectory in the source subtree, XCOPY looks for a parallel directory in the target tree. The pathnames must match except for the beginnings, which reflect the top of the tree. In the example, when XCOPY finds C:\EMAIL\INB, it looks for A:\INB. When XCOPY finds C:\EMAIL\HOLD\SHELVE, it looks for A:\HOLD\SHELVE. If XCOPY finds a parallel directory, it copies all the selected files to this directory, overwriting existing files as necessary.

If XCOPY doesn't find a target directory parallel to the source directory, it *creates a parallel directory* and copies the source files to this new directory. You can see in the figure that XCOPY created A:\TICKLER and A:\HOLD\SHELVE.

If XCOPY finds a source directory with no files to be copied, it does not look for or create a parallel target directory unless you specify the /E switch. The /E switch causes XCOPY to make the two directory trees parallel. You might use this switch if you are trying to keep your home computer "in sync" with your office computer, for example.

Suppose you want to back up your entire fixed disk using XCOPY instead of BACKUP. You have determined that the entire subtree starting at C:\CLASSES\HIST101 will fit on one diskette. The following command will copy the subtree, including empty subdirectories.

```
C>XCOPY C:\CLASSES\HIST101 A:\ /S /V /E
```

To add modified files and new subdirectories to the diskette created in the previous command, you could enter:

```
C>XCOPY C:\CLASSES\HIST101 A:\ /S /V /E /M
```

In both of these cases, you might want to include the /P switch to screen out files that don't need to be backed up.

Suppose you need to send a set of files to the home office via diskette. They are contained in the C:\ADMIN\ACCOUNTS subtree, which has several subdirectories. You could create the necessary diskette, maintaining the tree structure, with this command:

```
C>XCOPY C:\ADMIN\ACCOUNTS A:\ /S /V
```

Suppose you have received a diskette from a vendor that is structured into a root directory and several subdirectories, some of which are empty. You can copy the entire tree from drive A: to the current directory on drive C: with this command:

```
C>XCOPY A: /S /V /E
```

The complete format of XCOPY is shown below:

Format (external):
XCOPY source [target] [/V] [/A] [/M] [/D] [/S] [/E] [/W]

The /W (wait) switch causes XCOPY to prompt you for any diskettes. Without /W, XCOPY assumes the diskettes were inserted before the XCOPY command was entered, and it gets right to work. If you don't have a fixed disk, you must start the XCOPY command with the DOS program diskette in one of your drives. If you want the chance to start the program and then replace the DOS disk with either the source or the target diskette, use the /W switch. You might also include /W if you put XCOPY in a batch file; this serves as a reminder that an XCOPY operation is about to occur. You'll learn about batch files in Chapter 10.

Suppose you use XCOPY as your backup system. You have determined that the subtree starting at C:\NOVEL will fill half a diskette, leaving room for new and modified files to be added as the week progresses.

(a) It's Monday morning. Write a command to back up the entire tree—including empty subdirectories—to the diskette in drive A:.
C>_

(b) It's Tuesday. Write a command to back up only modified files to the diskette in A:. Clear the archive attributes of each copied file.
C>_

(c) On Wednesday your hard disk crashes. You get it repaired and use MD to create the C:\NOVEL subdirectory. Restore the C:\NOVEL subtree from the backup diskette.
C>_

(a) `C>XCOPY \NOVEL A: /V /E`
(b) `C>XCOPY \NOVEL A: /V /E /M`
(c) `C>XCOPY A: \NOVEL /V /E`

Here are some error messages you might encounter with XCOPY.

This message appears when XCOPY attempts to overwrite a Read/Only file:

```
Access denied
```

Figure 9.15 shows a sample job in which several files were successfully copied, then a Read/Only file was encountered. The `Access denied` message was displayed and the job terminated. You might also see the access denied message if the source and target files are accidentally the same.

```
C>XCOPY A:*.*

Reading source file(s)...
A:CHAP01
A:CHAP02
A:CHAP03
A:CHAP04

Access denied
        3 File(s) copied

C>_
```

Figure 9.15. Trying to Overwrite a Read/Only File

You'll see this message when a directory is included in both the source and the target trees:

```
Cannot perform a cyclic copy
```

For example, refer back to Figure 9.14. If the source directory was EMAIL, the target directory was SHELVE, and the /S switch was used, then SHELVE is in both trees and XCOPY could not proceed.

You'll see this message if you specify a DOS devicename such as PRN as either the source or target:

```
Cannot XCOPY from/to a reserved device
```

Filenames and directory names look alike. Most of the time, DOS can tell the difference by the context or by looking in the directory to see which type of entry the name has. However, when an XCOPY command specifies a target name that doesn't appear in the target directory, XCOPY doesn't know whether the name is a filename or a directory name.

```
Does name specify a file name
or a directory name on the target
(F = file, D = directory)?_
```

You must enter F or D to tell XCOPY how to treat the name.

This message appears in any situation where XCOPY is trying to create a directory on the target drive and cannot do so:

```
Unable to create directory
```

Perhaps a file with the same name already exists in the parent directory (you can't have both). Perhaps the disk is full, or the root directory is the parent directory and it's full. Perhaps the specified directory name is a devicename. You'll have to figure out what the problem is and correct it before re-entering the XCOPY command.

(a) Suppose you encounter this interaction:

```
C>XCOPY A:*.* /S /V /E
Reading source file...
PARTTIME.DAT
FULLTIME.DAT
TEMP.DAT
DATAMGR.EXE
Access denied
C>_
```

What's wrong?
How can you fix it?

(b) Suppose you encounter this interaction:

```
C>XCOPY C:*.DAT A:DATBAK /S /M
Does DATBAK  specify a file name
or a directory name on the target
(F = file, D = directory)?D
Unable to create target directory
C>_
```

What could be wrong?
A. The diskette in A: is full
B. The root directory of the diskette in A: is full
C. There is already a DATBAK directory on A:

(c) Suppose you have this interaction:

```
C>XCOPY C:*.DAT COM1 /S /M
Does COM1 specify a file name
or a directory name on the target
(F = file, D = directory)D
Unable to create target directory
C>_
```

What's wrong?
How can you fix it?

(a) DATAMGR.EXE is a Read/Only file; use ATTRIB to remove the Read/Only status and re-enter the XCOPY command
(b) A, B
(c) COM1 is a devicename and cannot be used as a directory name; re-enter the command using another directory name

---

Upgrading and Replacing Files

One more copy function gives you some features you might occasionally find useful. The REPLACE command compares the source and target directories and does one of two things: either it copies only matching files, or it copies only nonmatching files.

Let's look at the matching-files function first. This function is designed to help you upgrade versions of an application when you receive new copies from the vendor. Figure 9.16 shows how it works. The source diskette contains a new version of SORTER.EXE. Five copies of the previous version reside in various directories on the fixed disk. REPLACE seeks out and overwrites every existing copy. Thus, REPLACE makes it easy to upgrade your software, even if you have several versions of it on the fixed disk.

The command to upgrade the SORTER.EXE application is:

```
C>REPLACE A:SORTER.EXE C:\ /S
```

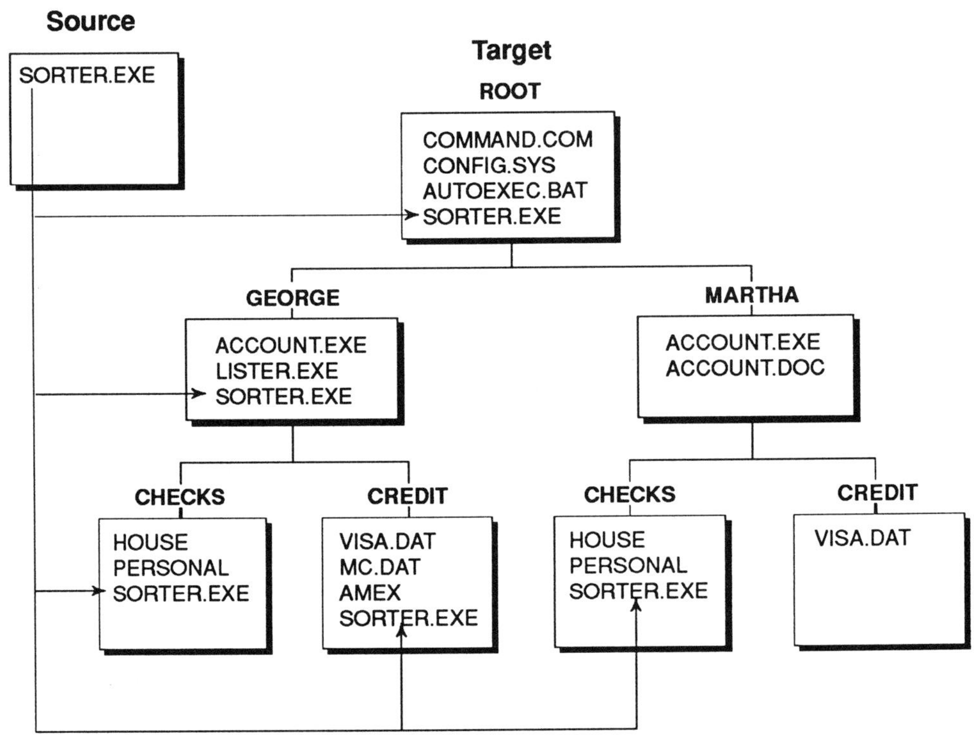

Figure 9.16. Upgrading Several Copies of a File with REPLACE

The /S switch causes all subdirectories of the target directory to be examined. Since we specified the root directory of C:, the entire fixed disk was examined.

If the source directory contains several files for upgrading, you can use a global filespec, as in:

```
C>REPLACE A:*.* C:\ /S
```

Figure 9.17 shows such a replace interaction. In the example, the source disk contained three upgraded files: GRAPH.EXE, GRAPHOUT.EXE, and DRAWGR.EXE. You can see that DOS found several copies of these programs on the fixed disk. All the files were replaced automatically.

✔ Suppose you receive a diskette containing upgrades to your word processing program. Several files are involved. You have several copies of the word

```
C>REPLACE A:*.* C:\ /S
 Replacing C:\SITCOM\JIMPROPS\GRAPH.EXE
 Replacing C:\SITCOM\GRAPH.EXE
 Replacing C:\SITCOM\DRAWGR.EXE
 Replacing C:\DOS\DRAWGR.EXE
 Replacing C:\DOS\GRAPH\GRAPH.EXE
 Replacing C:\DOS\GRAPH\GRAPHOUT.EXE
 Replacing C:\DOS\GRAPH\DRAWGR.EXE
 Replacing C:\DRAWGR.EXE
 Replacing C:\DOSBOOK\GRAPH.EXE
9 file(s) replaced
C>_
```

Figure 9.17. Upgrading Multiple Files with REPLACE

processing program on your fixed disk. Write a command to upgrade all the copies on your fixed disk. (The upgrade diskette is in drive A:.)

```
C>_
```

```
C>REPLACE A:*.* C:\ /S
```

The /A (add) switch reverses the function of REPLACE. It copies only files that don't exist in the target directory. This function helps you replace files that you erased or are missing for some other reason.

Figure 9.18 shows a REPLACE /A interaction. Only two directories are involved; you can't use REPLACE /A with /S. DOS found three files in the source directory that didn't exist in the target directory and added them.

Suppose you erased seven files from your current directory and now you have changed your mind. You have a complete backup copy of the directory

```
C>REPLACE C:*.* A: /A

 Adding A:\PLAY.OUT

 Adding A:\PROPOSAL

 Adding A:\CHAP01.BAK

3 file(s) added

C>_
```

Figure 9.18. Adding Files with REPLACE

made with XCOPY. It contains the files you want to replace. Write a command to copy only the missing files from drive A: to the current directory.

```
C>_
```

```
C>REPLACE A:*.* C: /A
```

Here is the complete format of the REPLACE command:

Format (external):
REPLACE source [target] [/A] [/S] [/P] [/W] [/R]

You must specify a source filespec. A drivename or pathname is not enough. If you omit the filespec, you'll see the message `No files found`.

If you omit the target, the current directory is assumed. You can specify a drivename and/or a pathname for the target. No filespec is permitted. REPLACE treats a filespec as a pathname and tells you `Path not found`.

The /A switch reverses the function of the command, causing missing files to be copied. You cannot use /A with /S. The /S switch causes the entire subtree to be searched for files to replace.

The /P switch causes each replacement or addition to be prompted with a message like this

```
Replace C:\SITCOM\JIMPROPS\GRAPH.EXE? (Y/N)_
```

or

```
Add C:\GRAPH.EXE? (Y/N)_
```

You might find this switch handy to prevent some copies from being overwritten or to copy only some of the missing files.

The /W switch gives you a chance to change the target diskette before starting the directory search. This switch is useful if you must start with your DOS diskette in the source or target drive in order to access the REPLACE program. It's also helpful when the REPLACE command is included in a batch file where you might forget to insert the correct diskette before starting the job. You'll learn about batch jobs in Chapter 10.

The /R switch lets REPLACE overwrite Read/Only files. Ordinarily, REPLACE terminates with an `Access denied` message just as XCOPY does if it tries to overwrite a Read/Only file. But in the software upgrade situation, you frequently need to upgrade program files that have been protected on the fixed disk. This is a case where you want to override the protection. The /R switch lets you do that. Without /R, you would have to go through each directory yourself and turn off the protection with ATTRIB -R before REPLACE could work. That would cause the same work and hassle that REPLACE was designed to prevent. The /R switch lets you avoid the hassle.

Notice there is no /V switch with REPLACE. You can verify copies with the VERIFY command, which you'll learn in Chapter 11.

(a) Write a command to replace all the missing files in the current directory. Use the prompt feature.

```
C>_
```

(b) Write a command to replace all matching files, including Read/Only files. Use drive A: as the source and drive B: as the target. Use both the wait feature and the prompt feature.

```
A>_
```

(*a*) `C>REPLACE A:*.* /A /P`
(*b*) `A>REPLACE A:*.* B: /P /R /W`

Note

Most of the commands you have learned in this chapter perform directory searches. In some cases, such as REPLACE, the command searches an entire tree for files to copy or overwrite. The behavior of these commands can be incorrect or even dangerous when used on directories manipulated by APPEND, JOIN, SUBST, and ASSIGN. If you avoid these commands, you won't have any problems. If you must manipulate directories, consult your DOS reference manual to find out exactly what the pitfalls are and how to overcome them.

Exercises

Do Part A of these exercises if you have a fixed-disk system. Do Part B if you have a two-diskette system and no fixed disk.

Part A (For Fixed-Disk Systems)

What You Should Do	***How the Computer Responds***
1. If necessary, enter a PATH command so your DOS external programs are available from any directory.	1. Records and uses whatever path you specify.
2. Run CHKDSK on the default drive by entering this command: `CHKDSK`	2. Displays directory and FAT information about the default drive and memory size information. (If any problems are identified, deal with them after you have completed these exercises.)
3. Now use CHKDSK to check for noncontiguous blocks in the files in the current directory by entering this command: `CHKDSK *.*`	3. Displays noncontiguous block information as well as information about the drive and memory. (If noncontiguous blocks are identified, don't try to fix them now. Wait until you have completed this set of exercises.)

4. Now try backing up your practice files. Select a target diskette that contains no useful information. BACKUP will delete any files on this diskette.	4.
a. Make the directory containing your practice files the default directory.	a. Switches to the indicated directory.
b. Enter this command: `C>BACKUP C:*.* A:`	b. Instructs you to insert the target diskette in A:.
c. Insert the target diskette and strike any key.	c. Backs up all the files from the source directory to the target diskette. Lists the files on the screen as it backs them up.
5. Now get a directory of the backup diskette.	5. Shows the diskette label as BACKUP 001 and the files as BACKUP.001 and CONTROL.001.
6. Now delete PRESBACK from your current directory.	6. Deletes the file as requested.
7. Restore PRESBACK from the backup diskette by entering this command: `C>RESTORE A: C:PRESBACK`	7. Finds and restores the indicated file.
8. Now delete the backup files from drive A:.	8.
a. Remove their Read/Only status by entering this command: `C>ATTRIB A:*.* -R`	a. Removes the Read/Only status as requested.
b. Delete all files by entering this com mand: `C>DEL A:*.*`	b. Asks for confirmation, then deletes all files on drive A:.

9. Now try backing up the same files with XCOPY using the prompt feature. Enter this command:

```
C>XCOPY *.* A: /P
```

Confirm each filespec as it is displayed.

9. Displays each filespec and asks you to confirm or deny it.

10. Again, erase PRESBACK from the source directory.

10. Erases the file as requested.

11. Now use REPLACE to restore PRESBACK to the current directory by entering this command:

```
C>REPLACE A: C:*.* /A
```

11. Selects the PRESBACK file for restoration.

12. Go on to Chapter Ten.

Part B (For Two-Diskette Systems)

What You Should Do / ***How the Computer Responds***

1. Put the DOS diskette containing CHKDSK.COM in drive A:.

1. Awaits your instructions.

2. Run CHKDSK on the default drive by entering this command:

```
A>CHKDSK
```

2. Displays directory and FAT information about the default drive and memory size information. (If any problems are identified, don't deal with them now. Wait until you have completed this set of exercises.)

3. Now use CHKDSK to check for noncontiguous blocks in the files in the current directory by entering this command:

```
A>CHKDSK *.*
```

3. Displays noncontiguous block information as well as information about the drive and memory. (If noncontiguous blocks are identified, don't try to fix them now. Wait until you have completed this set of exercises.)

4. Now try backing up your practice files. Select a target diskette that contains no useful information. BACKUP will delete any files on this diskette.
   a. Make sure the diskette in drive A: contains BACKUP.COM. If not, insert the correct diskette in drive A:.
   b. Enter this command:

```
A>BACKUP A:*.* B:
```

   c. Put the diskette containing your practice files in drive A:. Put a blank or reusable diskette in drive B:. Then strike any key.

4.
   a. Follows your instructions.
   b. Instructs you to insert the source diskette in drive A: and the target diskette in drive B:.
   c. Backs up all the files from the source directory to the target diskette. Lists the files on the screen as it backs them up.

5. Now get a directory of the backup diskette.

5. Shows the diskette label as BACKUP 001 and the files as BACKUP.001 and CONTROL.001.

6. Now delete PRESBACK from your current directory.

6. Deletes the file as requested.

7. Restore PRESBACK from the backup diskette.
   a. Put the DOS diskette in drive A:.
   b. Enter this command:

```
A>RESTORE B: A:PRESBACK /W
```

   c. When instructed to, insert your exercise diskette in drive A:.

7. Finds and restores the indicated file. Tells you when to insert the target diskette in drive A:.

8. Now delete the backup files from drive B:.
   a. Insert the DOS diskette in drive A:.
   b. Remove the Read/Only status of the backup files by entering this command:

```
A>ATTRIB B:*.* -R
```

8.
   a. Waits for your command.
   b. Removes the Read/Only status as requested.

c. Delete all the backup files by entering this command:

```
C>DEL B:*.*
```

c. Asks for confirmation, then deletes all files on drive B:.

9. Now try backing up the same files with XCOPY using the prompt feature.
   a. Enter this command:

```
C>XCOPY *.* B: /P /W
```

   b. Switch diskettes in drive A: and press any key.
   c. Confirm each filespec as it is displayed.

9. Tells you when to exchange diskettes. Displays each filespec and asks you to confirm or deny it.

10. Again, erase PRESBACK from the source directory.

10. Erases the file as requested.

11. Now use REPLACE to restore PRESBACK to the current directory.
   a. Put the DOS diskette in drive A:.
   b. Enter this command:

```
A>REPLACE B: A:*.* /A /W
```

   c. Put the exercise diskette in drive A: and press any character key.

11. Tells you when to switch diskettes. Select the PRESBACK file for restoration.

What If It Doesn't Work?

1. All the commands explained in this chapter are external. Thus, the program files must be available. If they are on your fixed disk, be sure to enter the appropriate PATH command so they can be accessed no matter what the default directory is. If they are on diskette, you may need to keep switching diskettes to access first the program, then the data diskette. Be sure to use the /W switch wherever appropriate to give yourself time to

switch diskettes before the program starts accessing files. If you have two DOS diskettes, some of the programs are probably on your second DOS diskette, which you haven't used much before this chapter.

2. CHKDSK should work on any disk that has been formatted. If you can't make it work at first, try again with another diskette.

3. If BACKUP or RESTORE doesn't work, you probably didn't enter the command correctly. Try again. If your version of DOS is not 3.3, BACKUP and RESTORE will work differently from the way we use them in these exercises.

4. If you can't delete backup files, you didn't remove the Read/Only status. Check the Read/Only status with ATTRIB.

5. If XCOPY or REPLACE doesn't work, you probably entered the command incorrectly, or the wrong diskettes are in the drives. Check the diskettes and enter the command again.

10

Batch Processing

You can submit a series of DOS commands at one time by placing them in a BAT file and asking DOS to execute the file. You will learn how to do that in this chapter. You will learn how to create a batch file and how to use one. In addition, you will learn a new set of commands that can be used for special effects within batch files.

When you have finished this chapter, you will be able to:

- Create a BAT file
- Use the PAUSE command
- Use the REM command
- Use the ECHO command
- Use @ to suppress command display
- Use the CLS command
- Use dummy parameters in a batch file
- Identify the functions of the CALL, SHIFT, GOTO, FOR, and IF commands
- Execute a batch file
- Supply dummy parameters
- Use the SET command to establish values for dummy parameters
- Abort a batch run
- Create an AUTOEXEC.BAT file
- Interpret error messages associated with batch files

What Is a Batch File?

A batch file is an ASCII file with extension BAT that contains one or more DOS commands. For example, here is a file to display three directories in a row. The filespec is DIRS.BAT.

```
DIR A:
DIR B:
DIR C:
```

To execute this batch file, you enter this command:

```
C>DIRS
```

The response looks like this:

```
C>DIRS
C>DIR A:
 Volume in drive A is WORK DISK 1
 Directory of A:\
       .
       .
       .
C>DIR B:
 Volume in drive B is WORK DISK 2
 Directory of B:\
       .
       .
       .
C>DIR C:
 Volume in drive C is HARD DISK
 Directory of C:\
       .
       .
       .
C>
C>_
```

Using batch files saves you from having to type and retype commands you use often. For example, suppose you want to repeat this procedure with 20 diskettes:

```
C>FORMAT B: /S /V
C>COPY A:*.* B:
```

Rather than type these two commands 20 times, you prepare a BAT file and simply execute it 20 times.

(a) What does a batch file contain?
(b) How are batch files used?
  A. To keep all DOS external commands together on disk
  B. To run jobs without having to respond to questions and directions
  C. To avoid having to retype a frequently used series of commands

---

(a) DOS commands
(b) C

To create a batch file, simply use COPY CON: or your word processor to make an ASCII file containing the DOS commands you want to use. The file must be named with extension BAT. When you enter a command such as GETDISK, DOS looks first to see if it is an internal command. Then it looks for GETDISK.COM, then GETDISK.EXE, and finally GETDISK.BAT. Therefore, your batch file should not have the same filename as any internal or external program, or it will never be found.

Figure 10.1 shows how to use COPY CON: to prepare a BAT file for the DIRS function. Remember that F6 ends the file and displays ^Z on the screen.

```
C>COPY CON: D.BAT
DIR A:
DIR B:
DIR C:
^Z
        1 File(s) copied

C>_
```

Figure 10.1. Using COPY CON: to Create a Batch File

(a) Which of these are good batch filespecs?
A. FREE.BAT
B. NEW.COM
C. LEXTBAT
D. TYPE.BAT
E. HOLD.BAT
F. MERGE.DOC
(b) What command would copy all nonprogram files from drive A: to drive B:?
(c) What might you call the above file?
(d) True or false? External commands should not be used as batch filenames.

(a) A, E (B, C, and F have a BAT extension, and D uses an internal command as the filename)
*(b) COPY *.* B:*
DEL B:.COM*
DEL B:.BAT*
DEL B:.EXE*
(c) We'd call it something like COPYTEXT.BAT or TEXTCOPY.BAT; you probably called it something else
(d) True

Executing Batch Jobs

To execute a batch file, simply enter the filename (no extension). Of course, the BAT file must be in the current directory, in the directory you specify, or in the program search path. For example, suppose drive A: contains MERGE.BAT. To execute that file, you would enter:

```
A>MERGE
```

If MERGE.BAT is on a nondefault directory on drive C: instead, you could enter a command like this:

```
A>C:\BATCHES\MERGE
```

But if MERGE.BAT is in any directory in the program search path, you don't have to worry about specifying the correct directory.

If the DOS programs being executed require individual responses, you'll have to enter them as usual. You can't build them into the batch file directly. Suppose you execute MAKECOPY.BAT, which contains these commands:

```
DEL B:*.*
COPY *.* B:
```

Figure 10.2 shows how this batch job looks when it is run. First the system asks you to confirm the deletion of all files on drive B:. You must respond to this question before the batch job continues. After the erasure takes place, the copies are made automatically.

You can automate the answers to a batch file by redirecting the input to a disk file that contains the needed answers in the exact sequence. For example, you could create a file named DELANS that contains one line:

```
Y
```

Now you can run MAKECOPY with this command:

```
C>MAKECOPY <DELANS
```

When the DEL command wants an answer, DOS goes to DELANS instead of the keyboard. Thus, a Y is automatically supplied as the answer.

```
C>MAKECOPY

C>DEL B:*.*
Are you sure (Y/N)?Y

C>COPY *.* B:
COMMAND.COM
ANSI.SYS
AUTOEXEC.32
CONFIG.320
AUTOEXEC.BAT
QEMM.COM

C>_
```

Figure 10.2. Responding to Messages in a Batch File

Suppose the A: diskette contains SECOND.BAT and HALF.BAT and the B: diskette contains THRU.BAT. No PATH command has been entered.

(a) Write a command to execute SECOND.BAT.

```
C>_
```

(b) Write a command to execute THRU.BAT.

```
C>_
```

(c) Which statements are true about batch files?

A. You must respond to messages just as if you were entering the commands one at a time

B. Messages are suppressed by DOS

C. You can redirect message answers to a disk file

(a) `C>SECOND`

(b) `A>B:THRU`

(c) *A, C*

You can use several of the control functions while a batch job is running. You can echo print, suspend the job, and cancel the current command or the job.

To cancel the job, press Ctrl-Break. DOS asks you this question:

```
Terminate batch job (Y/N)?_
```

You must differentiate between the current command and the whole job. If you want to terminate only the current command, enter N. If you want to terminate the entire batch job (all the remaining commands), enter Y.

Suppose you are running a batch job called TYPALL.

(a) How can you suspend the job long enough to look at the current display?

(b) Suppose the command TYPE FIRST is currently executing. How can you cancel the command and go on to the next command in the batch? What do you enter after `Terminate batch job (Y/N)`?

(c) Suppose you want to cancel the entire batch job. What keys do you press? What do you enter after `Terminate batch job (Y/N)`?

(a) *Ctrl-NumLock (or Pause)*
(b) *Press Ctrl-Break; N*
(c) *Ctrl-Break; Y*

Here are a few sample batch job requests showing some of the messages you might see. In this example, the LOADDISK.BAT file is not in the default directory and not in the search path.

```
C>LOADDISK
Bad command or file name
C>_
```

In the next example, we terminated the first command when we realized that we had installed the wrong two diskettes. Because we had changed the diskette in drive A:, DOS couldn't find the COMPDISK.BAT file when it wanted to, and so it asked for the diskette containing the batch file.

```
A>COMPDISK
A>DISKCOMP A: B:
Insert FIRST diskette in drive A:
Insert SECOND diskette in drive B:
Press any key when ready...
Comparing 9 sectors per track, 2 side(s)
Compare error on
Side 0, track 0

Compare error on
Side 1, track 0

Compare error on
Side 0, track 1

Compare error on
Side 1, track 1

Com^C
Terminate batch job (Y/N)?N
A>
Insert disk with batch file
and strike any key when ready. . .
```

You can also get the usual error messages associated with each of the individual commands. For example, if you try to execute an external command whose COM or EXE file is not available, you'll get this message:

```
Bad command or file name
```

(a) Suppose you run a batch job that involves removing the diskette containing the batch file. You see this message:

```
Insert disk with batch file
and strike any key when ready. . ._
```

What should you do?

A. Put any DOS diskette in the appropriate drive and hit a character key
B. Put a diskette containing the batch file in the appropriate drive and hit a character key
C. Press Ctrl-Break to get rid of the message

(b) Suppose you have this interaction:

```
C>COMPRESS
Bad command or file name
C>_
```

What's wrong?

A. There's no COMPRESS.COM or COMPRESS.EXE file in the current directory or in the program search path
B. There's no internal command called COMPRESS
C. There's no COMPRESS.BAT file in the current directory or in the program search path
D. All of the above

(c) Suppose you have this interaction:

```
C>COMPRESS
C>FORMAT A:
Bad command or file name
C>_
```

What's wrong?

A. There's no COMPRESS program file in the current directory or in the program search path

B. You can't reference an external program from a batch file
C. There's no FORMAT program file in the current directory or in the program search path

---

(a) B
(b) D
(c) C

When you prepare a batch file, write the commands in the order you want DOS to execute them. You can include any standard DOS commands. Now try writing some batch files.

(a) Write a batch file to get a directory of the default drive, sort the directory in alphabetical order, and display it one page at a time. (This can all be done in one command with piping. The advantage of a batch file is to give yourself a shorter command to type.)
What would you call this batch file?
(b) Write a file to clean up a diskette whose files have become fragmented. Start by creating a temporary subdirectory on another drive. Then copy all the files from the diskette being cleaned up to that directory. Delete all the files on the original diskette, then copy the files back to it again. Finally, erase and remove the temporary subdirectory.
What would you call this batch file?
(c) Write a file to write protect all the program files in the default directory—that is, all files with extension COM, EXE, or BAT. For confirmation, since ATTRIB doesn't confirm itself, display the attributes of all files in the directory.
What would you call this batch file?

(a)
```
DIR | SORT | MORE
```
We'd call this file D.BAT so we could get a sorted, paged directory by entering the single letter D

(b)
```
MD C:\WORKAREA
COPY B:*.* C:\WORKAREA /V
DEL B:*.*
COPY C:\WORKAREA B: /V
DEL C:\WORKAREA\*.*
RD C:\WORKAREA
```

You might have used different drives as appropriate for your computer. You might have written out MKDIR and RMDIR; you might have used any valid name for the temporary subdirectory; you could have used BACKUP and RESTORE, XCOPY, or REPLACE to copy the files. You could have used FORMAT instead of DEL to remove all the files from drive B:; we would call this file CLEANUP.BAT.

(c)
```
ATTRIB +R *.COM
ATTRIB +R *.EXE
ATTRIB +R *.BAT
ATTRIB *.*
```
We would call this file PROGPROT.BAT

DOS includes several facilities that are useful in batch files: the internal commands CLS, REM, PAUSE, ECHO, GOTO, CALL, FOR, IF and SHIFT; the AUTOEXEC.BAT file; and dummy parameters. The remainder of this chapter deals with these features.

Displaying Messages

Your batch file's displays will be more attractive and readable if you clear the old messages from the screen before starting the job, especially if your first command won't generate enough output to push old messages off the screen. You can do this with the CLS (clear screen) command. Its format is:

Format (internal):
CLS

You can use CLS anytime with DOS, but it has little use outside a batch job (unless you want to hide your work from someone). But you may want to use CLS frequently within batch jobs—not only at the beginning, but also between other commands.

(a) Add a command to this batch file to erase the screen before executing the MD command.

```
MD C:\WORKAREA
COPY B:*.* C:\WORKAREA /V
DEL B:*.*
```

```
COPY C:\WORKAREA B: /V
DEL C:\WORKAREA\*.*
RD C:\WORKAREA
```

(b) For the above job to work, does CLS.COM need to be available on the default directory or search path?

(a) Put CLS before the MD command
(b) No—CLS is an internal command

A batch job's display looks better without the prompts and commands, so that all you see is the command output. ECHO OFF suppresses the prompts and commands. Compare the two interactions shown in Figure 10.3, both of which were based on the same batch file. We added ECHO OFF as the first command in the file on the right, but not on the left.

The ECHO OFF command itself is displayed, but no other prompts or commands are displayed until the batch job finishes and control returns to COMMAND. Notice that the output of CHKDSK is displayed, however. The standard outputs for all commands are displayed even with ECHO OFF.

If any command yields error messages, these messages are displayed. Use ECHO OFF carefully. It can be confusing to get an error message without being able to see the command that caused the error.

```
C>CHK
C>CHKDSK A:
Volume BACKUP    001 created May 17, 1990 1:16p

   362496 bytes total disk space
        0 bytes in 1 hidden files
    50176 bytes in 10 user files
   312320 bytes availible on disk

   654336 bytes total memory
   555568 bytes free

C>CHKDSK C:
Volume FIXED DISK created December 12, 1989 4:09p

 25600000 bytes total disk space
    53248 bytes in 2 hidden files
    32768 bytes in 10 directories
  8429568 bytes in 481 user files
 17084416 bytes availible on disk

   654336 bytes total memory
   555568 bytes free

C>_
```

```
C>CHK                    <---- ECHO OFF added
C>ECHO OFF
Volume BACKUP    001 created May 17, 1990 1:16p

   362496 bytes total disk space
        0 bytes in 1 hidden files
    50176 bytes in 10 user files
   312320 bytes availible on disk

   654336 bytes total memory
   555568 bytes free
Volume FIXED DISK created December 12, 1989 4:09p

 25600000 bytes total disk space
    53248 bytes in 2 hidden files
    32768 bytes in 10 directories
  8429568 bytes in 481 user files
 17084416 bytes availible on disk

   654336 bytes total memory
   555568 bytes free

C>_
```

Figure 10.3. Effect of ECHO OFF

(a) With ECHO OFF, what DOS messages are displayed?
   A. Prompts
   B. Normal command output
   C. Error messages
   D. Commands

(b) If you use both CLS and ECHO OFF in a batch file, which would you put first? Why?

(a) B, C

(b) ECHO OFF; because CLS erases the ECHO OFF command too, leaving the screen clear for command output

---

Another way to prevent a command from being displayed is to precede it with an "at" sign (@). This suppresses only the individual command. For example, suppose you want to echo most of the commands in the following batch file, but you want to suppress the COPY command. You could create the job like this:

```
DIR A:
DIR B:
DIR C:
@COPY C:LASER.SET COM1:
```

Even when you turn ECHO OFF, the ECHO OFF command itself is displayed. To suppress the display of this command also, use @ECHO OFF.

Create a batch file that creates a subdirectory named C:\SORTER and copies all files from drive A: to the new subdirectory. Suppress all prompts and commands.

```
@ECHO OFF
MD C:\SORTER
COPY A:*.* C:\SORTER
```

You can add your own messages to a batch job. Messages are especially helpful for jobs that other people will use or that you yourself will use only once in a while.

DOS gives you two ways to insert messages in a batch file: REM and ECHO. They have slightly different effects.

REM (for REMarks) causes no processing. When ECHO is on, the REM command appears on the screen next to the command prompt, then DOS goes on to the next command in the batch file. When ECHO is off, the REM command is suppressed along with all other commands; you don't see the message on the screen. Thus, you can use REM with ECHO OFF to document your batch file without the documentation appearing on the screen. You only see the remarks when you type or print the batch file.

Here's an example:

```
@ECHO OFF
CLS
REM   THIS BATCH JOB SETS THE WRITE
REM   PROTECT ATTRIBUTES TO PROTECT
REM   ALL THE PROGRAM FILES IN THE
REM   DEFAULT DIRECTORY.
ATTRIB +R *.COM
ATTRIB +R *.EXE
ATTRIB +R *.BAT
ATTRIB *.*
```

Since ECHO is turned off before the REM commands, they do not appear on the screen. If we eliminated the ECHO OFF command, the output from this batch job would appear as shown in Figure 10.4. As you can see, REM is not the most attractive way to display a message in a batch job.

Unlike REM, the ECHO command does cause processing; whatever follows the word ECHO (except the words ON and OFF) is displayed as output. The ECHO messages are displayed even when ECHO is OFF. In fact, they look even stranger than REM messages when ECHO is ON. Here's an example:

```
ECHO OFF
ECHO I'M WRITE PROTECTING ALL COM, EXE, AND BAT FILES
ATTRIB +R *.COM
ATTRIB +R *.EXE
ATTRIB +R *.BAT
ATTRIB *.*
```

```
C>PROGPROT

C>REM  THIS BATCH JOB SETS THE WRITE

C>REM  PROTECT ATTRIBUTES TO PROTECT

C>REM  ALL THE PROGRAM FILES IN THE

C>REM  DEFAULT DIRECTORY.

C>ATTRIB +R *.COM

C>ATTRIB +R *.EXE

C>ATTRIB +R *.BAT

C>ATTRIB *.*
  A    R   C:\HSG.EXE
  A    R   C:\GRAB.EXE
  A    R   C:\WINGRAB.EXE
  A    R   C:\WGLIG.EXE
  A        C:\HS.DAT
  A        C:\HS.FDT
  A        C:\HS.GDT
  A        C:\HS.PDT
  A        C:\HS.PSD
  A    R   C:\PROGPROT.BAT
  A        C:\HS.CFG
  A        C:\READ.ME

C>_
```

Figure 10.4. Displaying REM Messages

Figure 10.5 shows how the batch file looks when executed with the ECHO OFF command. Figure 10.6 shows how it looks if we delete the ECHO OFF command. You see both the ECHO OFF command and its output; hence you see the same message twice. ECHO messages are definitely intended to be used with ECHO OFF or with @ECHO.

```
C>PROGPROT

C>ECHO OFF
I'M WRITE PROTECTING ALL THE COM, EXE, AND BAT FILES
  A     R  C:\HSG.EXE
  A     R  C:\GRAB.EXE
  A     R  C:\WINGRAB.EXE
  A     R  C:\WGLIG.EXE
  A        C:\HS.DAT
  A        C:\HS.FDT
  A        C:\HS.GDT
  A        C:\HS.PDT
  A        C:\HS.PSD
  A     R  C:\PROGPROT.BAT
  A        C:\HS.CFG
  A        C:\READ.ME

C>_
```

Figure 10.5. ECHO Messages with ECHO OFF

(a) Match these commands with their descriptions.
  A. REM — 1. Message is displayed when ECHO is OFF
  B. ECHO — 2. Message is suppressed when ECHO is OFF
  3. Message is displayed twice when ECHO is ON

(b) How might you use these commands with ECHO OFF?
  A. REM — 1. To get input from the keyboard
  B. ECHO — 2. To document the batch file without displaying any messages
  3. To display messages on the screen

(c) True or false? ECHO messages work best with ECHO OFF or @.

(a) A—2; B—1,3
(b) A—2; B—3
(c) True

```
C>PROGPROT

C>ECHO I'M WRITE PROTECTING ALL COM, EXE, AND BAT FILES
I'M WRITE PROTECTING ALL COM, EXE, AND BAT FILES

C>ATTRIB +R *.COM

C>ATTRIB +R *.EXE

C>ATTRIB +R *.BAT

C>ATTRIB *.*
  A    R  C:\HSG.EXE
  A    R  C:\GRAB.EXE
  A    R  C:\WINGRAB.EXE
  A    R  C:\WGLIG.EXE
  A       C:\HS.DAT
  A       C:\HS.FDT
  A       C:\HS.GDT
  A       C:\HS.PDT
  A       C:\HS.PSD
  A    R  C:\PROGPROT.BAT
  A       C:\HS.CFG
  A       C:\READ.ME

C>_
```

Figure 10.6. ECHO Messages with ECHO ON

The complete format of the ECHO command is:

Format (internal):
ECHO [OFF | ON | message]

The OFF operand turns off the echo function. The ON operand turns it back on. You may find this ON useful occasionally. The message operand is displayed as it is. If you enter ECHO with no operands, DOS tells you whether ECHO is ON or OFF. (You ought to be able to tell this anyway by whether you can see the command prompt.) If you turn ECHO OFF during a batch file, it is automatically turned ON again at the end of the job. Thus, you get a command prompt for your next command.

The complete format of the REM command is:

Format (internal):
REM [remark]

The remark can be up to 123 characters long. (The total length of any DOS command, including the command name, can be 127 characters.)

(a) You wrote this batch file earlier. Now add commands to turn echo off, clear the screen, and display `Please wait...` while the sorted directory is being prepared.

```
DIR | SORT | MORE
```

(b) You also wrote the following batch file earlier. Adapt it to do these things:

1. Suppress prompts and commands
2. Display the message `These are the files on the diskette` before displaying the output of the first COPY command
3. Clear the screen and display the message `Answer Y to the following question if you want to delete all the files on the diskette; otherwise, press Ctrl-Break now before starting the DEL command`
4. Clear the screen and display `Now I'll put the files back on the diskette` before the second COPY command
5. Also add some nondisplayable commands to the file to explain what it does.

```
MD C:\WORKAREA
COPY B:*.* C:\WORKAREA /V
DEL B:*.*
COPY C:\WORKAREA B: /V
DEL C:\WORKAREA\*.*
RD C:\WORKAREA
```

(a)
```
@ECHO OFF
CLS
ECHO Please wait...
DIR | SORT | MORE
```

(b)
```
@ECHO OFF
CLS
REM  THIS BATCH JOB CLEANS UP FRAGMENTED
REM  FILES ON A DISKETTE BY COPYING THEM
REM  TO A TEMPORARY STORAGE AREA, DELETING
REM  THEM FROM THE SOURCE DISKETTE, THEN
REM  COPYING THEM BACK AGAIN.
MD C:\WORKAREA
ECHO These are the files on the diskette
COPY B:*.* C:\WORKAREA /V
CLS
ECHO Answer Y to the following question if you
ECHO want to delete all the files on the diskette;
ECHO otherwise, press Ctrl-Break now
DEL B:*.*
ECHO Now I'll put the files back on the diskette
COPY C:\WORKAREA B: /V
DEL C:\WORKAREA\*.*
RD C:\WORKAREA
```

Letting the User Respond

You know that some DOS commands display a message and wait for a response. You can make your batch jobs do the same thing by coding the PAUSE command. If you code PAUSE with no operand, it will cause the system to display this message

```
Strike a key when ready...
```

then wait for the user to respond.

If you put a comment after PAUSE, the comment is displayed before the `Strike a key` message, but only if ECHO is ON. Thus, if you code `PAUSE Please switch the diskette in drive B:`, the user will see:

```
C>PAUSE Please switch the diskette in drive B:
Strike a key when ready...
```

The comment may be up to 121 characters long. If you need longer comments, or if ECHO is OFF, use ECHO commands before the PAUSE command.

Here is the batch file you created in the previous frame. Revise it so the user has a chance to put the desired diskette in drive B: before the first COPY operation.

```
@ECHO OFF
CLS
REM  THIS BATCH JOB CLEANS UP FRAGMENTED
REM  FILES ON A DISKETTE BY COPYING THEM
REM  TO A TEMPORARY STORAGE AREA, DELETING
REM  THEM FROM THE SOURCE DISKETTE, THEN
REM  COPYING THEM BACK AGAIN.
MD C:\WORKAREA
ECHO These are the files on the diskette
COPY B:*.* C:\WORKAREA /V
CLS
ECHO Answer Y to the following question if you
ECHO want to delete all the files on the diskette;
ECHO otherwise, press Ctrl-Break now
DEL B:*.*
ECHO Now I'll put the files back on the diskette
COPY C:\WORKAREA B: /V
DEL C:\WORKAREA\*.*
RD C:\WORKAREA
```

Add these commands between MD and ECHO:

```
ECHO Please put the diskette to be cleaned in drive B:
PAUSE
```

Here's an example of a batch file (DUPDISK.BAT) that uses REM, ECHO, and PAUSE. This file copies all files from one disk in drive A: to another in the same drive. It would be used in a fixed-disk system.

```
@ECHO OFF
REM   This copies all user files from one diskette to another.
MD C:\TEMPDIR
ECHO Insert diskette to be copied into drive A:
PAUSE
COPY A:*.* C:\TEMPDIR /V
```

```
ECHO Please insert new formatted disk now
PAUSE
COPY C:\TEMPDIR\*.* A: /V
DEL C:\TEMPDIR\*.*
RMDIR C:\TEMPDIR
ECHO The files are now all on the new diskette
```

The first ECHO command turns off commands, so the REM command serves only as internal documentation; it never appears on the screen. The second ECHO causes a message to be displayed before PAUSE. If we included this message in the PAUSE command (or in a REM command), it wouldn't appear. So the user wouldn't know it is time to insert a diskette to be copied. After the files are copied to a temporary subdirectory, another ECHO-PAUSE combination asks the user to insert the target diskette. The files are then copied back to that diskette and erased from the temporary directory, which is removed. The final ECHO command tells the user the result.

Figure 10.7 shows the displayed output for one use of DUPDISK.BAT.

(a) What command, if any, could you use in a batch file to suppress the command output?
(b) What command in the batch file generates the `Are you sure` message?
(c) Write a message to precede `Are you sure` telling the user what's happening.

(a) There is no command to do this (however, you can redirect command output to the devicename NUL to get rid of it)
(b) `DEL C:\TEMPDIR\*.*`
(c) `ECHO If all the files were copied, press Y to erase them from the temporary directory`

Note Generous use of ECHO, REM, and PAUSE can make your batch jobs more useful to you and others. Don't skimp on these facilities.

Using Dummy Parameters

You can design a batch file to receive operands when it is executed. To do this, you put dummy parameters in the file. The dummy parameters can be a

```
C>DUPDISK
Insert diskette to be copied into drive A:
Strike a key when ready . . .
A:COMMAND.COM
A:ANSI.SYS
A:SUTOEXEC.32
A:CONFIG.320
A:AUTOEXEC.BAT
A:QEMM.COM
A:MOUSE.COM
A:HOT.BAT
A:BACKUP.LOG
A:F10ANSW.SCR
       10 File(s) copied
Please insert new formatted disk now
Strike a key when ready . . .
C:\TEMPDIR\COMMAND.COM
C:\TEMPDIR\ANSI.SYS
C:\TEMPDIR\SUTOEXEC.32
C:\TEMPDIR\CONFIG.320
C:\TEMPDIR\AUTOEXEC.BAT
C:\TEMPDIR\QEMM.COM
C:\TEMPDIR\MOUSE.COM
C:\TEMPDIR\HOT.BAT
C:\TEMPDIR\BACKUP.LOG
C:\TEMPDIR\F10ANSW.SCR
       10 File(s) copied
Answer Y to the following question
Are you sure (Y/N)?Y
The files are now all on the new diskette

C>_
```

Figure 10.7. Output of DUPDISK.BAT

single digit preceded by a percent sign, as in %0 through %9, or a word surrounded by percent signs, as in %filespec1%. Use dummy parameters in place of command operands such as filespecs, drivenames, and switches.

For example, suppose you want to set up a batch job called MOVE to move any file from drive A: to drive C:. You can code the job this way:

```
COPY A:%1 C: /V
DEL A:%1
```

To execute this command, you would enter the MOVE command followed by a value for %1, like this:

```
C>MOVE NEWJOB.DAT
```

DOS substitutes the operand (NEWJOB.DAT) everywhere that %1 occurs in the batch file. Thus, the job that is executed in our example is:

```
COPY A:NEWJOB C: /V
DEL A:NEWJOB
```

(a) Suppose we enter `C>MOVE DOLLARS.DAT`. Write the commands that are executed.

(b) Write a command to use MOVE to transfer QUESTB from drive A: to drive C:.

`C>_`

(a) `COPY A:DOLLARS.DAT C: /V`
`DEL A:DOLLARS.DAT`

(b) `C>MOVE QUESTB`

When you enter a batch command, the numbered dummy parameters are always assigned to the parts of the command as shown in Figure 10.8. Thus, the %0 parameter, if used, always refers to the command name itself. %1 always refers to the first operand, %2 to the second operand, and so on.

```
DISKIT   A:  B:  C:  D:   ...
  ↑      ↑   ↑   ↑   ↑
  %0     %1  %2  %3  %4   ...
```

Figure 10.8. Numbering Batch Parameters

You will rarely, if ever, use %0 in a batch file. If you use the numbered parameters at all, you'll start with %1. It makes no sense to skip %1 and start with %2 or a higher number, because it would be very awkward to code the command to execute the job. So always use the numbered dummy parameters in order, except that you can skip %0.

(a) What does the %0 parameter always refer to?
Use this command for Questions b and c:

```
c>GETFILE B:DOLLARS B:CENTS
```

(b) What value will be used for %1?
(c) What value will be used for %2?
(d) Here is an incorrectly coded BAT file:

```
COPY %4 + %5 + %6 %9
TYPE %9
```

What is wrong with this file?

(a) The batch command name
(b) B:DOLLARS
(c) B:CENTS
(d) It should use %1 through %4, not %4, %5, %6 and %9

If you ever need to use more than nine numbered parameters in a batch file, look up the SHIFT command in your DOS manual. SHIFT shifts all the operands one place to the left, so the tenth operand becomes %9. You can have as many numbered operands as you'd like by using SHIFT, but only ten are available at a time. (Don't try to use SHIFT without reading about it in your DOS manual first.)

(a) Code a batch file to eliminate a directory. The batch file should erase all files in the directory, then remove the directory. The pathname will be supplied when the batch job is executed.

(b) Code a batch file to sort an input file, creating an output file. Then print the sorted file. Both filespecs will be supplied when the batch file is executed.

(c) What DOS command lets you use more than nine numbered dummy parameters in a batch file?

(a)
```
DEL %1\*.*
RD %1
```
(b)
```
SORT <%1 >%2
PRINT %2
```
(c) *SHIFT*

You can also use named parameters in a batch job. There is no limit to the number of named parameters you can use. Enclose each one in percent signs, as in %FILESPEC1%.

When DOS encounters a named parameter, it looks in the DOS environment for a value for the parameter. You can use the SET command to store values for named parameters in the environment. For example, to establish a value for FILESPEC1, you would enter this command:

```
C>SET FILESPEC1=C:\NOVEL\CHAP10
```

This value remains in the environment until you change it with another SET command or reboot. Therefore, each time you run a batch job that refers to %FILESPEC1%, DOS will substitute the value C:\NOVEL\CHAP10.

Named parameters have several advantages over numbered parameters. You can set a value to be used with several batch jobs; you don't have to keep re-entering it. Also, using more than nine parameters per job is not as awkward.

You can see what your current environment values are by entering SET with no operands. You can remove a parameter from the environment by nullifying its value. For example, to remove FILESPEC1 from the environment, you would enter:

```
C>SET FILESPEC1=
```

(a) Write a batch job named MOVEIT to move a file or group of files from the current directory to drive A:. Use a named parameter for the filespec.

(b) Now enter a command to establish the filespec as C:*.SYS.

C>_

(c) Now enter a command to run your batch job.

C>_

(d) Write a command to find and display all the parameter values currently stored in the DOS environment.

C>_

(e) Write a command to delete the filespec parameter you stored in Question (b).

C>_

(a) `COPY %FILESPEC% A:`
`DEL %FILESPEC%`

(b) `C>SET FILESPEC=C:\*.SYS`

(c) `C>MOVEIT`

(d) `C>SET`

(e) `C>SET FILESPEC=`

Logic Commands

DOS offers several commands that control what happens next in a batch file. We'll overview them here, but if you want to use these commands, you'll need to study them in your DOS manual. They make your batch files much more complex, so avoid these commands unless you really need them.

The FOR command sets up a loop that repeats another DOS command several times with different operands. Here are some examples:

```
FOR %%D IN (A: B: C:) DO DIR %%D
```

%%D is a variable operand. DOS sets it first to A:, then to B:, then to C:. So this command results in DIR A:, then DIR B:, then DIR C:.

Like all the batch commands, FOR can be used as a regular command outside a batch file. You might find it handy for repeating a command for a set of files or directories. The format is slightly different when used outside the batch file. Use only one percent sign in front of the variable name instead of two. For example, to use the above FOR command at the command prompt, you would enter:

```
C>FOR %D IN (A: B: C:) DO DIR %D
```

Suppose you want to print a group of files with unrelated names. You could enter this command:

```
C>FOR %F IN (JOHN-V1 TED-MAC GREENS GROUNDS.BAK) PRINT %F
```

Here are some more examples of the FOR command.

```
FOR %%F IN (PRODUCTS SERVICES PASSTHRU) DO SORT %%F >>LISTING
```

This sorts three files and adds them to the file named LISTING.

```
FOR %%S IN ("SILVER" "GOLD") DO FIND %%S PRODUCTS
```

This finds all the lines in PRODUCTS that contain either SILVER or GOLD.

The CALL command executes a batch file. It's a handy way of executing one batch file from within another batch file. When the called batch file terminates, DOS goes back to the first batch file, to the line following CALL. Suppose you have a batch job called GETDISK that asks the user for a specific disk and makes sure the correct disk is installed. You want to use GETDISK to get a diskette named PROGMASTER in drive A: before making a duplicate copy of the diskette. You could create this job:

```
SET DISKNAME=PROGMASTER
CALL GETDISK
DISKCOPY A: B:
```

CALL works well with other batch commands, such as FOR. In this case, CALL lets you execute a complete routine in the FOR command instead of just one command. For example, suppose you want to execute a job named ORG on four different files. You could enter this command:

```
C>FOR %F IN (JOHN-V1 TED-MAC GREENS GROUNDS.BAK) CALL ORG %F
```

The IF command executes another command only if a condition is true. Here are some examples:

```
IF EXIST B:\COMMAND.COM ECHO This disk is bootable
```

This command displays the message `This disk is bootable` only if B:\ contains a file named COMMAND.COM.

This command erases all files in the current directory only if a Y has been entered as the first operand of the invoking command. (The double equal sign is required here.)

```
IF %1==Y DEL *.*
```

You could use an IF command to determine whether to do a particular action in a batch job.

Every command issues a number, called an exit code, as it terminates. The exit code indicates whether the command was successful or not. All commands issue a 0 if the command was successful, and a higher number otherwise. The IF ERRORLEVEL command tests the exit code of the preceding command. This command would call the batch job named NOGOOD if the exit code of the preceding command was higher than 0.

```
IF ERRORLEVEL 1 CALL NOGOOD
```

The GOTO command skips to someplace else in the batch job. It's usually used with the IF command. Here is an example:

```
IF EXIST LISTING GOTO SKIPIT
   FOR %%D IN (A: B: C:) DO DIR ON %%D >>LISTING
   GOTO END
:SKIPIT
   ECHO LISTING file exists. Please use a different directory.
:END
```

This example checks for the existence of a file named LISTING. If it exists, DOS jumps down to the line starting with :SKIPIT. Thus the ECHO command is the next one executed. However, if no LISTING exists, it drops down to the FOR command, which places the directories of A:, B:, and C: in a file named LISTING. Then the GOTO END command jumps to the last line in the file.

As you can imagine, these four logic commands, combined with dummy parameters and SHIFT, give you the ability to do quite complex programming in a batch file. But as we've said before, the simpler your batch files, the better. So don't use these commands unless you have to. And if you do use them, look them up in your DOS manual first.

Identify the function of each command:

(a) FOR	A. Skips to another line in the batch file
(b) GOTO	B. Terminates the batch job before reaching the end
(c) IF	C. Repeats a DOS command with different parameters
(d) CALL	D. Executes a DOS command only if a condition is met
	E. Executes another batch file
	F. Displays a message to the user

(a) C
(b) A
(c) D
(d) E

The AUTOEXEC.BAT Facility

Normally, when you boot DOS, the date and time are set and then DOS waits for your first command. But you can set up the DOS boot disk to execute a batch file automatically as soon as it's booted. All you need to do is place a file named AUTOEXEC.BAT in the root directory of the boot disk.

Suppose you want to set a search path to include both your diskette drives each time you boot. In addition, you want to use your automatic clock program, GETTIME. You could put the following AUTOEXEC.BAT file on your boot disk:

```
ECHO OFF
CLS
PATH A:;B:
GETTIME
```

In the next two chapters you will learn many commands that alter the DOS environment that are appropriate in AUTOEXEC.BAT files.

When DOS finds and executes AUTOEXEC.BAT, it no longer gets the date and time automatically. If your system always knows the correct date and time anyway, you'll find this a convenience. If not, and you need to set the date and time each time you boot, then you should include the DATE and TIME commands in the AUTOEXEC.BAT file. You'll learn both commands in Chapter 11.

(a) Suppose you have a fixed disk with all your program files in directory PROGRAMS and all your batch files in directory BATCHES. Both of these directories branch off C:\. Create a batch file, to be executed automatically during the boot procedure, that will set a search path that includes these two directories.
(b) What would you name the above file?
(c) Where would you place it?

(a) `PATH C:\PROGRAMS;C:\BATCHES`
(b) AUTOEXEC.BAT
(c) The root directory of C:

Exercises

These exercises let you practice creating and using simple batch files.

What You Should Do	*How the Computer Responds*

1. Use COPY CON: or your word processor to create an ASCII file named D.BAT containing these commands:
`ECHO OFF`
`REM This job displays a sorted`
`REM directory`
`CLS`
`DIR %1 | SORT | MORE`
`ECHO Good-bye`
	1. Creates the file as directed.

2. Now enter the simple command D.	2. Displays a sorted directory one page at a time. Then says `Good-bye`.
3. Enter D followed by the name of one of your drives or directories, as in `D A:` or `D \DOS`.	3. Displays a sorted directory of the designated drive or directory.

4. Enter `D C*.*`.

4. Displays a sorted directory of all files starting with C.

5. Use DIR to see if your boot disk has a file called AUTOEXEC.BAT. If so, skip to Step 8; do not perform Step 6 or you will erase the contents of your current AUTOEXEC.BAT, which could be extremely inconvenient.

5. Displays the directory as requested.

6. Use COPY CON: or your word processor to create an ASCII file named AUTOEXEC.BAT. Be sure to put it in the root directory of the disk you boot from. It should contain:

```
ECHO OFF
CLS
PATH A:\;B:\;C:\;C:\DOS
```

(or whatever path works for your system)

```
ECHO Don't forget to set the date
  and time
```

6. Follows your instructions.

7. Now reboot using the disk containing AUTOEXEC.BAT.

7. Clears the screen, sets the path (you won't see any messages), and displays the `Don't forget` message.

8. If any of the batch files in this chapter look useful to you, now's a good time to put them in your system.

8. Follows your instructions.

What If It Doesn't Work?

1. If DOS can't find your first batch file (D.BAT), be sure to put it in the current directory or in one of the directories in your search path.
2. If DOS can't find AUTOEXEC.BAT, be sure to put it in the root directory of your boot disk.

3. If DOS has trouble reading and understanding either batch job, make sure each is in ASCII format. If you created them with COPY CON:, they are automatically in the correct format. If you created the files with your word processor, they might not be in the correct format. Check the documentation for your word processor to see how to create a file in ASCII format. Try TYPEing or PRINTing the file to see what it looks like.

4. Check all the commands in the file to make sure you didn't misspell anything or leave anything out.

5. If you still can't make it work, get help. Using batch files is an important aspect of DOS—especially AUTOEXEC.BAT.

11

Altering the Environment (Part I)

Your personal computer has a default environment set by the operating system. In this chapter, you'll learn to use DOS commands to alter that environment. You'll learn to change the system's date and time, make it verify each write-to-disk operation, make it respond to Ctrl-Break more often, and add other details to the environment.

When you complete this chapter, you will be able to:

- Change the date and time for your system
- Verify write operations originated by any program
- Cause DOS to check for Ctrl-Break more often
- Change the standard I/O device
- Add more information to the DOS prompt
- Modify the appearance of information on your monitor
- Establish communications characteristics for your COM ports
- Change the print size on your printer
- Set up the environment for the PRINT command
- Print graphics screens with PrtSc

Changing the Date and Time

The DATE and TIME commands invoke the same functions you are familiar with from booting. Here are the formats:

Format (internal):	**Format (internal):**
DATE [date]	TIME [time]

If you enter DATE with no operand, DOS responds:

`Current date is Mon 6-5-89` (or whatever date DOS thinks it is)
`Enter new date (mm-dd-yy):_`

The displayed date includes the day of the week. The date format, shown as `mm-dd-yy` in our example, depends on the country your computer is set up for. (You'll learn how to change the country in Chapter 12.) You can change the date by entering a new one in the indicated format or leave it alone by just pressing Enter.

TIME is very similar to DATE. If you enter TIME with no operand, DOS responds:

`Current time is 5:15:29.32` (or whatever time DOS thinks it is)
`Enter new time:_`

Like the date, you can change the time or leave it alone.

If you want to change the date or time without checking the current value, you can enter the command with the appropriate date or time as an operand. Suppose you want to change the date and time to August 1, 1995 at 7 A.M. You could enter:

```
C>DATE 8-1-95
C>TIME 7
C>_
```

Notice that DOS doesn't acknowledge the new date or time, other than to display a prompt for the next command. A lack of error messages means that DOS accepted the operand.

When you enter the date and time, the system clock is reset. Therefore, once you have set the correct date and time, they should stay correct even after rebooting.

(a) **Review.** Which of the following are valid DOS dates (USA format)?

A. MAR 1, 1989	D. 6-10-16
B. 3-1-89	E. 12-21-1979
C. 3-1-1989	F. 1-1-2106

(b) **Review.** Which of the following are valid DOS times (USA format)?

A. 12	F. 0
B. 23:01	G. 21.4.36
C. 23-01	H. 7:2:1.20
D. 16.5	I. 7/2/1.20
E. 6.59.16.01	

(c) Write a command to review the current date.

`C>_`

(d) Write a command to review the current time.

`C>_`

(e) Write a command to change the time to midnight.

`C>_`

(f) Write a command to change the date to January 1, 2001.

`C>_`

(a) B, C (A is in the wrong format; D, E, and F have illegal years)

(b) A, B, F, H (C uses a hyphen instead of a colon; D uses a period instead of a colon; E uses periods instead of colons; G uses periods instead of colons; I uses slashes instead of colons)

(c) `C>DATE`

(d) `C>TIME`

(e) `C>TIME 0`

(f) `C>DATE 1-1-2001`

Verifying Write Operations

The best computers in the world sometimes experience errors when writing data on external media such as disks. Power fluctuations and user error can cause writing problems, but the most common problems are caused by minor flaws in the media and by hardware malfunctions.

If you're concerned about the accuracy of the information you record, you can use DOS's verification feature. You've already seen how to use /V with various DOS commands that make copies. You can also turn verification on for *all* write operations. DOS then rereads, verifies, and corrects if necessary, everything it writes on disk, no matter which command or application is writing it. This slows down the writing process considerably. Thus, you might want to use it when writing program files, which can't be edited, but not when writing data files, which can always be corrected if a mistake creeps in. If you have repeated problems with your system, you might want to use this verification technique for all write operations until you can locate the source of the problem and have it corrected.

Verification is controlled with the VERIFY command. Here's the format:

Format (internal):
VERIFY [ON | OFF]

You turn verification on with the command VERIFY ON. You turn it off again with the command VERIFY OFF. You can check whether it's on or off by entering VERIFY without an operand. DOS will respond with `VERIFY is on` or `VERIFY is off`. When you boot DOS, VERIFY is automatically OFF. If you'll be verifying everything, you can include the VERIFY command in your AUTOEXEC.BAT file.

Note You must enter the whole word VERIFY to avoid confusion with the VER (version) command.

(a) Write a command to check if the VERIFY feature is on or off.

`C>_`

(b) Write a command to turn verification on.

`C>_`

(a) `C>VERIFY`
(b) `C>VERIFY ON`

Increasing Break Points

Earlier you learned to terminate a program using Ctrl-Break. However, Ctrl-Break terminates a program only when it reads information from the keyboard or writes information to the screen or some external device such as the printer. Some programs work for long periods of time without reading from the keyboard or writing to the screen or printer, so you can't interrupt them.

If you wish to have DOS check for a Ctrl-Break more often, you can use the BREAK command. This slows your programs down slightly, because checking for Ctrl-Break takes time. The BREAK command is similar to VERIFY in format:

Format (external):
BREAK [ON | OFF]

When you boot DOS, BREAK is OFF. Like VERIFY, you can use BREAK three ways:

BREAK	Displays whether BREAK is ON or OFF
BREAK ON	Turns the BREAK feature ON
BREAK OFF	Turns the BREAK feature OFF

Even with the BREAK feature OFF, Ctrl-Break still terminates a program eventually, but it might take a little longer. Some programs cannot be broken into at all, whether BREAK is on or off.

(a) Why would you want to have the BREAK feature off?
(b) Write a command to find out whether BREAK is ON or OFF.
```
C>_
```
(c) Write a command to turn the BREAK feature OFF.
```
C>_
```

(a) Having the computer check for Ctrl-Break more often slows down processing; if you want programs to run as fast as possible, keep the BREAK feature off
(b) `C>BREAK`
(c) `C>BREAK OFF`

Changing the Standard I/O Device

DOS recognizes your keyboard as the standard input device and your monitor as the standard output device. The combination of keyboard and monitor is known as the *console*. The console is the standard input/output (I/O) device with DOS. As you know, you can redirect input or output of a specific command, as necessary.

All the DOS programs and most applications use the standard I/O device. When you want to enter a command, you use the keyboard. Messages appear on the monitor, even if other output goes to the printer or disk.

You can change the standard I/O device using the CTTY command.

Format (external):
CTTY [devicename]

Devicename can be AUX, COMn, or CON. You can change to any device capable of both input and output. For example, CTTY AUX changes the standard I/O device to the auxiliary port. Don't change it to an output-only device, such as a printer, or you won't be able to enter any more commands, and you'll have to boot to clear the devicename (even rebooting won't work since the keyboard can't send the signals to the computer). CTTY CON restores the console as the standard I/O device.

(a) Suppose you have a communications adapter, known to DOS as COM1. Write a command to use the I/O device hooked up to the communications adapter via telephone as the standard I/O device.

C>_

(b) Now write a command to re-establish the console as the standard I/O device without booting.

C>_

Where would you enter this command?

(a) `A>CTTY COM1`
(b) `CTTY CON;` *through* *COM1*

Changing the DOS Prompt

You might want to show a different system prompt on your screen. For example, you can display the current time in the system prompt. Or you can show the current directory, which is a tremendous help. The PROMPT command lets you change the prompt.

Format (external):

PROMPT [prompt text]

Your prompt can include any letters or numbers, as well as special characters. To use regular letters or numbers, just type them in the command. Here's an example:

```
C>PROMPT Enter data here
Enter data here_
```

The new prompt remains until you change it again or reboot.

```
Enter data herePROMPT GOOD MORNING!
GOOD MORNING!_
```

You can reset the default prompt by specifying PROMPT with no operands.

(a) Write a command to use COMMAND= as the prompt.
`C>_`

(b) Write a command to re-establish the default prompt.
`COMMAND=_`

(a) `C>PROMPT COMMAND=`
(b) `COMMAND=PROMPT`

A useful prompt gives information to the user. The default prompt, for example, shows the default drive. You can include special information in prompts by using the special codes shown in Figure 11.1.

The default prompt is ng, producing the current drive followed by >. If you enter

C>PROMPT TG

DOS responds with

`12:14:23.06>_` (or whatever the current time is)

and continues to use that new prompt until you change it or reboot. If you enter

```
C>PROMPT $P$_
```

DOS shows the default current directory name, including drive, then starts a new line for your entry.

The special characters and standard characters, including spaces, can be used in any combination. Figure 11.2 shows an example in which we create a prompt containing the time and date on the first line and the phrase `Enter command here` on the second.

Code	Meaning
$B	Vertical bar (|)
$D	The current date
$E	Escape character
$G	Greater than character (>)
$H	Backspace (erases previous character; could be used with time, for example, to erase hundredths)
$L	Less than character (<)
$N	Current disk drive
$P	Current drive and directory
$Q	Equal sign (=)
$T	The current time
$V	The current DOS version
$$	Dollar sign ($)
$_	New line (carriage return and line feed)

Figure 11.1. PROMPT Codes

Perhaps the most useful prompt displays the default directory followed by >, as in:

```
C>PROMPT $P$G
C:\DOS>_
```

This is the prompt you're most likely to use. From now on, we'll use this prompt in our examples.

Whatever prompt you like to work with, you'll probably want to put the necessary PROMPT command in your AUTOEXEC.BAT file so the prompt you like comes up every time you start up DOS.

```
C>PROMPT $T  $D$_Enter command here

19:13:58.91  Sun  6-04-1989
Enter command here_
```

Figure 11.2. Sample PROMPT Interaction

(a) Write a command to change the system prompt to:

```
DATE=(current date)   TIME=(current time)
C>_
```

(b) Write a command to show the time on one line and the current default directory followed by > on the next line.

```
C>_
```

(c) Write a command to re-establish the standard DOS prompt.

```
C>_
```

(a) `C>PROMPT DATE=$D    TIME=$T`

(b) `C>PROMPT $T$_$P$G`

(c) `C>PROMPT` *or* `C>PROMPT $N$G`

Modifying Your Monitor Display

Suppose your monitor display is not centered. What can you do? Or suppose your monitor is capable of several display modes: color, monochrome, 40 or 80 characters per line, 25 or 43 lines per screen, and so forth. How can you select the monitor features you want? The MODE command solves these problems.

Here's the basic MODE format for monitor control:

Format (external):
MODE n

The value of n tells DOS how to set the monitor. Figure 11.3 shows all the valid values for n. If your system has only a monochrome board, you can use only MONO. If your system has only a color/graphics board, you can use any value except MONO. If your system has both types of monitor, all values are valid. Use the MODE command to switch between the two types. To use your monochrome monitor as the console monitor, enter `MODE MONO`. To use your graphics monitor as the console monitor, enter `MODE CO80` or whatever value is appropriate.

On a graphics monitor, you might want to display the directory in large characters so it can be read from across the desk. You do this with MODE 40, MODE BW40, or MODE CO40. You will see larger characters immediately on a new screen. The larger characters will be used in any applications you run, perhaps making menus unreadable, so use this feature wisely. You can switch back to 80 characters at any time with MODE 80, MODE BW80, or MODE CO80.

40	Use 40 characters per line (large text)
80	Use 80 characters per line (normal text)
BW40	Use 40 characters per line and disable color
BW80	Use 80 characters per line and disable color
CO40	Use 40 characters per line and enable color
CO80	Use 80 characters per line and enable color
MONO	Use the monochrome monitor as the console monitor

Figure 11.3. Valid Monitor Values for MODE

Selecting BWxx or COxx may not make any difference on your monitor. It won't affect your DOS screen, which is always in monochrome. It might affect some of your applications. Try it out and see.

Select the true statements.

(a) MODE MONO can be used only with a monochrome adapter.
(b) You can see your DOS commands in color if you enter MODE CO40 or MODE CO80.
(c) You can switch a graphics monitor to large type (40 characters per line) by entering MODE 40.
(d) The character size (40 or 80 characters per line) affects DOS commands only, not applications.

a, c

You can also use the MODE command to adjust the display on a color/graphics monitor. Here's the format:

Format (TSR):
MODE [n],m[,T]

The valid values for n are the same as before; just use one that selects the display mode you want. You can omit it to retain the current display mode. The allowable values for m are R and L to specify whether the display is to be shifted to the right or left. If you specify T as well, you'll see a test line that will help you adjust the display. Figure 11.4 shows an example in which we shift the display left on the screen.

As long as you answer N to the question `Do you see the rightmost 9,` DOS shifts the screen to the left and repeats the question. Keep saying N until the screen is positioned on the monitor the way you like it. When you finally press Y, the display remains at that position until you change it again or reboot. If you enter MODE 80,R,T, you'll see the same test line, but DOS asks `Do you see the leftmost 0?` You can practice with these until you get a nicely centered display.

Some screens cannot be shifted. Others can be shifted within limits. The message `Unable to shift screen left/right` means that the display cannot be shifted in the indicated direction.

```
0123456789012345678901234567890123456789012345678901234567890123456789012345678

Do you see the rightmost 9? (y/n)
```

Figure 11.4. Shifting the Display with MODE

(a) Suppose you want to move the display on your monochrome monitor to the right. Write the command.

`C:\DOS>_`

(b) Suppose you want to adjust the 40-character color display to the left. Write the command.

`C:\DOS>_`

(*a*) `C:\DOS>MODE MONO,R,T`
(*b*) `C:\DOS>MODE CO40,L,T` *or* `MODE 40,L,T`

Controlling the Serial Ports

You can use MODE to establish the asynchronous communications characteristics of your serial ports, if necessary. You use MODE to set the baud rate, parity style, and so forth, for data that DOS sends to the port. If your port is hooked up to a modem and you use a telecommunications software package with the modem, then the software probably establishes the communications characteristics, and you don't need to do it with MODE. The same is probably true if you have a serial mouse or joystick that is controlled by software. But if you have a serial printer that you want DOS to use for its printing (screen prints, echo prints, and PRINT commands), then you must use MODE to tell DOS how to use the COM port. Some of your applications might also require the MODE command in order to use the printer correctly. In most cases, you'll want to include MODE commands in batch files.

Here's the format of the MODE command to control a serial port:

Format (external):
MODE COMx[:]baud-rate[,parity,data-bits,stop-bits,P]

The COM operand and the baud-rate are required. The other operands have default values that will be used if you don't include them. Figure 11.5 shows the possible values for each operand except P, and shows the defaults where appropriate.

Suppose your serial printer on COM1 runs at 9600 baud, uses even parity, 7 data-bits, and 1 stop-bit. You could enter this command:

```
C:\DOS>MODE COM1:9600
```

If your printer uses no parity, 8 data-bits, and 2 stop-bits, you would enter this command:

```
C:\DOS>MODE COM1:9600,N,8,2
```

To find out which operands to enter, just look in your printer manual. DOS identifies operands in this particular form of the MODE command by

Operand	Allowable Values	Default
baud-rate	110, 150, 300, 600, 1200, 2400, 4800, 9600, 19200 (PS/2 only) *Note:* These can be abbreviated as 11, 15, 30, 60, 12, 24, 48, 96, and 19	none
parity	N (none); E (even); O (odd)	E
data-bits	7, 8	7
stop-bits	1, 2	2 for 110 baud 1 for all others

Figure 11.5. MODE Serial Port Values

counting commas. So if you leave out the parity and data-bits operands but include the stop-bits, you must be sure to enter the correct number of commas before the stop-bits operand:

```
C:\DOS>MODE COM1:9600,,,2
```

The P operand tells DOS to keep trying if the printer is unavailable. Without P, DOS abandons a print job if the printer is unavailable (off-line, out of paper, turned off, busy, and so forth) after a certain amount of time. With P, DOS keeps trying. If you have trouble with DOS not printing or not completing jobs on the serial printer, try using the P operand. If you have trouble with DOS hanging up on print jobs when the printer is not available, so that you have to reboot to clear it, try removing the P operand.

DOS automatically sends screen prints and echo printing to LPT1 if you don't tell it otherwise. If you want them sent to your serial printer, then you need to enter this command:

```
C:\DOS>MODE LPT1=COM1
```

This substitutes COM1 for LPT1 in all printing functions, so that you will no longer be able to reach LPT1 if you need to. To cancel the reassignment enter:

```
C:\DOS>MODE LPT1
```

Suppose your only printer is an Apple Laserwriter attached to COM2 (not COM1). It requires 9600 baud, no parity checking, 8 data-bits, and 1 stop-bit. Continuous retry is advisable.

(a) Write a command to establish the serial port characteristics for this printer.
`C:\DOS>_`

(b) Write a command to redirect all print output from LPT1 to this printer.
`C:\DOS>_`

(c) Write a command to undo the printer rerouting in Question b so that your parallel printer is used.
`C:\DOS>_`

(a) `C:\DOS>MODE COM2:9600,N,8,1,P`
(b) `C:\DOS>MODE LPT1=COM1`
(c) `C:\DOS>MODE LPT1`

Modifying Printer Characteristics

The MODE command can control the output of a parallel printer too. DOS prints either 80 or 132 characters per line and either 6 or 8 lines per inch. Unless instructed to do otherwise, DOS will print 80 characters per line and six lines per inch. This is a very readable format. Some printers can print up to 132 characters per line, however. Here's the format for the MODE command to establish the printer spacing:

Format (TSR):
MODE LPTn[:] [c][,l],[P]

You must specify the printer as LPT1, LPT2, or LPT3. The colon is optional. The value of c (characters per line) must be 80 or 132. The value of l (lines per inch) must be 6 or 8. P causes continual retry, as with serial printers.

Figure 11.6 shows an echo print of a series of commands that reset the printer spacing on a standard dot matrix printer.

If your printer is capable of switching print sizes, you probably will do so only for long print jobs where you want to conserve some paper. For your everyday work, the default mode is usually preferable.

```
B:\>DIR*.

 Volume in drive B is BACKUP   002
 Directory of B:\

PROCESS          5376  11-30-88    9:53a
PROCESS5         6912  12-01-88   10:53a
NEWLIST            82   2-26-89   11:05a
PRESBACK          180   5-25-89   12:38p
PRESIDEN          180   5-26-89   12:38p
PRESSORT           65   2-26-89   11:34a
PRESCOPY          180   5-25-89   12:38p
        7 Files(s)  327680 bytes free

B:\>MODE LPT1:132

LPT1: SET FOR 132

B:\>DIR *.

 Volume in drive B is BACKUP   002
 Directory of B:\

PROCESS          5376  11-30-88    9:53a
PROCESS5         6912  12-01-88   10:53a
NEWLIST            82   2-26-89   11:05a
PRESBACK          180   5-25-89   12:38p
PRESIDEN          180   5-26-89   12:38p
PRESSORT           65   2-26-89   11:34a
PRESCOPY          180   5-25-89   12:38p
        7 Files(s)  327680 bytes free

B:\>MODE LPT1:,8

Printer lines per inch set

B:\>DIR *.

 Volume in drive B is BACKUP   002
 Directory of B:\

PROCESS          5376  11-30-88    9:53a
PROCESS5         6912  12-01-88   10:53a
NEWLIST            82   2-26-89   11:05a
PRESBACK          180   5-25-89   12:38p
PRESIDEN          180   5-26-89   12:38p
PRESSORT           65   2-26-89   11:34a
PRESCOPY          180   5-25-89   12:38p
        7 Files(s)  327680 bytes free

B:\>
```

Figure 11.6. MODE Print Size Commands

(a) Write a command to use 132 characters per line on your printer.

```
C:\DOS>_
```

(b) Write a command to use 132 characters per line and eight lines per inch on your printer.

```
C:\DOS>_
```

(c) Adapt your above command for continuous retry.

```
C:\DOS>_
```

(a) `C:\DOS>MODE LPT1: 132`

(b) `C:\DOS>MODE LPT1: 132,8`

(c) `C:\DOS>MODE LPT1: 132,8,P`

You can control the print environment by including special operands the first time you enter the PRINT command. These operands can be in any sequence.

You have already learned to use the PRINT command to establish a print queue, add files to it with /P, cancel files from it with /C, and terminate the entire queue with /T. As you have used it, PRINT uses a number of default values in establishing a print environment. You can change that environment by specifying the appropriate options in the PRINT command the first time you use it.

The first time you use PRINT after booting, DOS loads part of the program into memory. The options you'll learn here can be specified only the first time you use PRINT. Figure 11.7 shows the print environment options, their default values, and the values you can specify.

Once you decide what your printer needs, you can include the appropriate PRINT command in your AUTOEXEC.BAT file to set up the printer as soon as you boot.

/D:devicename names the device. If you include /D, DOS won't ask you to confirm the device when PRINT is first used. PRINT /D:PRN SAMPLE results in immediate printing of SAMPLE on the PRN: device.

/B:buffer-size specifies the size of the print buffer. This is a memory area where DOS stores the data that's printing. The buffer size is not the same as the printer's own internal memory, which DOS can't control. By default, DOS uses a 512-byte print buffer. If you do a lot of printing, you could specify /B:1024 or /B:2048 to make printing more efficient. However, the more space you allocate to the print buffer, the less space is available to run programs.

Switch	Allowable Value	Default
/D:devicename	Any print devicename	LPT1:
/Q:queue-size	1 - 32	10
/B:buffer-size	1 - 32767	512
/S:timeslice	1 - 255	8
/U:busytick	1 - 255	1
/M:maxtick	1 - 255	2

Figure 11.7. PRINT Environment Options

/Q:queue-size changes the queue size from the default of 10. If you find this default limit inconvenient, you might want to increase it. But doing so takes more space away from available memory, so don't increase the queue size if you don't need to.

We explore the remaining options a little later.

(a) Write the first PRINT command since booting. It should establish LPT1 as the device, set up a queue size of 15, and start printing MICHAEL.LET.
`C:\DOS>_`
(b) Write a command to set a queue size of 8, a buffer of 1024, and PRN as the default device. The command will be in the AUTOEXEC.BAT file, so it won't actually print anything.

(a) `C:\DOS>PRINT /D:LPT1: /Q:15 MICHAEL.LET`
(b) `PRINT /D:PRN: /Q:8 /B:1024`

As you know, PRINT lets you continue with other work at your computer while printing takes place. To do this, PRINT shares time with whatever else you are doing. The total time is divided into *timeslices* that are regulated by the system's internal clock. Timeslices and other factors are regulated by *clockticks*. Three PRINT options can change DOS's default settings for print timesharing.

/S:timeslice specifies how often PRINT gets a timeslice. PRINT gets one timeslice out of the number of slices specified; your other work gets the remainder. The smaller the number, the more often PRINT gets a slice. The default is 8, meaning that PRINT gets one out of every eight timeslices. You can specify a number between 1 and 255. To give PRINT more priority, assign a number smaller than 8. To give PRINT less priority, assign a number larger than 8. The setting /S:1 gives the printer the greatest priority, greatly slowing down whatever else you are doing. The setting /S:255 gives your other work the greatest priority; the print job will be very slow, with long pauses.

/U:busytick specifies the number of clockticks that PRINT will wait until the print device is available. The default is 1, meaning that the printer must be available immediately. PRINT loses its timeslice if it has to wait longer than specified. You can speed up a print job (but slow down your other work) by specifying /U: greater than 1.

/M:maxtick specifies the size of the timeslice. The default is 2 clockticks, but you can specify a number from 1 to 255 to give less or more priority to the printer. You can speed up the print job (but slow down your other work) by specifying /M: greater than 2.

You probably won't use these PRINT functions much until you are more familiar with DOS. The first example below gives priority to the printer, the second gives less priority to PRINT than to your other work.

```
PRINT /S:4 /U:4 /M:2
PRINT /S:12 /U:1 /M:1
```

Don't forget that you can't adjust these variables "on the fly." Once you set them, they are fixed until you reboot.

(a) All other variables being equal, which of these commands will print documents fastest?

A. `PRINT /S:8 /U:1 /M:2`

B. `PRINT /S:4 /U:10 /M:100`

C. `PRINT /S:20 /U:1 /M:1`

(b) Write a PRINT command to be included in your AUTOEXEC.BAT file to set the default device to LPT2 and to give PRINT 1 out of every 4 timeslices. Leave other values at their default settings.

(a) B
(b) `PRINT /D:LPT2 /S:4`

Printing Graphics

The GRAPHICS command pertains only to systems with color/graphics adapters and graphics printers. It allows you to print graphics screens with the PrtSc key. Ordinarily, PrtSc can handle screens only in text mode. If you want to be able to print graphics screens with PrtSc, enter the GRAPHICS command, as in this example:

```
C:\DOS>GRAPHICS
```

This establishes graphics print mode. Then, any time you press Shift-PrtSc, DOS prints the screen, including graphics. If the screen is in text mode, the screen is printed in under 30 seconds; a graphics screen can take up to three minutes, even more with some printers. The graphics screens are printed as follows, according to the type of printer and adapter:

- In the 320 X 200 color graphics mode, the screen contents are printed in up to four patterns or shades of gray.
- In the 640 X 200 color graphics mode, the screen is also printed in shades of gray, but sideways on the paper. The upper right corner of the screen is printed on the upper left corner of the paper.

(a) Which color graphics mode is printed sideways on the paper?
(b) Which mode is printed faster—text or color graphics?
(c) What keys are pressed to start screen printing?
(d) Write a command to allow a graphics screen to be printed on a graphics printer.
`C:\DOS>_`

(*a*) *640 X 240*
(*b*) *Text*
(*c*) *Shift-PrtSc*
(*d*) `C:\DOS>GRAPHICS`

Additional options are available for the GRAPHICS command. Here's the complete format:

Format (external):
GRAPHICS [printer type] [/R] [/B]

Printer type specifies the type of printer; if you omit it, GRAPHICS is assumed. Figure 11.8 shows the valid values. You specify the value that matches your printer and ribbon types.

The /R (reverse) option, which you can use with or without a printer type, reverses the graphics, printing black as black and white as white. The default is to print black as white and white as black, so the dark background of a screen is light on a screen print. You'll want to use /R when a realistic screen print (white letters on a dark background) is necessary.

The /B (background) switch can be specified only with COLOR4 or COLOR8; it specifies that the background color is to be printed. Otherwise, the background color is omitted in a screen print.

Suppose you have an RGB ribbon on a color printer. You want background colors printed as well. You could use this command before PrtSc:

```
C:\DOS>GRAPHICS COLOR4 /B
```

To make your compact printer print black for black, you'd use this command:

```
C:\DOS>GRAPHICS COMPACT /R
```

To reset your printer to the standard graphics printer, use the command:

```
C:\DOS>GRAPHICS
```

The GRAPHICS command requires 3K in addition to the memory used by DOS, reducing the amount of memory available for running programs.

(a) Write a command to allow graphics screen prints in full color, including background on an IBM Personal Color printer with CMY ribbon.

```
C:\DOS>_
```

(b) Write a command to cause black to print as black and white as white on a standard graphics printer. Include the background color.

```
C:\DOS>_
```

(a) `C:\DOS>GRAPHICS COLOR8 /B`
(b) `C:\DOS>GRAPHICS /R /B`

COLOR1	Color printer with one-color ribbon
COLOR4	Color printer with RBG ribbon
COLOR8	Color printer with CMY ribbon
COMPACT	Compact printer
GRAPHICS	Graphics printer and IBM ProPrinter
THERMAL	PC Convertible Thermal printer

Figure 11.8. Valid Printer Types for the GRAPHICS Command

All the commands you have learned in this chapter are particularly suited to an AUTOEXEC.BAT file. For example, suppose you like to have VERIFY and BREAK on at all times, you like to use a 40-character display, you like to include the default directory in the prompt, you have a graphics printer and frequently make graphics screen prints, and you prefer PRINT output to go to LPT2 with very low priority. This is the AUTOEXEC.BAT file you might use:

```
ECHO OFF
CLS
```

```
VERIFY ON
BREAK ON
MODE CO40
PROMPT $P$G
GRAPHICS
PRINT /D:LPT2 /S:255 /U:1 /M:1
DATE
TIME
```

Notice we included the DATE and TIME commands in this AUTOEXEC.BAT file. Remember these commands are suppressed when the boot disk contains AUTOEXEC.BAT. If they aren't set automatically from a clock/calendar, then you should include these two commands in your AUTOEXEC.BAT file.

Suppose you like to work with VERIFY on but BREAK off. You prefer to use your only printer most efficiently—132 characters per line, eight lines per inch. It is a graphics printer and you have a graphics adapter. For a prompt, you prefer:

```
What do you want?
```

You prefer giving your printer the highest possible priority. You do not have a clock/calendar. Write your AUTOEXEC.BAT file.

Here's one example. The command sequence can vary.

```
ECHO OFF
CLS
VERIFY ON
MODE LPT1 132 8 P
GRAPHICS
PROMPT What do you want?
PRINT /D:PRN /S:1 /U:255 /M:255
DATE
TIME
```

Exercises

What You Should Do	*How the Computer Responds*
1. Modify the time. a. Check the time. b. Change it to 2 P.M. c. Check the time again. d. Reset it to the correct time.	1. Displays and changes the time as requested.
2. Modify the date. a. Check the date. b. Change it to March 15, 1990. c. Check the date again. d. Reset it to the correct date.	2. Displays and changes the date as requested.
3. Change the prompt. a. Use this prompt message: `QUICKLY==>` b. Reset the normal prompt.	3. Changes the prompt as requested.
4. Modify the print output, if possible. a. Print the PRESDENT file. b. Set the printer for 132 characters per line and print the file again. c. Compare printouts, then reset the printer.	4. Prints the PRESDENT file at normal size, then prints it at reduced size, if possible.
5. Modify the display. a. Set the display for 40 characters. b. Display a directory. c. Reset the display to 80 characters.	5. Displays the directory in large characters if possible. Then returns to the normal character size.

What If It Doesn't Work?

1. If you have trouble with DATE and TIME, just try again. Remember to use 24-hour time.

2. If you have trouble with PROMPT, try this: `PROMPT QUICKLY$Q$Q$G`. To reset it, just enter `PROMPT`.

3. Many letter-quality printers can't handle 132 characters per line, so don't worry if your printer can't do this.

4. The color/graphics adapter is necessary to change the display mode on a monitor. Try using MODE to shift the display if yours is off-center.

12

Altering the Environment (Part II)

In this chapter you'll learn more ways to modify the DOS environment. You'll learn to define a CONFIG.SYS file to set parameters before AUTOEXEC.BAT is executed. You'll learn to define a RAM drive to increase the efficiency of your system. You'll also learn to change the country setup for your keyboard, monitor, and printer. And you'll learn more about the SET command.

When you complete this chapter, you will be able to:

- Create a CONFIG.SYS file containing statements that control the DOS environment
- Create and use RAM drives
- State which commands are used to establish a non-USA environment for your system
- Store variables in the environment with the SET command

System Configuration

Every time you boot your system, DOS searches in the root directory for a file called CONFIG.SYS. If it isn't there, DOS sets default values that control the DOS environment. You can create a CONFIG.SYS file to set different values.

You create a CONFIG.SYS file just like you create any ASCII text file. You can use any editor or word processor capable of producing an ASCII file, or you can use COPY CON:.

The DOS programs don't require a CONFIG.SYS file to operate correctly. Many applications, however, require nondefault settings for configuration values. The information you need in order to set up the environment correctly should be included in the application's documentation.

One value you can set in CONFIG.SYS is BREAK, which controls how often DOS checks for the Ctrl-Break key. The default BREAK status is OFF. Instead of using the BREAK command, as you would in an AUTOEXEC.BAT file, you simply specify BREAK ON.

```
C:\DOS>COPY CON: C:\CONFIG.SYS
BREAK ON
^Z
C:\DOS>_
```

The root directory of the fixed disk now contains a file named CONFIG.SYS containing BREAK ON. Whenever you boot from the fixed disk, the BREAK function is turned on. If you don't want it on, you can still use the standard BREAK command to turn it off.

What's the difference between CONFIG.SYS and AUTOEXEC.BAT? CONFIG.SYS is executed first and can influence AUTOEXEC.BAT. The statements in CONFIG.SYS are not displayed as AUTOEXEC.BAT commands are when ECHO is ON. But there are very few statements you can put in CONFIG.SYS, while AUTOEXEC.BAT is nearly unlimited.

(a) A CONFIG.SYS file takes effect:
  A. When it is created
  B. When the system is booted
  C. When a COPY command is used

(b) If the boot disk does not contain a CONFIG.SYS file or an AUTOEXEC.BAT file, what is the status of BREAK after booting?

(c) Write a CONFIG.SYS statement to turn on the BREAK status.

(a) B
(b) Off
(c) `BREAK ON`

Several configuration commands have to do with files and memory space. DOS uses memory buffers to move data between disks and memory. The more buffers you specify, up to a practical limit, the faster your disk access will be. DOS allocates a default number of buffers, from 2 to 15, based on the configuration of your disk drives and the amount of memory you have. Some programs, especially those that do a great deal of random access, are made more efficient by allocating more buffers. If you use a database package, allocating 10 or more buffers speeds it up. If you work with subdirectories, from 10 to 25 buffers may help. However, if you use too many buffers, you may slow DOS down since it has to search them all to locate data. Also, each buffer removes more than .5K of space from available memory.

You can specify from 1 to 99 buffers; many software manuals give recommendations for their programs. BUFFERS=30, which requests 30 buffers, is just right for most fixed-disk systems, if the memory space (nearly 16K) is available.

Many programs require that several files be available at once. Complex programs such as WordStar 2000 or WordPerfect need to work with up to 20 files at a time. An accounting package may need as many as 40. Every open file needs a small memory area (39 bytes) for the file's *handle* (control information about the file). By default, DOS creates eight file areas. You can raise that limit, up to 99, with the FILES statement. If the CONFIG.SYS file contains a statement like FILES=20, the file limit is set to the indicated number. If an application needs more than the default amount, its documentation should tell you how many to allocate. Leaving space for more file handles than you need doesn't do much harm, since each one takes up only 39 bytes.

Some older programs require File Control Blocks (FCBS) rather than file handles. FCBS are created with the FCBS statement, as in FCBS=30. Your application documentation will tell you if you need to use the FCBS statement in a CONFIG.SYS file, and it should show you the statement you need.

(a) Write a configuration statement to set the number of buffers to 12.
(b) Write a configuration statement that will allow 16 files to be open at once.

(a) `BUFFERS=12`
(b) `FILES=16`

DOS generally uses COMMAND.COM in the root directory of the boot drive as its command processor. Some systems use their own command processor instead. They must use a CONFIG.SYS file that includes SHELL=filespec, specifying the name of the command processor to be used. For example, if you have a shell called PROCESS.EXE, you would include this statement in your CONFIG.SYS file:

```
SHELL=C:\PROCESS.EXE
```

You can also use the SHELL statement to tell DOS where to find COMMAND.COM if it's not on the root directory of the boot drive. If you override the default shell, you'll probably also need the SET COMSPEC command in your AUTOEXEC.BAT file. SET COMSPEC is discussed later in this chapter.

The LASTDRIVE statement tells DOS the highest lettered drive it can accept in commands. The default value is E. You can use LASTDRIVE to pretend you have more drives than you really do. This allows you to create imaginary drives with SUBST beyond drive E:. Some of your applications might also require LASTDRIVE, as described in their documentation. To allocate the maximum number of drives, you would include this statement in your CONFIG.SYS file:

```
LASTDRIVE=Z:
```

Identify the appropriate configuration statement for each of the following:
(a) Tell DOS you have more drives than you really do
(b) Allocate extra disk buffers
(c) Cause DOS to check for Ctrl-Break more often
(d) Specify a command processor other than (boot drive):\COMMAND.COM
(e) Allocate buffers for file handles
(f) Allocate extra FCBs
(g) Allow you to specify 12 pathname substitutions

(a) LASTDRIVE
(b) BUFFERS
(c) BREAK
(d) SHELL
(e) FILES
(f) FCBs
(g) LASTDRIVE

Specifying Device Drivers

DOS needs device drivers to support any peripheral devices, including the screen, the keyboard, the disk drives, and the printer. A device driver is a program that sends data to or receives data from a peripheral device. All the standard device drivers are loaded automatically when you boot the system, and you don't have to worry about them. You can use the DEVICE statement in the CONFIG.SYS file to load other device drivers, as specified in your device manuals. DOS includes several device drivers you might need under certain circumstances. Your hardware, such as a mouse or a digitizer, might have its own driver.

Suppose you want to install the driver that came with your mouse. It's on C:\MOUSE and it's called PMOUSE.SYS. Here's how you would install it:

```
DEVICE=C:\MOUSE\PMOUSE.SYS
```

The DOS diskette includes a device driver called ANSI.SYS, which lets DOS use "Extended Screen and Keyboard Control." These are features that give an application better control over such screen facilities as background and foreground color, flashing, highlighting, cursor location, and so forth. You might have applications that require the ANSI.SYS driver to be installed; their documentation should tell you to install it. You can also use the ANSI.SYS features yourself in your PROMPT command. You could create a flashing red prompt, for example. If you're interested in learning more about customizing your prompt with the ANSI.SYS features, look up these capabilities in your DOS reference manual. To install the ANSI.SYS driver, include this statement in your CONFIG.SYS file:

```
DEVICE=ANSI.SYS
```

If the ANSI.SYS file is not located in the root directory of the boot drive, be sure to include the correct path in the filespec.

(a) What configuration statement lets you specify a device driver?
(b) Write a CONFIG.SYS statement to include a driver for your digitizer. The driver is called DIGIT.SYS and is located in C:\DRAW.
(c) What does the ANSI.SYS driver do?
  A. Allows use of ANSI codes instead of ASCII codes
  B. Allows use of the "Extended Screen and Keyboard Control" features
  C. Allows use of nonstandard disk formats

(d) Write a CONFIG.SYS statement to install the ANSI.SYS driver. It is located in C:\DOS.

(a) *DEVICE*
(b) `DEVICE=C:\DRAW\DIGIT.SYS`
(c) *B*
(d) `DEVICE=C:\DOS\ANSI.SYS`

Using a Virtual Disk

RAMDRIVE.SYS is a device driver that lets you turn part of your memory into virtual drives. (Earlier versions of DOS call this facility VDISK.SYS.) A virtual drive is an area of memory set aside to be used like a disk drive. Of course, it isn't really a disk drive; you lose all the data here when the machine loses power. DOS can access memory much faster than a disk, so programs that do a lot of disk access run much faster when you use a RAM drive. You can copy a program, such as a word processor, to a RAM drive area and make it the default drive. You'll actually see the difference in performance. Of course, your system must have plenty of memory, since space being used as a RAM drive is not free for other uses. However you can put the RAM drive into extended memory (above 1MB), which is ordinarily not used by DOS.

For example, suppose you frequently sort a file using the SORT program. When SORT.EXE and the file you sort are both on diskettes, the operation takes 80 seconds. If you place SORT.EXE and the file in a RAM drive, the operation is completed in about one second.

Again, a virtual drive isn't actually a disk drive; when the machine is rebooted or loses power, any data in memory, including the RAM drive, is lost. If you use a RAM drive, be sure to copy any files to be saved to actual disks before turning off the computer or rebooting. Since you could lose all your work in a power outage, many experts recommend that you don't put data files in a RAM drive, just programs. Since your program files are already recorded on disk, you don't need to worry about losing the RAM drive copy. You won't experience as much time savings with your data files on actual disks, but you also don't take the chance of losing a day's work. If you do put your data files in a RAM drive, copy them to a real disk at least once per hour.

Suppose your system has 512K. You could set up a 128K RAM drive. When you use CHKDSK, you'll see that the system still has 512K memory, but only 384K is free. You can still run most applications. If your application requires 390K of memory to run, you must be sure not to create RAM drives that leave less free memory than that, or you'll get an `Out of memory` message.

DOS lets you create as many RAM drives as you need; they are lettered in sequence after your real drives.

(a) Suppose your system has 256K memory, one diskette drive, and one-fixed disk drive.
   A. Can you specify a RAM drive?
   B. If so, what would its name be?

(b) Suppose your system has 640K of memory and two diskette drives.
   A. Can you create three RAM drives of 100K each?
   B. If so, what would their names be?
   C. How much memory would be free (ignoring buffer space, FASTOPEN space, TSRs, PRINT, MODE, and the like for now)?

(a) A—yes; B—D

(b) A—yes; B—C, D, E; C—about 340K

Suppose you have created a CONFIG.SYS file containing the statement `DEVICE=RAMDRIVE.SYS`. When you reboot the fixed-disk system, you'll see the message shown in Figure 12.1. Notice the RAM drive has been assigned the name D:. The buffer size tells you the size of the RAM drive; 64K is the default. The sector size tells you the size of each sector in the RAM drive; 128 bytes is the default. The default number of entries in the root directory is 64. You can specify different values for all these factors with the RAMDRIVE statement.

Here is the format of the RAMDRIVE statement:

Format (CONFIG.SYS statement):

DEVICE=RAMDRIVE.SYS [buffer-size] [sector-size] [directory-size] [/E]

The buffer size is specified in kilobytes. The minimum memory DOS needs outside the RAM drive is 64K. You can specify any size between one and the available memory size in your system. To create a RAM drive of 240K, you would place this statement in your CONFIG.SYS file:

```
DEVICE=RAMDRIVE.SYS 240
```

DOS might adjust what you specify, if necessary. If your specification leaves less than 64K of available memory, DOS decreases the RAM drive size, perhaps even eliminating it.

Here's a sample CONFIG.SYS file for a system with 320K.

```
DEVICE=RAMDRIVE.SYS 128
DEVICE=RAMDRIVE.SYS 128
DEVICE=RAMDRIVE.SYS 32
```

When the system boots, RAMDRIVE creates two RAM drives. Then there is only 64K left, so an error message is generated and the third RAM drive is not installed. If you really need three RAM drives, you have to rework the sizes to leave 64K memory for DOS.

```
Microsoft RAMdrive version 2.01 virtual disk D:
    Disk size: 64k
    Sector size: 512 bytes
    Allocation unit: 1 sectors
    Directory entries: 64
```

Figure 12.1. RAMDRIVE Message at Boot Time

(a) Write a configuration statement to set up a 96K RAM drive.
(b) Your system has 640K. Write statements to set up two RAM drives, each with 100K.

(a) `DEVICE=RAMDRIVE.SYS 96`

(b) `DEVICE=RAMDRIVE.SYS 100`
`DEVICE=RAMDRIVE.SYS 100`

In the DEVICE statement that sets up the RAM drive, you can also specify the sector size as 128, 256, or 512. DOS uses 512 as the default on RAM drives. You might as well use the default size unless you have reason not to. A larger sector size works better with large files; a smaller size works better with small files.

You can also specify the number of directory entries for a RAM drive, from 12 to 512. The default is 64. RAMDRIVE uses one directory entry to hold a label for the virtual disk; you can insert this label later with the LABEL command.

The directory takes up storage space just as files do. The more entries you specify (each entry takes up 32 bytes), the more drive space you use. There's a relationship between directory entries and sector size because DOS won't use just part of a sector for directory entries. Say your sector size is 128 bytes and you request 75 directory entries, 2400 bytes altogether. That's 18 complete sectors plus part of a nineteenth. DOS will make the entire nineteenth sector into directory entries, so you actually get 76 entries, not 75, for a total directory size of 2432 bytes. The message you see reflects the amount allocated, not what you requested.

If you request too many directory entries to fit in your RAM drive, the directory request is scaled down until it fits. Just allow enough space for the programs you want to run or the files you want to store.

The /E option tells RAMDRIVE to use extended memory—at or beyond the 1MB level. If you have an AT or PS/2 with more than 1MB of memory, you'll want to use /E to put your RAM drives in the extended memory. Most software doesn't use this memory, so the RAM drives won't decrease available memory by much—a nice advantage. (In extended memory, 768 bytes of available memory are taken up by control information for the RAM drives.)

(a) Write a CONFIG.SYS statement to establish a RAM drive with 128K, with 256-byte sectors, and 20 directory entries.

(b) Assume your system has 256K of memory. Write a CONFIG.SYS statement to establish the largest possible RAM drive with the largest possible sectors. Allocate only one sector to directory entries.

(c) What option tells DOS to place a RAM drive above the 1MB level?

(a) `DEVICE=RAMDRIVE.SYS 128 256 20`

(b) `DEVICE=RAMDRIVE.SYS 192 512 16` *(Any number less than 17 would allocate one sector to the directory and would get you 16 directory entries)*
(c) */E*

A RAM drive speeds up the operation of almost any program that performs a lot of disk I/O. Any word processor, for example, runs faster if it is in a RAM drive space. If you place both the word processor program and the files to be worked on in a RAM drive, the process is even smoother. You won't hear any disk accesses at all. A process that takes 10 seconds on a diskette may take only a fraction of a second on a RAM drive.

One popular word processor takes 20 to 25 seconds to bring up and open a file on disk. If the word processor files and any existing files to be edited are first copied to a RAM drive, a file is brought up and opened in only five seconds. And such operations as search-and-replace, scrolling, and spell-checking are much more efficient.

You must keep various factors in mind when planning the size of a RAM drive. Your application, such as the word processor, requires a certain amount of available memory. The documentation for each application should tell you how much it requires. DOS takes up a certain amount of available memory (depending on how many buffers you have allocated, what memory resident programs you have started up, and so on). Any TSR programs, such as MODE or PRINT, that you want to have in memory also take up space.

Figure 12.2 shows an interaction demonstrating a RAM drive session. You can see the message from the DEVICE=RAMDRIVE.SYS statement in the CONFIG.SYS file at boot time. Then AUTOEXEC.BAT copied all the necessary word processing files into the RAM drive. Next we copied the file we want to edit (PRACTICE) into the drive. Then we started up the word processor and edited the file. At the end of the session, before shutting down, we copied the edited file back to the real drive.

Suppose your system has two diskette drives and 640K of memory. Your word processor files, which all start with WP, take up 90K on disk. The files you edit take up about 80K. The word processor requires 123K of memory. After starting up all your TSRs and allocating buffers and so forth, CHKDSK shows you have 328K of available memory.

(a) What size RAM drive can you use?
(b) Write a command to set up the RAM drive.
(c) After booting the system, you need to place the word processor program files in the RAM drive. Write the command.

```
A:\>_
```

(d) While working with the word processor in the RAM drive, you create a new file called CANDID.BIO and then exit the word processor. Write a command to save the new file before you shut down.

`C:\>_`

(a) 220K is available; you need a minimum of 170K

(b) We chose to give 200K to the RAM drive with this statement:

`DEVICE=RAMDRIVE.SYS 200` *(you could use different buffer, sector, and directory sizes)*

Microsoft RAMdrive Version 2.01 virtual disk D: Disk size: 64k Sector size: 512 bytes Allocation unit: 1 sectors Directory entries: 64	This message results from the Device statement in CONFIG.SYS
C:\DOS>COPY C:\CX5\CX*.* D: C:CX.EXE C:CX.MSG C:CX.DCT 3 File(s) copied	This command copies the word processing program to the RAM drive
C:\DOS>COPY C:\TEXTS\PRACTICE D: 1 File(s) copied	This command copies the text file to be edited to the RAM drive
C:\DOS>D: D:\>	This command makes the RAM drive the default drive
. . .	Use the word processor to edit PRACTICE
D:\>COPY PRACTICE C:\TEXTS	Save PRACTICE on a real disk

Figure 12.2. Using a RAM Drive

(c) `A:\>COPY WP*.* C:`
(d) `C:\>COPY CANDID.BIO A:`

Other DOS Drivers

The DRIVER.SYS driver gives you control over an external diskette device. If you have external diskette devices (not A: or B:), you'll need to use this driver. Check your diskette hardware manual and/or DOS reference manual for the exact details on how to use DRIVER.SYS.

The IBMCACHE.SYS driver is available only if you have a PS/2 model 50, 60, or 80. It is a hidden file, so you won't see it in your directory. It creates a buffer in memory to cache (store) fixed disk data to reduce the number of disk accesses required and greatly speed up fixed disk operations. If you have one of the above PS/2 models, you will probably want to use IBMCACHE.SYS. You must run a program called IBMCACHE to install the driver. IBMCACHE is a menu-driven program, something like FDISK. Check your DOS manual for details.

Match the drivers with their descriptions.

(a) DRIVER.SYS	A. Available only with certain models of the PS/2
(b) IBMCACHE.SYS	B. Manages external diskette units
	C. Makes fixed disk operations faster

(a) B
(b) A, C

Country and Language Formats

DOS was developed in the United States and, by default, it uses formats appropriate to that country. If you use your system in a different country, you can do several things to adapt DOS.

The COUNTRY statement in CONFIG.SYS affects the date and time formats. It also provides information to applications about numeric formats (the decimal point and thousands separator), sort sequence (how to alphabetize such characters as â, à, and å), and currency symbols. Here's the format:

Format (CONFIG.SYS Statement):
COUNTRY=xxx[,,filespec]

Figure 12.3 lists the country codes. If you want to use the Swedish formats, for example, you would include the following statement in your CONFIG.SYS file:

```
COUNTRY=046
```

After rebooting, your date and time formats would look like this:

```
Current date is Wed  1992-01-15
Enter new date (yy-mm-dd):
Current time is 18.12.26,32
Enter new time:
```

DOS needs the COUNTRY.SYS file to obtain the country information. If the information isn't in the root directory of the boot disk, then you need to include a filespec in the COUNTRY statement to tell DOS where to find the

Arabic	785	Italy	039
Australia	061	Latin America	003
Belgium	032	Netherlands	031
Canada-English	001	Norway	047
Canada-French	002	Portugal	351
Denmark	045	Spain	034
Finland	358	Sweden	046
France	033	Switzerland	041
Germany	049	United Kingdom	044
Israel	972	United States	001

Figure 12.3. Country Codes

country information. The filespec must be preceded by two commas, as in this example:

```
COUNTRY=044,,C:\DOS\COUNTRY.SYS
```

Suppose you live in Canada. You want to use French-Canadian conventions with DOS and with your applications. Your COUNTRY.SYS file is in C:\SYSFILES. Write the CONFIG.SYS statement you would need.

```
COUNTRY=002,,C:\SYSFILES\COUNTRY.SYS
```

Your monitor display and printers have *codepages* built into them. A codepage is a table that tells the device what character to issue for each of the 256 possible values of a byte. For example, in the US codepage, code 157 is displayed or printed as ¥. In the multilingual and Nordic codepages, the same code yields Ø. In the Portuguese and Canadian-French codepage, the same code produces Ù.

When DOS displays or prints data, it sends numeric codes to the monitor or printer. How those codes are interpreted depends on the codepage that is installed in the device. Usually the codepage depends on the country where you buy the hardware. If you buy a printer in the USA, it will probably have the US codepage built in. If you buy a monitor in Portugal, it will have the Portuguese codepage built in.

Many printers and monitors are able to use different codepages than the built-in ones. You can download software codepages. Thus even though you bought your system in the USA, you can display and print files prepared in Nordic languages. DOS has five software codepages available, as shown in Figure 12.4. You can download a single codepage or set up your system to switch back and forth between several codepages.

The monitors that can handle software codepages are EGA, VGA, and LCD. The older monochrome and CGA monitors are not capable of doing this. The printers that can handle software codepages are the IBM ProPrinter Model 4201 and its compatibles, and the IBM Quietwriter III Model 5202 and its compatibles. If you don't have one of those models, the best thing to do is try switching codepages on your printer and see if it works.

Downloading a software codepage is not a simple task. It requires careful coordination of several CONFIG.SYS statements and DOS commands. We will overview the necessary facilities here. If you actually need to do this, check with your DOS reference manual for more details.

In your CONFIG.SYS file, you need:

- The COUNTRY statement, as discussed earlier, to establish the desired country formats and to tell DOS where COUNTRY.SYS is.
- A DEVICE=DISPLAY.SYS statement with operands to tell DOS which codepage is the monitor hardware codepage and to allocate buffers for every software codepage you want to use with the monitor. (The DISPLAY.SYS file, provided by DOS, must be available at boot time.)
- A DEVICE=PRINTER.SYS statement with operands to tell DOS which codepage is the printer hardware codepage and to allocate buffers for every software codepage you want to use with the printer. (The PRINTER.SYS file, provided by DOS, must be available at boot time.)

After booting, you need these commands:

- MODE CON: CODEPAGE PREPARE must be used to prepare the various codepages you want to use on the monitor. You can only prepare as many codepages as you allocated buffers for in the DEVICE=DISPLAY.SYS statement. The EGA.CPI or LCD.CPI file, provided by DOS, must be available when this command is executed.
- MODE LPTn: CODEPAGE PREPARE does the same thing for printer codepages. The 4201.CPI or 5202.CPI file, provided by DOS, must be available when this command is executed.
- MODE CON: CODEPAGE SELECT downloads a codepage to the monitor. The codepage must have been prepared first.
- MODE LPTn: CODEPAGE SELECT downloads a codepage to the printer. The codepage must have been prepared first.
- NLSFUNC (National Language Support FUNCtions) loads the CHCP program into memory as a resident program. You must execute NLSFUNC before you can execute CHCP.

Canada-French	863
Multilingual	850
Norway and Denmark	865
Portugal	860
United States	437

Figure 12.4. DOS Software Codepages

- CHCP (CHange CodePage) can be used instead of MODE...SELECT to download a codepage to all eligible devices at once. The codepages must have been prepared first and NLSFUNC must have been executed first.
- MODE device CODEPAGE REFRESH refreshes the software codepage after a hardware error (such as turning off the printer).

Match the statements/commands with their descriptions.

(a) MODE...PREPARE	A. Allocates buffers for codepages
(b) MODE...REFRESH	B. Prepares codepages before you can use them
(c) MODE...SELECT	C. Downloads one codepage to all the appropriate devices
(d) CHCP	D. Downloads one codepage to one device
(e) DEVICE=DISPLAY.SYS	E. Restores the software codepage after a hardware failure
(f) DEVICE=PRINTER.SYS	F. Prepares for the CHCP command
(g) NLSFUNC	

(a) B
(b) E
(c) D
(d) C
(e) A
(f) A
(g) F

Your keyboard also has a built-in codepage that determines what code is sent to DOS for each key you press. If you want to use a non-USA layout on a USA keyboard, you might need the KEYB command to tell DOS what keyboard layout you want to use and what monitor codepage it should be associated with.

Some CGA monitors in medium-resolution mode do not display international and graphic characters well. If you have problems with these characters looking smeared, enter the GRAFTABL command. This loads an alternate character set into the CGA monitor that displays more clearly. (If smeared graphics is a problem with your system, you'll probably want to put the GRAFTABL command in your AUTOEXEC.BAT file.)

There's also a command called SELECT that sets up your CONFIG.SYS and AUTOEXEC.BAT files for the country formats and keyboard layout of your choice. However, SELECT *reformats the target diskette,* eliminating your existing CONFIG.SYS and AUTOEXEC.BAT files as well as all other files on the diskette. Therefore don't use SELECT unless you are sure you know what you are doing. Most of the time, simply adding the necessary country statements and commands to your existing CONFIG.SYS and AUTOEXEC.BAT files is a safer procedure, especially if you have a fixed disk.

Be sure to look up these commands in your DOS reference manual if you decide to use them.

Match each command with its description.

(a) KEYB	A. Reformats the target diskette, destroying existing data
(b) GRAFTABL	B. Clears up some CGA displays
(c) SELECT	C. Specifies alternate keyboard layout and codepage
	D. Creates AUTOEXEC.BAT and CONFIG.SYS files with correct country statements and commands

---

(a) C
(b) B
(c) A, D

Adding to the Environment

The DOS environment is a set of parameters that affect all the work you do under DOS. Most of the time, you're not aware of the DOS environment; it's just there, working for you.

The PATH and PROMPT commands add parameters to the environment. So does the SET command, which adds any parameter you specify, even if DOS doesn't recognize the parameter or know how it will be used. You've already seen how to use SET to create a value for a dummy parameter used in batch files. You can also use SET to establish values for parameters used by applications. Any application program can look in the DOS environment for values for PATH, PROMPT, or any other parameter. For example, WordPerfect looks for a variable called WP containing any of its startup options. Suppose you always want to use these WordPerfect startup options: /R/NC/M-SETDIR. You would include this command in your AUTOEXEC.BAT file:

```
SET WP=/R/NC/M-SETDIR
```

DOS has no earthly idea what that parameter does, but it dutifully stores it in the environment.

Figure 12.5 shows the output when you use SET with no operands. A list of the environment variables is shown, including the standard environment variables, such as PATH and PROMPT, as well as any you may have set yourself.

COMSPEC is a standard DOS variable that tells DOS where to find the command processor. The example in the figure shows that COMMAND.COM is in C:\DOS. COMSPEC is a required variable; DOS cannot survive long without it. You can change the standard value with the SET command if you want DOS to use another shell. If you use the SHELL statement in CONFIG.SYS, you should also use SET COMSPEC in AUTOEXEC.BAT to specify the same filespec in both places.

```
C:\DOSBOOK> SET
COMSPEC=c:\dos\command.com
PROMPT=$p$g
PATH=C:\;C:\DOS;D:\HSG;D:\WS5;D:\WINDOWS

C:\DOSBOOK>_
```

Figure 12.5. Sample SET Display

(a) Write a command to see the environment variables PATH and COMSPEC.

```
C:\DOS>_
```

(b) Which of the commands below can change the display generated by SET?

A. PATH D. DEVICE
B. CHDIR E. SET
C. PROMPT F. COMSPEC

(a) `SET`
(b) A, C, E

Exercises

Much of the material covered in this chapter is specialized; you will be able to practice only some of the commands discussed in this chapter.

What You Should Do	*How the Computer Responds*
1. Modify BREAK status.	1.
a. Check the break status. (Enter BREAK with no operands.)	a. Displays BREAK is off.

b. Create a CONFIG.SYS file in the root directory of your boot drive. Use the append symbol (>>) so you don't erase an existing CONFIG.SYS file:
`COPY CON >>drive:\CONFIG.SYS`
`BREAK ON`
`^Z`
	b. Creates the CONFIG.SYS file according to your specifications.

c. Reboot.	c. Finds the CONFIG.SYS file and executes its statements.
d. Check your break status now.	d. Displays `BREAK is on`.
2. Check the environment variables.	2.
a. Enter SET.	a. Displays PATH and COMSPEC values.
b. Enter PROMPT TDG_	b. Creates and uses new prompt.
c. Check the environment again.	c. Displays PATH, COMSPEC, and PROMPT values.
d. Reset the prompt.	d. Restores the standard prompt.
3. Create a RAM drive.	3.

a. `COPY CON: >>drive:\CONFIG.SYS`
`DEVICE=path\RAMDRIVE.SYS 64`
`^Z`
	a. Creates the CONFIG.SYS file according to your specifications.

b. Use CHKDSK. Print the results with Shift-PrtSc.	b. Prints CHKDSK messages.
c. Reboot.	c. Shows RAM drive creation messages, including letter of RAM drive.

d. Use CHKDSK again to see how much memory is available now.

d. Displays less free memory (about 68,000 less; some is used for DOS purposes, such as directories and buffers).

4. Use SORT without the RAM drive:

```
SORT <path\PRESDENT >path\OUT
```

Time the sort.

4. Sorts PRESDENT and places OUT on disk.

5. Use the RAM drive.
   a. Copy SORT.EXE and PRESDENT to the RAM drive.
   b. Check its directory.
   c. Make the RAM drive the default.
   d. Enter the SORT command again and time it.
   e. Examine the output on the RAM drive. (Be sure to save the output to a real disk if you want to keep it.)

5.
   a. Copies the files as directed.
   b. Displays the directory of the RAM drive, showing the files you copied there.
   c. Shows the appropriate prompt.
   d. The SORT takes less time.
   e. Follows your instructions.

What If It Doesn't Work?

1. You shouldn't have any trouble with a CONFIG.SYS file or SET.

2. Feel free to erase any files created as you worked through this book.

3. If you have more space, create a larger RAM drive. Remember: You have to reboot to use a modified CONFIG.SYS file.

Index

G

H

Q

R

S

T

V